T0130679

Get the eBooks FREE!

(PDF, ePub, Kindle, and liveBook all included)

We believe that once you buy a book from us, you should be able to read it in any format we have available. To get electronic versions of this book at no additional cost to you, purchase and then register this book at the Manning website.

Go to https://www.manning.com/freebook and follow the instructions to complete your pBook registration.

That's it!
Thanks from Manning!

React Native in Action

React Native in Action

Developing iOS and Android apps with JavaScript

NADER DABIT

MANNING
SHELTER ISLAND

For online information and ordering of this and other Manning books, please visit www.manning.com. The publisher offers discounts on this book when ordered in quantity.

For more information, please contact

Special Sales Department
Manning Publications Co.
20 Baldwin Road
PO Box 761
Shelter Island, NY 11964
Email: orders@manning.com

Manning Publications Co.
20 Baldwin Road
PO Box 761
Shelter Island, NY 11964

Development editor:	Marina Michaels
Project editor:	Tiffany Taylor
Copy editor:	Tiffany Taylor
Proofreader:	Melody Dolab
Typesetter:	Happenstance Type-O-Rama
Cover designer:	Marija Tudor

ISBN: 9781617294051
Printed in the United States of America

brief contents

contents

preface

I've always been fascinated with the idea of mobile application development. Building mobile apps was one of the reasons I wanted to learn how to code. This fascination has lead me down many paths, from Objective-C to jQuery mobile to Cordova and now to React Native.

Because my career has centered around writing JavaScript, I've also always been drawn to technologies that increase my efficiency by using my existing skillset, allowing me to do more than just web development. Finding ways to be more efficient has been core to my career when choosing paths to follow and rabbit holes to dive into.

When React Native first landed, I knew that it was going to be something significant. There were already thousands of React and JavaScript developers in the world. React Native gave these developers a way to extend their existing skillset into the realm of mobile application development in a way that Cordova and other options didn't, and also appealed heavily to React developers who were at the time the most rapidly growing segment of all frontend developers. The framework also delivered a substantial increase in quality of applications that could be built versus other options available in the same space.

After writing my first application and shipping it to the app store, I had learned quite a bit and decided to start answering questions on Stack Overflow. I quickly realized that I had valuable knowledge I could share, while helping the community as well my career, so I began hanging out there more and more, answering questions.

I learned a lot while answering these questions, and eventually I made a conscious decision to specialize 100% in the React Native framework. I heard from many successful developers and consultants that specializing had helped them in their careers: they were more productive, got more business, and could demand a higher rate. So, I decided to try being a specialist for the first time in my career. This decision turned out to be great for me; I quickly began getting leads for consulting and, later, training.

I've watched the React Native framework grow from its infancy to what it is today and have seen many developers and companies rapidly increase their efficiency and productivity by taking advantage of what the framework has to offer. I think we're at an exciting time for React Native: many Fortune 500 companies and enterprises are picking it up, finally solidifying it as a first-class choice in their developer toolkits and giving more confidence to people who are considering betting their companies and applications on the framework. It will be exciting to watch the framework evolve and to see the new apps that will be shipped using React Native!

acknowledgments

This is the first time I've written a book. It has been a good learning experience, and also much more work than I anticipated. While I've been writing, my career has changed a couple of times and my obligations along with it, affecting the amount of time I could commit to the book. Nickie Buckner and Marina Michaels are the reason this book is complete. If it wasn't for them, it would have been in editing indefinitely; I was unable to rewrite a couple of chapters in a reasonable amount of time, and Nickie stepped up in a huge way to finish the book. Marina also did more than what was called for in helping the book make it the last 20% of the way as my time became increasingly constrained.

Thank you to my wife, Lilly, who worked overtime in addition to her already exceedingly high normal duties as I worked late nights in the office and sometimes at home to write this book. Thank you to my kids, Victor and Eli, who are awesome; I love them very much. And thank you to my parents for putting me in a position to be able to learn things and get second, third, and fourth chances at life.

My thanks go to many groups and individuals: to the React Native community and the React Native team (Jordan Walke, Christopher Chedeau, Adam Wolff, and everyone at Facebook over the years whom I didn't mention); to Monte Thakkar, who took over React Native Elements' open source while I was writing (and to all React Native Training open source contributors); to Eric Vicenti and Brent Vatne and all the people who have worked on Navigation and many other projects I use day to day; to Charlie Cheever, who has, with Expo, pushed the development of many React Native projects and, by extension, of Expo, and who has helped many open source projects; to Parasharum N, who has been committed to building things around React Native for years, now works on React Native at Facebook, and has always been a great asset to the community and ecosystem; to Peter Piekarczyk, Kevin Old, Lee Johnson, Gant Laborde, and Spencer Carli, who have consistently helped with the "React Native Radio" podcast; to Russ Davis and SchoolStatus, for the opportunity to learn React Native on the job, which is how I got started with it in the first place; to Orta Therox and the people at Artsy, for their commitment to the React Native community with their amazing blog and open source; to Leland Richardson, Devin Abbott, and the team at Airbnb, who gave React Native a fair shot and contributed extensively to the ecosystem even though the framework didn't work out for Airbnb in the long run; to the Wix team, who have contributed many amazing projects to the React Native open source ecosystem; to Mike Grabowski and Anna Lankauf, of Callstack, for being in charge of releasing React Native open source, for many contributions to the React Native open source ecosystem, and for collaborating with me on things over the years; and to Jason Brown for pushing amazing blog posts and teaching me about animations early on. I'm sure I left out many people, and if that person is you, I apologize and thank you for your contribution, as well.

Finally, I want to thank the people at Manning who made this book possible: publisher Marjan Bace and everyone behind the scenes on the editorial and production teams. My thanks also to the technical peer reviewers led by Aleksandar Dragosavljević: Alessandro Campeis, Andriy Kharchuk, Francesco Strazzullo, Gonzalo Barba López, Ian Lovell, Jason Rogers, Jose San Leandro, Joseph Tingsanchali, Markus Matzker, Matej Strašek, Mattias Lundell, Nickie Buckner, Olaoluwa Oluro, Owen Morris, Roger Sperberg, Stuart Rivero, Thomas Overby Hansen, Ubaldo Pescatore, and Zhuo Hong Wei. On the technical side, my thanks to Michiel Trimpe, who served as the book's technical editor; and Jason Rogers, who served as the book's technical proofreader.

about this book

React Native in Action was written to get you up and running with the React Native framework as quickly and seamlessly as possible. It uses a combination of real-world examples, discussions around APIs and development techniques, and a focus on learning things that will translate into real-world scenarios.

The book begins with an overview of React Native in chapter 1, following by a look at how React works in chapter 2. From chapter 3 through the end of the book, you build applications containing functionality you'll use to build applications in the real world. The book dives deep into topics such as data architecture, navigation, and animations, giving you a well-rounded understanding of how to build mobile apps using React Native.

The book is divided into 4 parts and 12 chapters:

- Part 1, "Getting Started with React Native":
  - Chapter 1 gets you up and running with React Native by going over what React Native is, how it works, its relationship with React, and when you might want to use React Native (and when you might not). This chapter includes an overview of React Native's components, which are at the core of React Native. It concludes with creating a small React Native project.
  - Chapter 2 covers state and props: what they are, how they work, and why they're important in React Native application development. It also covers the React Component specification and React lifecycle methods.
  - In chapter 3, you build your first React Native app—a todo app—from the ground up, and you'll learn about using the developer menu in iOS and Android to, among other things, debug your app.

- Part 2, "Developing Applications in React Native." With the basics covered, you can start adding features to your React Native app. The chapters in this part cover styling, navigation, animations, and elegant ways to handle data using data architectures (with a focus on Redux):

  - Chapters 4 and 5 teach you how to apply styles: either in line, with components, or in stylesheets that components can reference. Because React Native components are the main buildings blocks of your app's UI, chapter 4 spends some time teaching useful things you can do with the `View` component. Chapter 5 builds on the skills taught in chapter 4; it covers aspects of styling that are platform-specific, as well as some advanced techniques, including using flexbox to make it easier to lay out applications.

  - Chapter 6 shows how to use the two most-recommended and most-used navigation libraries: React Navigation and React Native Navigation. We'll walk through creating the three main types of navigators—tabs, stack, and drawer—and discuss how to control the navigation state.

  - Chapter 7 covers the four things you need to do to create animations, the four types of animatable components that ship with the Animated API, how to create custom animatable components, and several other useful skills.

  - In chapter 8, we explore handling data with data architectures. Because Redux is the most widely adopted method of handling data in the React ecosystem, you'll use it to build an app. Through doing so, you'll learn the skills needed to handle data. You'll see how to use the Context API and how to implement Redux with a React Native app by using reducers to hold the Redux state and delete items from the example app. You'll also learn how to use providers to pass global state to the rest of the app, how to use the `connect` function to access the example app from a child component, and how to use actions to add functionality.

- Part 3, "API Reference." React Native offers a wealth of APIs. The chapters in this part cover cross-platform APIs as well as APIs that are specific to the iOS and Android platforms:

  - Chapter 9 explores using React Native's cross-platform APIs: APIs that can be used on either iOS or Android to create alerts; detect whether the app is in the foreground, in the background, or inactive; persist, retrieve, and remove data; store and update text to the device clipboard; and perform a number of other useful features.

  - Chapters 10 and 11 look at React Native's APIs that are specific to either the iOS platform or the Android platform.

- Part 4, "Bringing It All Together." This part pulls together everything covered in the previous chapters—styling, navigation, animations, and some of the cross-platform components—into a single app:

- Chapter 12 starts by looking at the final design and walking through a basic overview of what the app will do. Then, you'll create a new React Native application and install the React Navigation library, dive deep into styling both the components as well as the navigation UI, work with data from external network resources by using the fetch API, and ultimately build out an application that allows users to view information about their favorite *Star Wars* characters.

Source code

This book contains many examples of source code, both in numbered listings and inline with normal text. In both cases, source code is formatted in a `fixed-width font like this` to separate it from ordinary text.

In many cases, the original source code has been reformatted; we've added line breaks and reworked indentation to accommodate the available page space in the book. In rare cases, even this was not enough, and listings include line-continuation markers (➥).

Additionally, comments in the source code have often been removed from the listings when the code is described in the text. Code annotations accompany many of the listings, highlighting important concepts.

Source code for the book's examples is available from the publisher's website at www.manning.com/books/react-native-in-action and on GitHub at https://github.com/dabit3/react-native-in-action.

Book forum

Purchase of *React Native in Action* includes free access to a private web forum run by Manning Publications where you can make comments about the book, ask technical questions, and receive help from the author and from other users. To access the forum, go to https://livebook.manning.com/#!/book/react-native-in-action/discussion. You can also learn more about Manning's forums and the rules of conduct at https://livebook.manning.com/#!/discussion.

Manning's commitment to our readers is to provide a venue where a meaningful dialogue between individual readers and between readers and the author can take place. It is not a commitment to any specific amount of participation on the part of the author, whose contribution to the forum remains voluntary (and unpaid). We suggest you try asking the author some challenging questions lest his interest stray! The forum and the archives of previous discussions will be accessible from the publisher's website as long as the book is in print.

about the author

Nader Dabit is a developer advocate at AWS Mobile, where he works on tools and services to allow developers to build full-stack web and mobile applications using their existing skillset. He is also the founder of React Native Training and the host of the "React Native Radio" podcast.

about the cover illustration

The figure on the cover of *React Native in Action* is captioned "Insulaire D'Amboine" or "Islander of Amboine." The illustration is taken from a nineteenth-century edition of Sylvain Maréchal's four-volume compendium of regional dress customs published in France. Each illustration is finely drawn and colored by hand. The rich variety of Maréchal's collection reminds us vividly of how culturally apart the world's towns and regions were just 200 years ago. Isolated from each other, people spoke different dialects and languages. Whether on city streets, in small towns, or in the countryside, it was easy to identify where they lived and what their trade or station in life was just by their dress.

Dress codes have changed since then and the diversity by region and class, so rich at the time, has faded away. It is now hard to tell apart the inhabitants of different continents, let alone different towns or regions. Perhaps we have traded cultural diversity for a more varied personal life—certainly for a more varied and fast-paced technological life.

At a time when it is hard to tell one computer book from another, Manning celebrates the inventiveness and initiative of the computer business with book covers based on the rich diversity of regional life of two centuries ago, brought back to life by Maréchal's pictures.

Part 1

Getting started with React Native

Chapter 1 will get you up and running by going over what React Native is, how it works, what its relationship with React is, and when you might want to use React Native (and when you might not). This chapter provides an overview of React Native's components, which are at the core of React Native. It concludes with creating a small React Native project.

Chapter 2 covers state and properties: what they are, how they work, and why they're important in React Native application development. It also covers the React Component specification and React lifecycle methods.

In chapter 3, you'll build your first React Native app—a Todo app—from the ground up. You'll also learn about using the developer menu in iOS and Android for, among other things, debugging apps.

Getting started with React Native

Native mobile application development can be complex. With the complicated environments, verbose frameworks, and long compilation times developers face, developing a quality native mobile application is no easy task. It's no wonder the market has seen its share of solutions come onto the scene that attempt to solve the problems that go along with native mobile application development and try to make it easier.

At the core of this complexity is the obstacle of cross-platform development. The various platforms are fundamentally different and don't share much of their development environments, APIs, or code. Because of this, we must have separate teams working on each platform, which is both expensive and inefficient.

But this is an exciting time in mobile application development. We're witnessing a new paradigm in the mobile development landscape, and React Native is on the forefront of this shift in how we build and engineer mobile applications. It's now possible to build native performing cross-platform apps as well as web applications with a single language and a single team. With the rise of mobile devices and the subsequent increase in demand for talent driving developer salaries higher and higher, React Native brings to the table the ability to deliver quality applications across all platforms at a fraction of the time and cost, while still delivering a high-quality user experience and a delightful developer experience.

1.1   *Introducing React and React Native*

React Native is a framework for building native mobile apps in JavaScript using the React JavaScript library; React Native code compiles to real native components. If you're not sure what React is, it's a JavaScript library open sourced by and used within Facebook. It was originally used to build user interfaces for web applications. It has since evolved and can now also be used to build server-side and mobile applications (using React Native).

React Native has a lot going for it. In addition to being backed and open sourced by Facebook, it also has a tremendous community of motivated people behind it. Facebook groups, with their millions of users, are powered by React Native as well as Facebook Ads Manager. Airbnb, Bloomberg, Tesla, Instagram, Ticketmaster, SoundCloud, Uber, Walmart, Amazon, and Microsoft are some of the other companies either investing in or using React Native in production.

With React Native, developers can build native views and access native platform-specific components using JavaScript. This sets React Native apart from other hybrid app frameworks like Cordova and Ionic, which package web views built using HTML and CSS into a native application. Instead, React Native takes JavaScript and compiles it into a true native application that can use platform-specific APIs and components. Alternatives like Xamarin take the same approach, but Xamarin apps are built using C#, not JavaScript. Many web developers have JavaScript experience, which helps ease the transition from web to mobile app development.

There are many benefits to choosing React Native as a mobile application framework. Because the application renders native components and APIs directly, speed and performance are much better than with hybrid frameworks such as Cordova and Ionic. With React Native, we're writing entire applications using a single programming language: JavaScript. We can reuse a lot of code, thereby reducing the time it takes to ship a cross-platform application. And hiring and finding quality JavaScript developers is much easier and cheaper than hiring Java, Objective C, or Swift developers, leading to an overall less-expensive process.

> **NOTE**   React Native applications are built using JavaScript and JSX. We'll discuss JSX in depth in this book, but for now think of it as a JavaScript syntax extension that looks like HTML or XML.

We'll dive much deeper into React in chapter 2. Until then, let's touch on a few core concepts as an introduction.

1.1.1 A basic React class

Components are the building blocks of a React or React Native application. The entry point of an application is a component that requires and is made of other components. These components may also require other components, and so on.

There are two main types of React Native components: *stateful* and *stateless*. Here's an example of a stateful component using an ES6 class:

```
class HelloWorld extends React.Component {
  constructor() {
    super()
    this.state = { name: 'Chris' }
  }

  render () {
    return (
      <SomeComponent />
    )
  }
}
```

And here's an example of a stateless component:

```
const HelloWorld = () => (
  <SomeComponent />
)
```

The main difference is that stateless components don't hook into any lifecycle methods and hold no state of their own, so any data to be rendered must be received as properties (props). We'll go through the lifecycle methods in depth in chapter 2, but for now let's take a first look at them and look at a class.

Listing 1.1 Creating a basic React Native class

```
import React from 'react'
import { View, Text, StyleSheet } from 'react-native'

class HelloWorld extends React.Component {
  constructor () {                       ◄──────  Constructor sets a state object
    super()                                        with a name property
    this.state = {
      name: 'React Native in Action'
    }
  }
  componentDidMount () {          ◄──  Final lifecycle method
    console.log('mounted..')
  }
  render () {          ◄──────────  Calls render()
    return (
      <View style={styles.container}>
        <Text>{this.state.name}</Text>
      </View>
    )
  }
}
```

```
  }

const styles = StyleSheet.create({
  container: {
    marginTop: 100,
    flex: 1
  }
})
```

> **NOTE** Something to keep in mind when we discuss the following methods is the concept of *mounting*. When a component is created, the React component lifecycle is instantiated, triggering the methods used in listing 1.1.

At the top of the file, you require `React` from `'react'`, as well as `View`, `Text`, and `StyleSheet` from `'react-native'`. `View` is the most fundamental building block for creating React Native components and the UI in general and can be thought of like a `div` in HTML. `Text` allows you to create text elements and is comparable to a `span` tag in HTML. `StyleSheet` lets you create style objects to use in an application. These two packages (`react` and `react-native`) are available as npm modules.

When the component first loads, you set a `state` object with the property `name` in the constructor. For data in a React Native application to be dynamic, it needs to be either set in the state or passed down as props. Here, you set the state in the constructor and can therefore change it if desired by calling

```
this.setState({
  name: 'Some Other Name'
})
```

which rerenders the component. Setting the variable in state allows you to update the value elsewhere in the component.

`render` is then called: it examines the props and state and then must return a single React Native element, `null`, or `false`. If you have multiple child elements, they must be wrapped in a parent element. Here, the components, styles, and data are combined to create what will be rendered to the UI.

The final method in the lifecycle is `componentDidMount`. If you need to do any API calls or AJAX requests to reset the state, this is usually the best place to do so. Finally, the UI is rendered to the device, and you can see the result.

1.1.2 *React lifecycle*

When a React Native class is created, methods are instantiated that you can hook into. These methods are called *lifecycle methods*, and we'll cover them in depth in chapter 2. The methods in listing 1.1 are `constructor`, `componentDidMount`, and `render`, but there are a few more, and they all have their own use cases.

Lifecycle methods happen in sync and help manage the state of components as well as execute code at each step of the way, if you wish. The only required lifecycle method is `render`; all the others are optional. When working with React Native, you're fundamentally working with the same lifecycle methods and specifications you'd use with React.

1.2   *What you'll learn*

In this book, we'll cover everything you need to know to build robust mobile applications for iOS and Android using the React Native framework. Because React Native is built using the React library, we'll begin in chapter 2 by covering and thoroughly explaining how React works.

We'll then cover styling, touching on most of the styling properties available in the framework. Because React Native uses flexbox for laying out the UI, we'll dive deep into how flexbox works and discuss all the flexbox properties. If you've used flexbox in CSS for layout on the web, all of this will be familiar to you, but keep in mind that the flexbox implementation used by React Native isn't 100% the same.

We'll then go through many of the native components that come with the framework out of the box and walk through how each of them works. In React Native, a component is basically a chunk of code that provides a specific functionality or UI element and can easily be used in the application. Components are covered extensively throughout this book because they're the building blocks of a React Native application.

There are many ways to implement navigation, each with its own nuances, pros, and cons. We'll discuss navigation in depth and cover how to build robust navigation using the most important of the navigation APIs. We'll cover not only the native navigation APIs that come out of the box with React Native, but also a couple of community projects available through npm.

Next, we'll discuss in depth both cross-platform and platform-specific APIs available in React Native and how they work. It will then be time for you to start working with data using network requests, AsyncStorage (a form of local storage), Firebase, and WebSocket. Then we'll dive into the different data architectures and how each of them works to handle the state of the application. Finally, we'll look at testing and a few different ways to test in React Native.

1.3   *What you should know*

To get the most out of this book, you should have beginner to intermediate knowledge of JavaScript. Much of your work will be done with the command line, so a basic understanding of how to use the command line is also needed. You should also understand what npm is and how it works on at least a fundamental level. If you'll be building in iOS, a basic understanding of Xcode is beneficial and will speed things along but isn't required. Similarly, if you're building for Android, a basic understanding of Android Studio will be beneficial but not required.

Fundamental knowledge of newer JavaScript features implemented in the ES2015 release of the JavaScript programming language is beneficial but not necessary. Some conceptual knowledge of MVC frameworks and single-page architecture is also good but not required.

1.4   Understanding how React Native works

Let's look at how React Native works by discussing JSX, the threading model, React, unidirectional data flow, and more.

1.4.1   JSX

React and React Native both encourage the use of JSX. JSX is basically a syntax extension to JavaScript that looks similar to XML. You can build React Native components without JSX, but JSX makes React and React Native a lot more readable and easier to maintain. JSX may seem strange at first, but it's extremely powerful, and most people grow to love it.

1.4.2   Threading

All JavaScript operations, when interacting with the native platform, are done in a separate thread, allowing the user interface as well as any animations to perform smoothly. This thread is where the React application lives, and where all API calls, touch events, and interactions are processed. When there's a change to a native-backed component, updates are batched and sent to the native side. This happens at the end of each iteration of the event loop. For most React Native applications, the business logic runs on the JavaScript thread.

1.4.3   React

A great feature of React Native is that it uses React. React is an open source JavaScript library that's also backed by Facebook. It was originally designed to build applications and solve problems on the web. This framework has become extremely popular since its release, with many established companies taking advantage of its quick rendering, maintainability, and declarative UI, among other things.

Traditional DOM manipulation is slow and expensive in terms of performance and should be minimized. React bypasses the traditional DOM with something called the *virtual DOM*: basically, a copy of the actual DOM in memory that only changes when comparing new versions of the virtual DOM to old versions of the virtual DOM. This minimizes the number of DOM operations required to achieve the new state.

1.4.4   Unidirectional data flow

React and React Native emphasize unidirectional, or one-way, data flow. Because of how React Native applications are built, this one-way data flow is easy to achieve.

1.4.5   Diffing

React takes the idea of diffing and applies it to native components. It takes your UI and sends the smallest amount of data to the main thread to render it with native components. The UI is declaratively rendered based on the state, and React uses diffing to send the necessary changes over the bridge.

1.4.6 *Thinking in components*

When building a UI in React Native, it's useful to think of your application as being composed of a collection of components. Thinking about how a page is set up, you already do this conceptually, but using concepts, names, or class names like *header*, *footer*, *body*, *sidebar*, and so on. With React Native, you can give these components names that make sense to you and other developers who may be using your code, making it easy to bring new people into a project or hand a project off to someone else.

Suppose a designer has handed you the example mockup shown in figure 1.1. Let's think of how to conceptualize this into components.

The first thing to do is to mentally break the UI elements into what they represent. The example mockup has a header bar, and within the header bar are a title and a

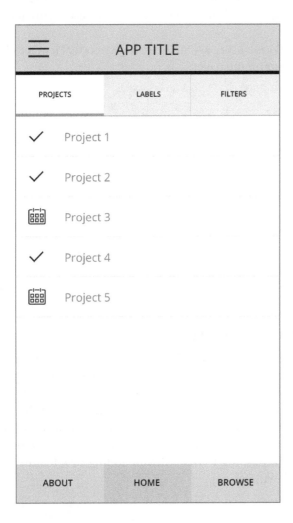

Figure 1.1   Example app design

menu button. Below the header is a tab bar, and within the tab bar are three individual tabs. Go through the rest of the mockup and think of what the other items are. These items you're identifying will be translated into components. This is the way you should think about composing a UI when working with React Native: break down common elements in the UI into reusable components, and define their interface accordingly. When you need an element in the future, it will be available for reuse.

Breaking UI elements into reusable components is good for code reuse and also makes your code declarative and understandable. For instance, instead of 12 lines of code implementing a footer, the element could be called `footer`. Looking at code built this way, it's much easier to reason about and know exactly what's going on.

Figure 1.2 shows how the design in figure 1.1 could be broken up as I just described. The names can be whatever makes sense to you. Some of the items are grouped together—I logically separated the items individually and grouped components conceptually.

Next, let's see how this would look using actual React Native code. First, let's look at how the main UI elements appear on the page:

```
<Header />
<TabBar />
<ProjectList />
<Footer />
```

Next, let's see how the child elements look:

```
TabBar:
      <TabBarItem  />
      <TabBarItem  />
      <TabBarItem />

ProjectList:
      // Add a Project component for each project in the list:
      <Project />
```

I've used the names declared in figure 1.2, but they could be whatever makes sense to you.

1.5   *Acknowledging React Native's strengths*

As discussed earlier, one of the main strengths React Native has going for it is that it uses React. React, like React Native, is an open source project backed by Facebook. As of the time of this writing, React has over 100,000 stars and more than 1,100 contributors on GitHub—that's a lot of interest and community involvement in the project, making it easier to bet on as a developer or as a project manager. Because React is developed, maintained, and used by Facebook, it has some of the most talented engineers in the world overseeing it, pushing it forward, and adding new features, and it probably won't be going away anytime soon.

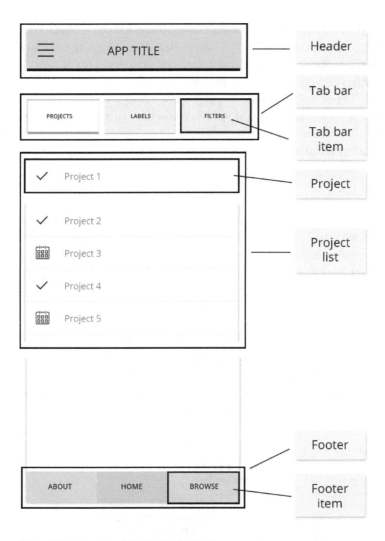

Figure 1.2 App structure broken down into separate components

1.5.1 *Developer availability*

With the rising cost and decreasing availability of native mobile developers, React Native enters the market with a key advantage over native development: it takes advantage of the wealth of existing talented web and JavaScript developers and gives them another platform on which to build without having to learn a new language.

1.5.2 *Developer productivity*

Traditionally, to build a cross-platform mobile application, you needed both an Android team and an iOS team. React Native allows you to build Android, iOS, and (soon) Windows applications using a single programming language, JavaScript, and possibly even a single team, dramatically decreasing development time and development cost while increasing productivity. As a native developer, the great thing about coming to a platform like this is the fact that you're no longer tied down to being only an Android or iOS developer, opening the door for a lot of opportunity. This is great news for JavaScript developers as well, allowing them to spend all their time in one state of mind when switching between web and mobile projects. It's also a win for teams who were traditionally split between Android and iOS, because they can now work together on a single codebase. To underscore these points, you can share your data architecture not only cross platform, but also on the web, if you're using something like Redux (discussed in chapter 12).

1.5.3 *Performance*

If you follow other cross-platform solutions, you're probably aware of solutions such as PhoneGap, Cordova, and Ionic. Although these are also viable solutions, the consensus is that performance hasn't yet caught up to the experience a native app delivers. This is where React Native also shines, because the performance is usually not noticeably different from that of a native mobile app built using Objective-C/Swift or Java.

1.5.4 *One-way data flow*

One-way data flow separates React and React Native from most other JavaScript frameworks and also any MVC framework. React incorporates a one-way data flow from top-level components all the way down (see figure 1.3). This makes applications much easier to reason about, because there's one source of truth for the data layer as opposed to having it scattered about the application. We'll look at this in more detail later in the book.

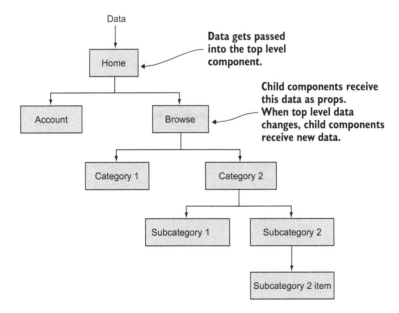

Figure 1.3   How one-way data flow works

1.5.5 *Developer experience*

The developer experience is a major win for React Native. If you've ever developed for the web, you're aware of the browser's snappy reload times. Web development has no compilation step: just refresh the screen, and your changes are there. This is a far cry from the long compile times of native development. One of the reasons Facebook decided to develop React Native was to overcome the lengthy compile times of the Facebook application when using native iOS and Android build tools. To make a small UI change or any other change, Facebook developers had to wait a long time while the program compiled to see the results. Long compilation times result in decreased productivity and increased developer cost. React Native solves this issue by giving you the quick reload times of the web, as well as Chrome and Safari debugging tools, making the debugging experience feel a lot like the web.

React Native also has something called *hot reloading* built in. What does this mean? Well, while developing an application, imagine having to click a few times into your app to get to the place you're developing. While using hot reloading, when you make a code change, you don't have to reload and click back through the app to get to the current state. Using this feature, you save the file, and the application reloads only the component you've changed, instantly giving you feedback and updating the current state of the UI.

1.5.6 *Transpilation*

Transpilation is typically when something known as a *transpiler* takes source code written in one programming language and produces the equivalent code in another language. With the rise of new ECMAScript features and standards, transpilation has spilled over to also include taking newer versions and yet-to-be-implemented features of certain languages, in this case JavaScript, and producing transpiled standard JavaScript, making the code usable by platforms that can only process older versions of the language.

React Native uses Babel to do this transpilation step, and it's built in by default. Babel is an open source tool that transpiles the most bleeding-edge JavaScript language features into code that can be used today. You don't have to wait for the bureaucratic process of language features being proposed, approved, and then implemented before you can use them. You can start using a feature as soon as it makes it into Babel, which is usually very quickly. JavaScript classes, arrow functions, and object destructuring are all examples of powerful ES2015 features that haven't made it into all browsers and runtimes yet; but with Babel and React Native, you can use them today with no worries about whether they will work. If you like using the latest language features, you can use the same transpilation process to develop web applications.

1.5.7 *Productivity and efficiency*

Native mobile development is becoming more and more expensive, so engineers who can deliver applications across platforms and stacks will become increasingly valuable and in demand. Once React Native—or something similar, if it comes along—makes developing desktop and web as well as mobile applications using a single framework mainstream, there will be a restructuring and rethinking of how engineering teams are organized. Instead of a developer being specialized in a certain platform, such as iOS or web, they'll oversee features across platforms. In this new era of cross-platform and cross-stack engineering teams, developers delivering native mobile, web, and desktop applications will be more productive and efficient and will therefore be able to demand a higher wage than a traditional web developer who can only deliver web applications.

Companies that are hiring developers for mobile development stand to benefit the most from using React Native. Having everything written in one language makes hiring a lot easier and less expensive. Productivity also soars when a team is all on the same page, working within a single technology, which simplifies collaboration and knowledge sharing.

1.5.8   Community

The React community, and by extension the React Native community, is one of the most open and helpful groups I've ever interacted with. When I've run into issues I couldn't resolve on my own by searching online or on Stack Overflow, I've reached out directly to either a team member or someone in the community and have had nothing but positive feedback and help.

1.5.9   Open source

React Native is open source. This offers a wealth of benefits. First, in addition to the Facebook team, hundreds of developers contribute to React Native. Bugs are pointed out much faster than in proprietary software, which has only the employees on a specific team working on bug fixes and improvements. Open source usually gets closer to what users want because the users can have a hand in making the software what they want it to be. Given the cost of purchasing proprietary software, licensing fees, and support costs, open source also wins when measuring price.

1.5.10   Immediate updates

Traditionally, when publishing new versions of an app, you're at the mercy of the app store approval process and schedule. This long, tedious process can take up to two weeks. Making a change, even if it's extremely small, is painful and requires releasing a new version of the application.

React Native, as well as hybrid application frameworks, allow you to deploy mobile app updates directly to the user's device, without going through an app store approval process. If you're used to the web and the rapid release cycle it offers, you can now do the same thing with React Native and other hybrid application frameworks.

1.5.11   Other solutions for building cross-platform mobile applications

React Native isn't the only option for building a cross-platform mobile application. Multiple other options are available, with the main ones being Cordova, Xamarin, and Flutter:

- *Cordova* is basically a native shell around a web application that allows the developer to access native APIs within the application. Unlike traditional web applications, Cordova apps can be deployed to the App Store and Google Play Store. The benefit of using something like Cordova is that there isn't much more to learn if you're already a web developer: you can use HTML, JavaScript, CSS, and your JavaScript framework of choice. The main drawback of Cordova is that you'll have a hard time matching the performance and smooth UI that React Native offers: you're relying on the DOM, because you're mainly working with web technologies.

- *Xamarin* is a framework that allows developers to build iOS, Android, Windows, and macOS applications using a single codebase written in C#. Xamarin compiles to a native app in different ways depending on the platform being targeted. Xamarin has a free tier that lets developers build and deploy mobile applications and a paid tier for larger or enterprise companies. Xamarin will probably appeal more to native developers because it doesn't have similarities to web technologies like React Native and Cordova.

- *Flutter* is a framework open sourced by Google that uses the Dart programming language to build applications that run on iOS and Android platforms.

1.6 React Native's drawbacks

Now that we've gone over the benefits of using React Native, let's look at a few reasons and circumstances where you may not want to choose the framework. First, React Native is still immature when compared to other platforms such as native iOS, Android, and Cordova. Feature parity isn't there yet with either native iOS or Cordova. Most functionality is now built in, but there may be times when you need functionality that isn't yet available, and this means you must dig into the native code to build it yourself, hire someone to do it, or not implement the feature.

Another thing to think about is the fact that you and/or your team must learn a completely new technology if you aren't familiar with React. Most people agree that React is easy to pick up; but if you're already proficient with Angular and Ionic, for example, and you have an application deadline coming up, it may be wise to go with what you already know instead of spending the time it takes to learn and train your team on a new tech. In addition to learning React and React Native, you must also become familiar with Xcode and the Android development environments, which can take some getting used to.

Finally, React Native is an abstraction built on top of existing platform APIs. When newer versions of iOS, Android, and other future platforms are released, there may be a time when React Native will be behind on new features, forcing you to either build custom implementations to interact with these new APIs or wait until React Native regains feature parity with the new release.

1.7 Creating and using basic components

Components are the fundamental building blocks of React Native, and they can vary in functionality and type. Examples of components in popular use cases include buttons, headers, footers, and navigation components. They can vary in type from an entire view, complete with its own state and functionality, to a single stateless component that receives all its props from its parent.

1.7.1   *An overview of components*

As I've said, the core of React Native is the concept of components. Components are collections of data and UI elements that make up views and, ultimately, applications. React Native has built-in components that are described as *native components* in this book, but you can also build custom components using the framework. We'll go into depth on how to build, create, and use components.

As mentioned earlier, React Native components are built using JSX. Table 1.1 shows a few basic examples of what JSX in React Native looks like versus HTML. As you can see, JSX looks similar to HTML or XML.

Table 1.1   JSX components vs. HTML elements

Component type	HTML	React Native JSX
Text	`<span>Hello World</span>`	`<Text>Hello World</Text>`

View	`<div>`
	   `<span>Hello World 2</span>`
	`</div>`
		`<View>`
		   `<Text>Hello World 2</Text>`
		`</View>`

Touchable highlight	`<button>`
	   `<span>Hello World 2</span>`
	`</button >`
		`<TouchableHighlight>`
		   `<Text>Hello World 2</Text>`
		`</TouchableHighlight>`

1.7.2   *Native components*

The framework offers native components out of the box, such as `View`, `Text`, and `Image`, among others. You can create components using these Native components as building blocks. For example, you can use the following markup to create a `Button` component using React Native `TouchableHighlight` and `Text` components.

Listing 1.4   Creating a `Button` component

```
import { Text, TouchableHighlight } from 'react-native'
const Button = () => (
  <TouchableHighlight>
    <Text>Hello World</Text>
  </TouchableHighlight>
)
export default Button
```

You can then import and use the new button.

Listing 1.5 Importing and using the `Button` component

```
import React from 'react'
import { Text, View } from 'react-native'
import Button from './components/Button'
const Home = () => (
  <View>
    <Text>Welcome to the Hello World Button!</Text>
    <Button />
  </View>
)
```

Next, we'll go through the fundamentals of what a component is, how components fit into the workflow, and common use cases and design patterns for building them.

1.7.3   Component composition

Components are usually composed using JSX, but they can also be composed using JavaScript. In this section, you'll create a component several different ways to see all the options. You'll be creating this component:

```
<MyComponent />
```

This component outputs "Hello World" to the screen. Now, let's see how to build this basic component. The only out-of-the-box components you'll use to build this custom component are the `View` and `Text` elements discussed earlier. Remember, a `View` component is similar to an HTML `<div>`, and a `Text` component is similar to an HTML `<span>`.

Let's look at a few ways to create a component. The entire application doesn't have to be consistent in its component definitions, but it's usually recommended that you stay consistent and follow the same pattern for defining classes throughout your application.

CREATECLASS SYNTAX (ES5, JSX)

This is the way to create a React Native component using ES5 syntax. You'll probably still see this syntax in use in some older documentation and examples, but it isn't being used in newer documentation and is now deprecated. We'll focus on the ES2015 class syntax for the rest of the book but will review the `createClass` syntax here in case you come across it in older code:

```
const React = require('react')
const ReactNative = require('react-native')
const { View, Text } = ReactNative

const MyComponent = React.createClass({
  render() {
    return (
      <View>
       <Text>Hello World</Text>
      </View>)
    }
})
```

CLASS SYNTAX (ES2015, JSX)

The main way to create stateful React Native components is using ES2015 classes. This is the way you'll create stateful components for the rest of the book and is now the approach recommended by the community and creators of React Native:

```
import  React from 'react'
import { View, Text } from 'react-native'

class  MyComponent extends React.Component {
  render() {
    return (
      <View>
        <Text>Hello World</Text>
      </View>)
  }
}
```

STATELESS (REUSABLE) COMPONENT (JSX)

Since the release of React 0.14, we've had the ability to create *stateless* components. We haven't yet dived into state, but just remember that stateless components are basically pure functions that can't mutate their own data and don't contain their own state. This syntax is much cleaner than the class or createClass syntax:

```
import React from 'react'
import { View, Text } from 'react-native'

const MyComponent = () => (
  <View>
    <Text>Hello World</Text>
  </View>
)

or

import React from 'react'
import { View, Text } from 'react-native'

function MyComponent () {
  return <View><Text>HELLO FROM STATELESS</Text></View>
}
```

CREATEELEMENT (JAVASCRIPT)

React.createElement is rarely used, and you'll probably never need to create a React Native element using this syntax. But it may come in handy if you ever need more control over how you're creating a component, or if you're reading someone else's code. It will also give you a look at how JavaScript compiles JSX. React.createElement takes a few arguments:

```
React.createElement(type, props, children) {}
```

Let's walk through them:

- type—The element you want to render
- props—Any properties you want the component to have
- children—Child components or text

In the following example, you pass in a view as the first argument to the first instance of React.createElement, an empty object as the second argument, and another element as the last argument. In the second instance, you pass in text as the first argument, an empty object as the second argument, and "Hello" as the final argument:

```
class MyComponent extends React.Component {
render() {
    return (
      React.createElement(View, {},
        React.createElement(Text, {}, "Hello")
      )
    )
  }
}
```

This is the same as declaring the component as follows:

```
class MyComponent extends React.Component {
  render () {
    return (
      <View>
        <Text>Hello</Text>
      </View>
    )
  }
}
```

1.7.4 Exportable components

Next, let's look at another, more in-depth implementation of a React Native component. You'll create an entire component that you can export and use in another file:

```
import React, { Component } from 'react'
import {
  Text,
  View
} from 'react-native'

class Home extends Component {
  render() {
    return (
      <View>
        <Text>Hello from Home</Text>
      </View>)
  }
}

export default Home
```

Let's go over all the pieces that make up this component and discuss what's going on.

IMPORTING

The following code imports React Native variable declarations:

```
import React, { Component } from 'react'
import {
    Text,
    View
} from 'react-native'
```

Here, you're importing React directly from the React library using a default import and importing `Component` from the React library using a named import. You're also using named imports to pull `Text` and `View` into your file.

The `import` statement using ES5 would look like this:

```
var React = require('react')
```

This statement without using named imports would look like this:

```
import React = from 'react'
const Component = React.Component
import ReactNative from 'react-native'
const Text = ReactNative.Text
const View = ReactNative.View
```

The `import` statement is used to import functions, objects, or variables that have been exported from another module, file, or script.

COMPONENT DECLARATION

The following code declares the component:

```
class Home extends Component { }
```

Here you're creating a new instance of a React Native `Component` class by extending it and naming it `Home`. Before, you declared `React.Component`; now you're just declaring `Component`, because you imported the `Component` element in the object destructuring statement, giving you access to `Component` as opposed to having to call `React.Component`.

THE RENDER METHOD

Next, look at the `render` method:

```
render() {
  return (
    <View>
      <Text>Hello from Home</Text>
    </View>)
}
```

The code for the component is executed in the `render` method, and the content after the `return` statement returns what's rendered on the screen. When the `render` method is called, it should return a single child element. Any variables or functions declared outside of the `render` function can be executed here. If you need to do any calculations, declare any variables using state or props, or run any functions that don't manipulate the state of the component, you can do so between the render method and the return statement.

EXPORTS

Now, you export the component to be used elsewhere in the application:

```
export default Home
```

If you want to use the component in the same file, you don't need to export it. After it's declared, you can use it in the file or export it to be used in another file. You may also use module.exports = 'Home', which is ES5 syntax.

1.7.5   *Combining components*

Let's look at how to combine components. First, create Home, Header, and Footer components in a single file. Begin by creating the Home component:

```
import React, { Component } from 'react'
import {
    Text,
    View
} from 'react-native'

class Home extends Component {
  render() {
    return (
      <View>

      </View>)
    }
  }
```

In the same file, below the Home class declaration, build out a Header component:

```
class Header extends Component {
    render() {
      return <View>
              <Text>HEADER</Text>
            </View>
    }
  }
```

This looks nice, but let's see how to rewrite Header into a stateless component. We'll discuss when and why it's good to use a stateless component versus a regular React Native class in depth later in the book. As you'll begin to see, the syntax and code are much cleaner when you use stateless components:

```
const Header = () => (
  <View>
    <Text>HEADER</Text>
  </View>
)
```

Now, insert Header into the Home component:

```
  class Home extends Component {
    render() {
```

```
      return (
       <View>
         <Header />
       </View>
      )
    }
 }
```

Create a `Footer` and a `Main` view, as well:

```
const Footer = () => (
  <View>
    <Text>Footer</Text>
  </View>
)

const Main = () => (
  <View>
    <Text> Main </Text>
  </View>
)
```

Now, drop those into your application:

```
class Home extends Component {
  render() {
    return (
      <View>
        <Header />
        <Main />
        <Footer />
      </View>
    )
  }
}
```

The code you just wrote is extremely declarative, meaning it's written in such a way that it describes what you want to do and is easy to understand in isolation. This is a high-level overview of how you'll create components and views in React Native, but should give you a good idea of how the basics work.

1.8   Creating a starter project

Now that we've gone over a lot of details about React Native, let's dig into some more code. We'll focus on building apps using the React Native CLI, but you can also use the Create React Native App CLI to create a new project.

1.8.1   Create React Native App CLI

You can create React Native projects using the Create React Native App CLI, a project generator that's maintained in the React Community GitHub repository, mainly by the Expo team. Expo created the React Native App project as a way to allow developers to get up and running with React Native without having to worry about installing all the native SDKs involved with running a React Native project using the CLI.

To create a new project using Create React Native App, first install the CLI:

```
npm install -g create-react-native-app
```

Here's how to create a new project using `create-react-native-app` from the command line:

```
create-react-native-app myProject
```

1.8.2 *React Native CLI*

Before we go any further, check this book's appendix to verify that you have the necessary tools installed on your machine. If you don't have the required SDKs installed, you won't be able to continue building your first project using the React Native CLI.

To get started with the React Native starter project and the React Native CLI, open the command line and then create and navigate to an empty directory. Once you're there, install the react-native CLI globally by typing the following:

```
npm install -g react-native-cli
```

After React Native is installed on your machine, you can initialize a new project by typing `react-native init` followed by the project name:

```
react-native init myProject
```

`myProject` can be any name you choose. The CLI will then spin up a new project in whatever directory you're in. Open the project in a text editor.

First, let's look at the main files and folders this process has generated for you:

- *android*—This folder contains all the Android platform-specific code and dependencies. You won't need to go into this folder unless you're implementing a custom bridge into Android or you install a plugin that calls for some type of deep configuration.
- *ios*—This folder contains all the iOS platform-specific code and dependencies. You won't need to go into this folder unless you're implementing a custom bridge into iOS or you install a plugin that calls for some type of deep configuration.
- *node_modules*—React Native uses *npm* (node package manager) to manage dependencies. These dependencies are identified and versioned in the .package. json file and stored in the node_modules folder. When you install any new packages from the npm/node ecosystem, they'll go here. These can be installed using either npm or yarn.
- *.flowconfig*—Flow (also open sourced by Facebook) offers type checking for JavaScript. Flow is like Typescript, if you're familiar with that. This file is the configuration for flow, if you choose to use it.
- *.gitignore*—This is the place to store any file paths you don't want in version control.

- *.watchmanconfig*—Watchman is a file watcher that React Native uses to watch files and record when they change. This is the configuration for Watchman. No changes to this will be needed except in rare use cases.
- *index.js*—This is the entry point of the application. In this file, App.js is imported and `AppRegistry.registerComponent` is called, initializing the app.
- *App.js*—This is the default main import used in index.js containing the base project. You can change it by deleting this file and replacing the main import in index.js.
- *package.json*—This file holds your npm configuration. When you npm install files, you can save them here as dependencies. You can also set up scripts to run different tasks.

The following listing shows App.js.

Listing 1.6   App.js

```
/**
 * Sample React Native App
 * https://github.com/facebook/react-native
 * @flow
 */

import React, { Component } from 'react';
import {
  Platform,
  StyleSheet,
  Text,
  View
} from 'react-native';

const instructions = Platform.select({
  ios: 'Press Cmd+R to reload,\n' +
    'Cmd+D or shake for dev menu',
  android: 'Double tap R on your keyboard to reload,\n' +
    'Shake or press menu button for dev menu',
});

export default class App extends Component<{}> {
  render() {
    return (
      <View style={styles.container}>
        <Text style={styles.welcome}>
          Welcome to React Native!
        </Text>
        <Text style={styles.instructions}>
          To get started, edit App.js
        </Text>
        <Text style={styles.instructions}>
          {instructions}
        </Text>
```

```
        </View>
    );
  }
}

const styles = StyleSheet.create({
  container: {
    flex: 1,
    justifyContent: 'center',
    alignItems: 'center',
    backgroundColor: '#F5FCFF',
  },
  welcome: {
    fontSize: 20,
    textAlign: 'center',
    margin: 10,
  },
  instructions: {
    textAlign: 'center',
    color: '#333333',
    marginBottom: 5,
  },
});
```

This code looks much like what we went over in the last section. There are a couple of new items you haven't yet seen:

```
StyleSheet
Platform
```

`Platform` is an API that allows you to detect the current type of operating system you're running on: web, iOS, or Android.

`StyleSheet` is an abstraction like CSS stylesheets. In React Native, you can declare styles either inline or using stylesheets. As you can see in the first view, a container style is declared:

```
<View style={styles.container}>
```

This corresponds directly to

```
container: {
    flex: 1,
    justifyContent: 'center',
    alignItems: 'center',
    backgroundColor: '#F5FCFF',
}
```

At the bottom of the index.js file, you see

```
AppRegistry.registerComponent('myProject', () => App);
```

This is the JavaScript entry point to running all React Native apps. In the index file is the only place you'll call this function. The root component of the app should register itself with `AppRegistry.registerComponent`. The native system can then load the bundle for the app and run the app when it's ready.

Now that we've gone over what's in the file, run the project in either your iOS simulator or your Android emulator (see figure 1.4). In the text element that contains "Welcome to React Native," enter "Welcome to Hello World!" or other text of your choice. Refresh the screen, and you should see your changes.

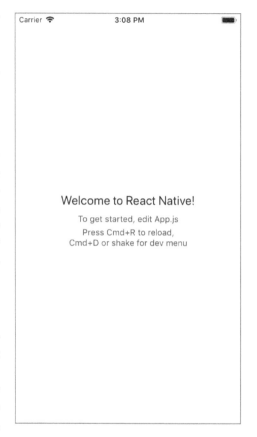

Welcome to React Native!

To get started, edit App.js
Press Cmd+R to reload,
Cmd+D or shake for dev menu

Figure 1.4   React Native starter project: what you should see after running the starter project on the emulator

Summary

- React Native is a framework for building native mobile apps in JavaScript using the React JavaScript library.
- Some of React Native's strengths are its performance, developer experience, ability to build cross platform with a single language, one-way data flow, and community. You may consider React Native over a hybrid mainly because of its performance, and over Native mainly because of the developer experience and cross-platform ability with a single language.
- JSX is a preprocessor step that adds an XML-like syntax to JavaScript. You can use JSX to create a UI in React Native.
- Components are the fundamental building blocks in React Native. They can vary in functionality and type. You can create custom components to implement common design elements.
- Components that require state or lifecycle methods need to be created using a JavaScript class by extending the `React.Component` class.
- Stateless components can be created with less boilerplate for components that don't need to keep up with their own state.
- Larger components can be created by combining smaller subcomponents.

Understanding React

2

Now that we've gone over the basics, it's time to dive into some other fundamental pieces that make up React and React Native. We'll discuss how to manage state and data, and how data is passed through an application. We'll also dive deeper by demonstrating how to pass properties (props) between components and how to manipulate these props from the top down.

After you're equipped with knowledge about state and props, we'll go deeper into how to use the built-in React lifecycle methods. These methods allow you to perform certain actions when a component is created or destroyed. Understanding them is key to understanding how React and React Native work and how to take full advantage of the framework. The lifecycle methods are also conceptually the biggest part of React and React Native.

NOTE   You'll see both React and React Native referenced in this chapter. Keep in mind that when I mention React, I'm talking not about things that are specific to React Native, but concepts that are related to both React and React Native. For example, state and props work the same in both React and React Native, as do the React lifecycle and the React component specifications.

2.1   Managing component data using state

One of the ways data is created and managed in a React or React Native component is by using state. Component state is declared when the component is created, and its structure is a plain JavaScript object. State can be updated within the component using a function called setState that we'll look at in depth shortly.

The other way data can be handled is by using props. Props are passed down as parameters when the component is created; unlike state, they can't be updated within the component.

2.1.1   Correctly manipulating component state

State is a collection of values that a component manages. React thinks of UIs as simple state machines. When the state of a component changes using the setState function, React rerenders the component. If any child components are inheriting this state as props, then all of the child components are rerendered as well.

When building an application using React Native, understanding how state works is fundamental because state determines how stateful components render and behave. Component state is what allows you to create components that are dynamic and interactive. The main point to understand when differentiating between state and props is that state is mutable, whereas props are immutable.

SETTING *INITIAL STATE*

State is initialized when a component is created either in the constructor or with a property initializer. Once the state is initialized, it's available in the component as this.state. The following listing shows an example.

Listing 2.1   Setting state with a property initializer

```
import React from 'react'

class MyComponent extends React.Component {
  state = {
    year: 2016,
    name: 'Nader Dabit',
    colors: ['blue']
  }

  render() {
    return (
      <View>
        <Text>My name is: { this.state.name }</Text>
```

```
            <Text>The year is: { this.state.year }</Text>
            <Text>My colors are { this.state.colors[0] }</Text>
          </View>
        )
      }
  }
}
```

The `constructor` function is called the moment a JavaScript class is instantiated, as shown in the next listing. This isn't a React lifecycle method, but a regular JavaScript class method.

Listing 2.2   Setting state with a constructor

```
import React {Component} from 'react'

class MyComponent extends Component {
  constructor(){
    super()
    this.state = {
      year: 2016,
      name: 'Nader Dabit',
      colors: ['blue']
    }
  }
  render() {
    return (
      <View>
        <Text>My name is: { this.state.name }</Text>
        <Text>The year is: { this.state.year }</Text>
        <Text>My colors are { this.state.colors[0] }</Text>
      </View>
    )
  }
}
```

The constructor and property initializer both work exactly the same, and which approach you use is based on preference.

UPDATING STATE

State can be updated by calling `this.setState(object)`, passing in an object with the new state you want to use. `setState` merges the previous state with the current state, so if you only pass in a single item (key-value pair), the rest of the state will remain the same, while the new item in the state will be overwritten.

Let's look at how to use `setState` (see listing 2.3). To do so, we'll introduce a new method, a touch handler called `onPress`. `onPress` can be called on a few types of "tappable" React Native components, but here you'll attach it to a `Text` component to get started with this basic example. You'll call a function called `updateYear` when the text is pressed, to update the state with `setState`. This function will be defined before the `render` function, because it's usually best practice to define any custom methods before the render method, but keep in mind that the order of the definition of the functions doesn't affect the actual functionality.

Listing 2.3   Updating state

```
import React {Component} from 'react'

class MyComponent extends Component {
    constructor(){
      super()
      this.state = {
        year: 2016,
      }
    }
    updateYear() {
      this.setState({
        year: 2017
      })
    }
    render() {
      return (
        <View>
          <Text
            onPress={() => this.updateYear()}>
            The year is: { this.state.year }
          </Text>
        </View>
      )
    }
  }
```

Figure 2.1 shows how the state is updated each time the text element in listing 2.3 is pressed. Every time `setState` is called, React will rerender the component (calling the `render` method again) and any child components. Calling `this.setState` is the way to change a state variable and trigger the `render` method again, because changing the state variable directly won't trigger a rerender of the component and therefore no changes will be visible in the UI. A common mistake for beginners is updating the state variable directly. For example, something like the following doesn't work when trying

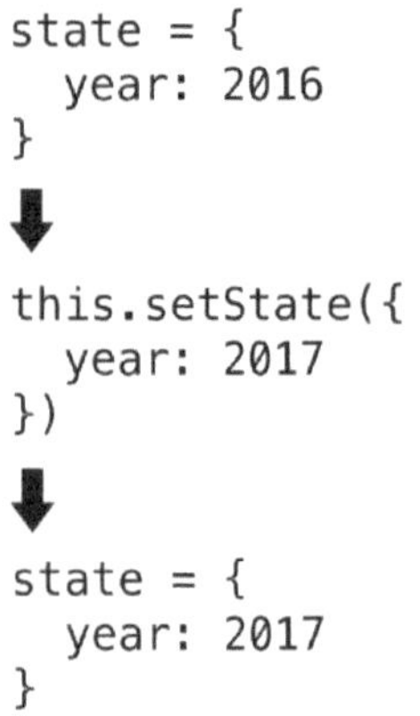

```
state = {
  year: 2016
}
```
⬇
```
this.setState({
  year: 2017
})
```
⬇
```
state = {
  year: 2017
}
```

Figure 2.1   The flow of `setState`, with arrows indicating when the text element is pressed. The state `year` property is initialized to 2016 in the constructor. Each time the text is pressed, the state `year` property is set to 2017.

to update state—the `state` object is updated, but the UI isn't updated because `set-State` isn't called and the component isn't rerendered:

```
class MyComponent extends Component {
  constructor(){
    super()
    this.state = {
      year: 2016,
    }
  }
  updateYear() {
    this.state.year = 2017
  }
  render() {
    return (
      <View>
        <Text
          onPress={() => this.updateYear()}>
          The year is: { this.state.year }
        </Text>
      </View>
    )
  }
}
```

But a method is available in React that can force an update once a state variable has been changed as in the previous snippet. This method is called `forceUpdate`; see listing 2.4. Calling `forceUpdate` causes `render` to be called on the component, triggering a rerendering of the UI. Using `forceUpdate` isn't usually necessary or recommended, but it's good to know about in case you run into it in examples or documentation. Most of the time, this rerendering can be handled using other methods such as calling `set-State` or passing in new props.

Listing 2.4   Forcing rerender with `forceUpdate`

```
class MyComponent extends Component {
  constructor(){
    super()
    this.state = {
      year: 2016
    }
  }
  updateYear() {
    this.state.year = 2017
  }
  update() {
    this.forceUpdate()
  }
  render() {
    return (
      <View>
```

```
      <Text onPress={ () => this.updateYear() }>
        The year is: { this.state.year }
      </Text>
      <Text
       onPress={ () => this. update () }>Force Update
      </Text>
    </View>
  )
  }
}
```

Now that we've gone over how to work with state using a basic string, let's look at a few other data types. You'll attach a Boolean, an array, and an object to the state and use it in the component. You'll also conditionally show a component based on a Boolean in the state.

Listing 2.5   State with other data types

```
class MyComponent extends Component {
    constructor(){
      super()
      this.state = {
        year: 2016,
        leapYear: true,
        topics: ['React', 'React Native', 'JavaScript'],
        info: {
          paperback: true,
          length: '335 pages',
          type: 'programming'
        }
      }
    }
    render() {
      let leapyear = <Text>This is not a leapyear!</Text>
      if (this.state.leapYear) {
        leapyear = <Text>This is a leapyear!</Text>
      }
      return (
        <View>
          <Text>{ this.state.year }</Text>
          <Text>Length: { this.state.info.length }</Text>
          <Text>Type: { this.state.info.type }</Text>
          { leapyear }
        </View>
      )
    }
}
```

2.2   *Managing component data using props*

Props (short for *properties*) are a component's inherited values or properties that have been passed down from a parent component. Props can be either static or dynamic values when they're declared, but when they're inherited they're immutable; they can only be altered by changing the initial values at the top level where they're declared and passed down. React's "Thinking in React" documentation says that props are best explained as "a way of passing data from parent to child." Table 2.1 highlights some of the differences and similarities between props and state.

Table 2.1 Props vs. state

Props	State
External data	Internal data
Immutable	Mutable
Inherited from a parent	Created in the component
Can be changed by a parent component	Can only be updated in the component
Can be passed down as props	Can be passed down as props
Can't change inside the component	Can change inside the component

A good way to explain how props work is to show an example. The following listing declares a book value and passes it down to a child component as a static prop.

Listing 2.6 Static props

```
class MyComponent extends Component {
  render() {
    return (
      <BookDisplay book="React Native in Action" />
    )
  }
}
class BookDisplay extends Component {
  render() {
    return (
      <View>
        <Text>{ this.props.book }</Text>
      </View>
    )
  }
}
```

This code creates two components: <MyComponent /> and <BookDisplay />. When you create <BookDisplay />, you pass in a property called book and set it to the string "React Native in Action". Anything passed as a property in this way is available on the child component as this.props.

You can also pass down literals as you would variables, by using curly braces and a string value as shown next.

Listing 2.7   Displaying static props

```
class MyComponent extends Component {
  render() {
    return (
      <BookDisplay book={"React Native in Action"} />
    )
  }
}
class BookDisplay extends Component {
  render() {
    return (
      <View>
        <Text>{ this.props.book }</Text>
      </View>
    )
  }
}
```

DYNAMIC PROPS

Next, pass a dynamic property to the component. In the `render` method, before the `return` statement, declare a variable `book` and pass it in as a prop.

Listing 2.8   Dynamic props

```
class MyComponent extends Component {
    render() {
      let book = 'React Native in Action'
      return (
        <BookDisplay book={ book } />
      )
    }
  }

class BookDisplay extends Component {
  render() {
    return (
      <View>
        <Text>{ this.props.book }</Text>
      </View>
    )
  }
}
```

Now, pass a dynamic property to the component using state.

Listing 2.9   Dynamic props using state

```
class MyComponent extends Component {
  constructor() {
    super()
    this.state = {
      book: 'React Native in Action'
```

```
      }
    }
  render() {
    return (
      <BookDisplay book={this.state.book} />
    )
  }
}
class BookDisplay extends Component {
  render() {
    return (
      <View>
        <Text>{ this.props.book }</Text>
      </View>
    )
  }
}
```

Next, let's look at how to update the state and, consequently, the value passed down as the prop to BookDisplay. Remember, props are immutable, so you'll change the state of the parent component (MyComponent), which will supply a new value to the Book-Display book prop and trigger a rerender of both the component and the child component. Breaking this idea into individual parts, here's what needs to be done:

1 Declare the state variable:

```
this.state = {
  book: 'React Native in Action'
}
```

2 Write a function that will update the state variable:

```
updateBook() {
  this.setState({
    book: 'Express in Action'
  })
}
```

3 Pass the function and the state down to the child component as props:

```
<BookDisplay
  updateBook={ () => this.updateBook() }
  book={ this.state.book } />
```

4 Attach the function to the touch handler in the child component:

```
<Text onPress={ this.props.updateBook }>
```

Now that you know the pieces you need, you can write the code to put this into action. You'll use the components from the previous examples and add the new functionality.

Listing 2.10 Updating dynamic props

```
class MyComponent extends Component {
  constructor(){
    super()
```

```
      this.state = {
        book: 'React Native in Action'
      }
    }
  updateBook() {
    this.setState({
    book: 'Express in Action'
    })
  }
  render() {
    return (
      <BookDisplay
       updateBook={ () => this.updateBook() }
       book={ this.state.book } />
    )
  }
}
class BookDisplay extends Component {
  render() {
    return (
      <View>
        <Text
         onPress={ this.props.updateBook }>
          { this.props.book }
        </Text>
      </View>
    )
  }
}
```

DESTRUCTURING PROPS AND STATE

Constantly referring to state and props as this.state and this.props can get repetitive, violating the DRY (don't repeat yourself) principle that many of us try to follow. To fix this, you can try using destructuring. *Destructuring* is a new JavaScript feature that was added as part of the ES2015 spec and is available in React Native applications. The basic idea is that you can take properties from an object and use them as variables in an app:

```
const person = { name: 'Jeff', age: 22 }

const { age } = person

console.log(age)    #22
```

Write a component using destructuring, as shown next.

Listing 2.11   Destructuring state and props

```
class MyComponent extends Component {
  constructor(){
    super()
    this.state = {
      book: 'React Native in Action'
    }
```

```
    }
    updateBook() {
      this.setState({ book: 'Express in Action' })
    }
    render() {
      const { book } = this.state
      return (
        <BookDisplay
          updateBook={ () => this.updateBook() }
          book={ book } />
      )
    }
  }
class BookDisplay extends Component {
    render() {
      const { book, updateBook } = this.props
      return (
        <View>
          <Text
            onPress={ updateBook }>
            { book }
          </Text>
        </View>
      )
    }
  }
```

You no longer have to refer to `this.state` or `this.props` in the component when referencing the book; instead, you've taken the book variable out of the state and the props and can reference the variable itself. This starts to make more sense and will keep your code cleaner as your state and props become larger and more complex.

PROPS WITH STATELESS COMPONENTS

Because stateless components only have to worry about props and don't have their own state, they can be extremely useful when creating reusable components. Let's see how props are used in a stateless component.

To access props using a stateless component, pass in `props` as the first argument to the function.

Listing 2.12 Props with stateless components

```
const BookDisplay = (props) => {
  const { book, updateBook } = props
  return (
    <View>
      <Text
        onPress={ updateBook }>
        { book }
      </Text>
    </View>
  )
}
```

You can also destructure props in the function argument.

Listing 2.13   Destructuring props in a stateless component

```
const BookDisplay = ({ updateBook, book }) => {
  return (
    <View>
      <Text
        onPress={ updateBook }>
        { book }
      </Text>
    </View>
  )
}
```

That looks much nicer and cleans up a lot of unnecessary code! You should use state-less components wherever you can, simplifying your codebase and logic.

> **NOTE** Stateless components are often referred to as *functional* components, because they can be written as functions in JavaScript.

PASSING ARRAYS AND OBJECTS AS PROPS

Other data types work exactly as you might expect. For example, to pass an array, you pass in the array as a prop. To pass an object, you pass in the object as a prop. Let's look at a basic example.

Listing 2.14   Passing other data types as props

```
class MyComponent extends Component {
  constructor(){
    super()
    this.state = {
      leapYear: true,
      info: {
        type: 'programming'
      }
    }
  }
  render() {
    return (
      <BookDisplay
        leapYear={ this.state.leapYear }
        info={ this.state.info }
        topics={['React', 'React Native', 'JavaScript']} />
    )
  }
}
const BookDisplay = (props) => {
  let leapyear
  let { topics } = props
  const { info } = props
  topics = topics.map((topic, i) => {
    return <Text>{ topic }</Text>
```

```
  })
  if (props.leapYear) {
    leapyear = <Text>This is a leapyear!</Text>
  }
  return (
    <View>
        { leapyear }
        <Text>Book type: { info.type }</Text>
        { topics }
    </View>
  )
}
```

2.3 React component specifications

When creating React and React Native components, you can hook into several specifications and lifecycle methods to control what's going on in your component. In this section, we'll discuss them and give you a good understanding of what each one does and when you should use them.

First we'll go over the basics of the component specifications. A component *specification* basically lays out how a component should react to different things happening in the lifecycle of the component. The specifications are as follows:

- render method
- constructor method
- statics object, used to define static methods available to a class

2.3.1 Using the render method to create a UI

The render method is the only method in the component specification that's required when creating a component. It must return either a single child element, null, or false. This child element can be a component you declared (such as a View or Text component), or another component you defined (maybe a Button component you created and imported into the file):

```
render() {
  return (
    <View>
      <Text>Hello</Text>
    </View>
  )
}
```

You can use the render method with or without parentheses. If you don't use parentheses, then the returned element must of course be on the same line as the return statement:

```
render() {
  return <View><Text>Hello</Text></View>
}
```

The render method can also return another component that was defined elsewhere:

```
render() {
   return <SomeComponent />
}
#or
render() {
   return (
      <SomeComponent />
   )
}
```

You can also check for conditionals in the render method, perform logic, and return components based on their value:

```
render() {
  if(something === true) {
    return <SomeComponent />
  } else return <SomeOtherComponent />
}
```

2.3.2   *Using property initializers and constructors*

State can be created in a constructor or using a *property initializer*. Property initializers are an ES7 specification to the JavaScript language, but they work out of the box with React Native. They provide a concise way to declare state in a React class:

```
class MyComponent extends React.Component {
   state = {
     someNumber: 1,
     someBoolean: false
   }
```

You can also use a constructor method to set the initial state when using classes. The concept of classes, as well as the constructor function, isn't specific to React or React Native; it's an ES2015 specification and is just syntactic sugar on top of JavaScript's existing prototype-based inheritance for creating and initializing an object created with a class. Other properties can also be set for a component class in the constructor by declaring them with the syntax this.property (property being the name of the property). The keyword this refers to the current class instance you're in:

```
constructor(){
  super()
  this.state = {
    someOtherNumber: 19,
    someOtherBoolean: true
  }
  this.name = 'Hello World'
  this.type = 'class'
  this.loaded = false
}
```

When using a constructor to create a React class, you must use the super keyword before you can use the this keyword, because you're extending another class. Also, if you need access to any props in the constructor, they must be passed as an argument to the constructor and the super call.

Setting the state based on props usually isn't good practice unless you're intentionally setting some type of seed data for the component's internal functionality, because the data will no longer be consistent across components if it's changed. State is only created when the component is first mounted or created. If you rerender the same component using different prop values, then any instances of that component that have already been mounted won't use the new prop values to update state.

The following example shows props being used to set state values within the constructor. Let's say you pass in "Nader Dabit" as the props to the component initially: the `fullName` property in the state will be "Nader Dabit". If the component is then rerendered with "Another Name", the constructor won't be called a second time, so the state value for `fullName` will remain "Nader Dabit":

```
constructor(props) {
    super(props)
    this.state = {
        fullName: props.first + ' ' + props.last,
    }
}
```

2.4 *React lifecycle methods*

Various methods are executed at specific points in a component's lifecycle: these are called the *lifecycle methods*. Understanding how they work is important because they allow you to perform specific actions at different points in the creation and destruction of a component. For example, suppose you wanted to make an API call that returned some data. You'd probably want to make sure the component was ready to render this data, so you'd make the API call once the component was mounted in a method called `componentDidMount`. In this section, we'll go over the lifecycle methods and explain how they work.

The life of a React component has three stages: creation (mounting), updating, and deletion (unmounting). During these three stages, you can hook into three sets of lifecycle methods:

- *Mounting (creation)*—When a component is created, a series of lifecycle methods are triggered and you have the option to hook into any or all of them: `constructor`, `getDerivedStateFromProps`, `render`, and `componentDidMount`. The one such method you've used so far is `render`, which renders and returns a UI.
- *Updating*—When a component updates, the update lifecycle methods are triggered: `getDerivedStateFromProps` (when props change), `shouldComponentUpdate`, `render`, `getSnapshotBeforeUpdate`, and `componentDidUpdate`. An update can happen in one of two ways:
  - When `setState` or `forceUpdate` is called within a component
  - When new props are passed down into the component
- *Unmounting*—When the component is unmounted (destroyed), a final lifecycle method is triggered: `componentWillUnmount`.

2.4.1   *The static getDerivedStateFromProps method*

getDerivedStateFromProps is a static class method that is called both when the component is created and when it receives new props. This method receives the new props and most up-to-date state as arguments and returns an object. The data in the object is updated to the state. The following listing shows an example.

Listing 2.15   `static getDerivedStateFromProps`

```
export default class App extends Component {
  state = {
    userLoggedIn: false
  }
  static getDerivedStateFromProps(nextProps, nextState) {
    if (nextProps.user.authenticated) {
      return {
        userLoggedIn: true
      }
    }
    return null
  }
  render() {
    return (
      <View style={styles.container}>
        {
          this.state.userLoggedIn && (
            <AuthenticatedComponent />>
          )
        }
      </View>
    );
  }
}
```

2.4.2   *The componentDidMount lifecycle method*

componentDidMount is called exactly once, just after the component has been loaded. This method is a good place to fetch data with AJAX calls, perform setTimeout functions, and integrate with other JavaScript frameworks.

Listing 2.16   `componentDidMount`

```
class MainComponent extends Component {
  constructor() {
    super()
    this.state = { loading: true, data: {} }
  }
  componentDidMount() {
     #simulate ajax call
    setTimeout(() => {
      this.setState({
        loading: false,
        data: {name: 'Nader Dabit', age: 35}
```

```
    })
  }, 2000)
}
render() {
  if(this.state.loading) {
    return <Text>Loading</Text>
  }
  const { name, age } = this.state.data
  return (
    <View>
      <Text>Name: {name}</Text>
      <Text>Age: {age}</Text>
    </View>
  )
}
}
```

2.4.3 *The shouldComponentUpdate lifecycle method*

shouldComponentUpdate returns a Boolean and lets you decide when a component renders. If you know the new state or props won't require the component or any of its children to render, you can return false. If you want the component to rerender, return true.

Listing 2.17 `shouldComponentUpdate`

```
class MainComponent extends Component {
  shouldComponentUpdate(nextProps, nextState) {
    if(nextProps.name !== this.props.name) {
      return true
    }
    return false
  }
  render() {
    return <SomeComponent />
  }
}
```

2.4.4 *The componentDidUpdate lifecycle method*

componentDidUpdate is invoked immediately after the component has been updated and rerendered. You get the previous state and previous props as arguments.

Listing 2.18 `componentDidUpdate`

```
class MainComponent extends Component {
  componentDidUpdate(prevProps, prevState) {
    if(prevState.showToggled === this.state.showToggled) {
      this.setState({
        showToggled: !showToggled
      })
    }
  }
}
```

```
  render() {
    return <SomeComponent />
  }
}
```

2.4.5   *The componentWillUnmount lifecycle method*

componentWillUnmount is called before the component is removed from the application. Here, you can perform any necessary cleanup, remove listeners, and remove timers that were set up in componentDidMount.

Listing 2.19   componentWillUnmount

```
class MainComponent extends Component {

  handleClick() {
    this._timeout = setTimeout(() => {
      this.openWidget();
    }, 2000);
  }
  componentWillUnmount() {
    clearTimeout(this._timeout);
  }
  render() {
    return <SomeComponent
           handleClick={() => this.handleClick()} />
  }
}
```

Summary

- State is a way to handle data in React components. Updating state rerenders the UI of the component and any child component relying on this data as props.
- Properties (props) are how data is passed down through a React Native application to child components. Updating props automatically updates any components receiving the same props.
- A React component specification is a group of methods and properties in a React component that specifies the declaration of the component. render is the only required method when creating a React component; all other methods and properties are optional.
- There are three main stages in a React component's lifecycle: creation (mounting), updating, and deletion (unmounting). Each has its own set of lifecycle methods.
- React lifecycle methods are available in a React component and are executed at specific points in the component's lifecycle. They control how the component functions and updates.

Building your first React Native app

3

When learning a new framework, technology, language, or concept, diving directly into the process by building a real app is a great way to jump-start the learning process. Now that you understand the basics of how React and React Native work, let's put these pieces together to make your first app: a todo app. Going through the process of building a small app and using the information we've gone over so far will be a good way to reinforce your understanding of how to use React Native.

You'll use some functionality in the app that we haven't yet covered in depth, and some styling nuances we've yet to discuss, but don't worry. Instead of going over these new ideas one by one now, you'll build the basic app and then learn about these concepts in detail in later chapters. Take this opportunity to play around with the app as you build it to learn as much as possible in the process: feel free to break and fix styles and components to see what happens.

3.1   *Laying out the todo app*

Let's get started building the todo app. It will be similar in style and functionality to the apps on the TodoMVC site (http://todomvc.com). Figure 3.1 shows how the app will look when you're finished, so you can conceptualize what components you need and how to structure them. As in chapter 1, figure 3.2 breaks the app into components and container components. Let's see how this will look in the app using a basic implementation of React Native components.

Listing 3.1   Basic todo app implementation

```
<View>
  <Heading />
  <Input />
  <TodoList />
  <Button />
  <TabBar />
</View>
```

The app will display a heading, a text input, a button, and a tab bar. When you add a todo, the app will add it to the array of todos and display the new todo beneath the input. Each todo will have two buttons: Done and Delete. The Done button will mark it as complete, and the Delete button will remove it from the array of todos. At the bottom of the screen, the tab bar will filter the todos based on whether they're complete or still active.

Figure 3.1   Todo app design

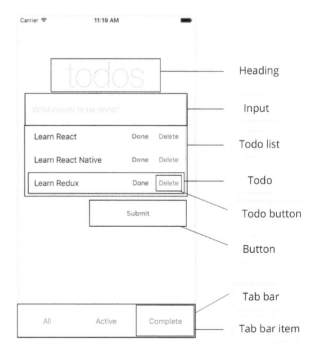

Figure 3.2   Todo app with descriptions

3.2 Coding the todo app

Let's get started coding the app. Create a new React Native project by typing `react-native init TodoApp` in your terminal (see figure 3.3). Now, go into your index file: if you're developing for iOS, open index.iOS.js; and if you're developing for Android, open index.Android.js. The code for both platforms will be the same.

> **NOTE** I'm using React Native version 0.51.0 for this example. Newer versions may have API changes, but nothing should be broken for building the todo app. You're welcome to use the most recent version of React Native, but if you run into issues, use the exact version I'm using here.

In the index file, import an `App` component (which you'll create soon), and delete the styling along with any extra components you're no longer using.

Listing 3.2 index.js

```
import React from 'react'
import { AppRegistry } from 'react-native'
import App from './app/App'

  const TodoApp = () => <App />

AppRegistry.registerComponent('TodoApp', () => TodoApp)
```

Here, you bring in `AppRegistry` from `react-native`. You also bring in the main `App` component, which you'll create next.

In the `AppRegistry` method, you initiate the application. `AppRegistry` is the JS entry point to running all React Native apps. It takes two arguments: the `appKey`, or the name of the application you defined when you initialized the app; and a function that returns the React Native component you want to use as the entry point of the app. In this case, you're returning the `TodoApp` component declared in listing 3.2.

Now, create a folder called app in the root of the application. In the app folder, create a file called App.js and add the basic code shown in the next listing.

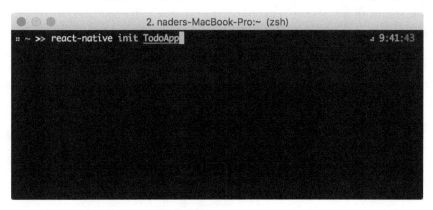

Figure 3.3   Initializing a new React Native app

Listing 3.3   Creating the App component

```
import React, { Component } from 'react'
import { View, ScrollView, StyleSheet } from 'react-native'

class App extends Component {
  render() {
    return (
      <View style={styles.container}>
        <ScrollView keyboardShouldPersistTaps='always'
                    style={styles.content}>
          <View/>
        </ScrollView>
      </View>
    )
  }
}

const styles = StyleSheet.create({
  container: {
    flex: 1,
    backgroundColor: '#f5f5f5'
  },
  content: {
    flex: 1,
    paddingTop: 60
  }
})

export default App
```

You import a new component called ScrollView, which wraps the platform Scroll-View and is basically a scrollable View component. A keyboardShouldPersistTaps prop of always is added: this prop will dismiss the keyboard if it's open and allow the UI to process any onPress events. You make sure both the ScrollView and the parent View of the ScrollView have a flex:1 value. flex:1 is a style value that makes the component fill the entire space of its parent container.

Now, set up an initial state for some of the values you'll need later. You need an array to keep your todos, which you'll name todos; a value to hold the current state of the TextInput that will add the todos, named inputValue; and a value to store the type of todo that you're currently viewing (All, Current, or Active), named type.

In App.js, before the render function, add a constructor and an initial state to the class, and initialize these values in the state.

Listing 3.4   Setting the initial state

```
...

class App extends Component {
  constructor() {
    super()
```

```
      this.state = {
        inputValue: '',
        todos: [],
        type: 'All'
      }
    }
    render() {
      ...
    }
}

...
```

Next, create the Heading component and give it some styling. In the app folder, create a file called Heading.js. This will be a stateless component.

```
import React from 'react'
import { View, Text, StyleSheet } from 'react-native'

const Heading = () => (
  <View style={styles.header}>
    <Text style={styles.headerText}>
      todos
    </Text>
  </View>
)

const styles = StyleSheet.create({
  header: {
    marginTop: 80
  },
  headerText: {
    textAlign: 'center',
    fontSize: 72,
    color: 'rgba(175, 47, 47, 0.25)',
    fontWeight: '100'
  }
})

export default Heading
```

Note that in the styling of headerText, you pass an rgba value to color. If you aren't familiar with RGBA, the first three values make up the RGB color values, and the last value represents the alpha or opacity (red, blue, green, alpha). You pass in an alpha value of 0.25, or 25%. You also set the font weight to 100, which will give the text a thinner weight and look.

Go back into App.js, bring in the Heading component, and place it in the Scroll-View, replacing the empty View you originally placed there.

Run the app to see the new heading and app layout: see figure 3.4. To run the app in iOS, use `react-native run-ios`. To run in Android, use `react-native run-android` in your terminal from the root of your React Native application.

Listing 3.6   Importing and using the `Heading` component

```
import React, { Component } from 'react'
import {View, ScrollView, StyleSheet} from 'react-native'
import Heading from './Heading'

class App extends Component {
  ...
  render() {
    return (
      <View style={styles.container}>
        <ScrollView
         keyboardShouldPersistTaps='always'
         style={styles.content}>
          <Heading />
        </ScrollView>
      </View>
    )
  }
}
...
```

Figure 3.4   Running the app

Next, create the TextInput component and give it some styling. In the app folder, create a file called Input.js.

Listing 3.7   Creating the TextInput component

```
import React from 'react'
import { View, TextInput, StyleSheet } from 'react-native'

const Input = () => (
  <View style={styles.inputContainer}>
    <TextInput
      style={styles.input}
      placeholder='What needs to be done?'
      placeholderTextColor='#CACACA'
      selectionColor='#666666' />
  </View>
)

const styles = StyleSheet.create({
  inputContainer: {
    marginLeft: 20,
    marginRight: 20,
    shadowOpacity: 0.2,
    shadowRadius: 3,
    shadowColor: '#000000',
    shadowOffset: { width: 2, height: 2 }
  },
  input: {
    height: 60,
    backgroundColor: '#ffffff',
    paddingLeft: 10,
    paddingRight: 10
  }
})
```

```
export default Input
```

You're using a new React Native component called TextInput here. If you're familiar with web development, this is similar to an HTML input. You also give both the TextInput and the outer View their own styling.

TextInput takes a few other props. Here, you specify a placeholder to show text before the user starts to type, a placeholderTextColor that styles the placeholder text, and a selectionColor that styles the cursor for the TextInput.

The next step, in section 3.4, will be to wire up a function to get the value of the TextInput and save it to the state of the App component. You'll also go into App.js and add a new function called inputChange below the constructor and above the render function. This function will update the state value of inputValue with the value passed in, and for now will also log out the value of inputValue for you to make sure the function is working by using console.log(). But to view console.log() statements in React Native, you first need to open the developer menu. Let's see how it works.

3.3   Opening the developer menu

The developer menu is a built-in menu available as a part of React Native; it gives you access to the main debugging tools you'll use. You can open it in the iOS simulator or in the Android emulator. In this section, I'll show you how to open and use the developer menu on both platforms.

> **NOTE**   If you aren't interested in the developer menu or want to skip this section for now, go to section 3.4 to continue building the todo app.

3.3.1   Opening the developer menu in the iOS simulator

While the project is running in the iOS simulator, you can open the developer menu in one of three ways:

- Press Cmd-D on the keyboard.
- Press Cmd-Ctrl-Z on the keyboard.
- Open the Hardware > Shake Gesture menu in the simulator options (see figure 3.5).

When you do, you should see the developer menu, shown in figure 3.6.

> **NOTE**   If Cmd-D or Cmd-Ctrl-Z doesn't open the menu, you may need to connect your hardware to the keyboard. To do this, go to Hardware > Keyboard > Connect Hardware Keyboard in your simulator menu.

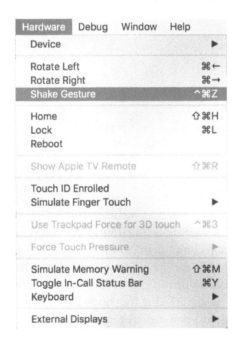

Figure 3.5   Manually opening the developer menu (iOS simulator)

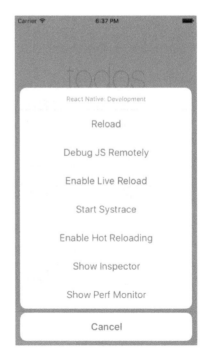

Figure 3.6   React Native developer menu (iOS simulator)

3.3.2 Opening the developer menu in the Android emulator

With the project open and running in the Android emulator, the developer menu can be opened in one of three ways:

- Press F2 on the keyboard.
- Press Cmd-M on the keyboard.
- Press the Hardware button (see figure 3.7).

When you do, you should see the developer menu shown in figure 3.8.

Figure 3.7   Manually opening the hardware menu (Android emulator)

Figure 3.8   React Native developer menu (Android emulator)

3.3.3 Using the developer menu

When the developer menu opens, you should see the following options:

- *Reload (iOS and Android)*—Reloads the app. This can also be done by pressing Cmd-R on the keyboard (iOS) or pressing R twice (Android).
- *Debug JS Remotely (iOS and Android)*—Opens the Chrome dev tools and gives you full debugging support through the browser (figure 3.9). Here, you have access not only to logging statements in your code, but also to breakpoints and whatever you're used to while debugging web apps (with the exception of the DOM). If you need to log any information or data in your app, this is usually the place to do so.

Figure 3.9   Debugging in Chrome

- *Enable Live Reload (iOS and Android)*—Enables live reload. When you make changes in your code, the entire app will reload and refresh in the simulator.
- *Start Systrace (iOS only)*—Systrace is a profiling tool. This will give you a good idea of where your time is being spent during each 16 ms frame while your app is running. Profiled code blocks are surrounded by start/end markers that are then visualized in a colorful chart format. Systrace can also be enabled manually from the command line in Android. If you want to learn more, check out the docs for a very comprehensive overview.
- *Enable Hot Reloading (iOS and Android)*—A great feature added in version .22 of React Native. It offers an amazing developer experience, giving you the ability to see your changes immediately as files are changed without losing the current state of the app. This is especially useful for making UI changes deep in your app without losing state. It's different than live reloading because it retains the current state of your app, only updating the components and state that have been changed (live reloading reloads the entire app, therefore losing the current state).
- *Toggle Inspector (iOS and Android)*—Brings up a property inspector similar to what you see in the Chrome dev tools. You can click an element and see where it is in the hierarchy of components, as well as any styling applied to the element (figure 3.10).

Figure 3.10   Using the inspector (left: iOS, right: Android)

- *Show Perf Monitor (iOS and Android)*—Brings up a small box in the upper-left corner of the app, giving some information about the app's performance. Here you'll see the amount of RAM being used and the number of frames per second at which the app is currently running. If you click the box, it will expand to show even more information (figure 3.11).
- *Dev Settings (Android emulator only)*—Brings up additional debugging options, including an easy way to toggle between the __DEV__ environment variable being true or false (figure 3.12).

Figure 3.11   Perf Monitor (left: iOS, right: Android)

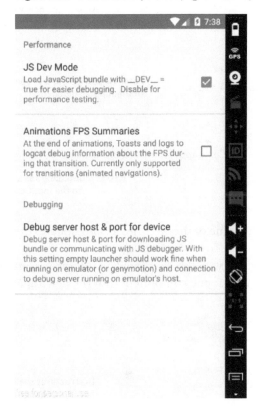

Figure 3.12   Dev Settings (Android emulator)

3.4   *Continuing building the todo app*

Now that you know how the developer menu works, open it and press Debug JS Remotely to open the Chrome dev tools. You're ready to start logging information to the JavaScript console.

You'll import the `Input` component into app/App.js and attach a method to `TextInput`, which you'll give as a prop to the `Input`. You'll also pass the `inputValue` stored on the state to `Input` as a prop.

Listing 3.8   Creating the `inputChange` function

```
...
import Heading from './Heading'
```

```
import Input from './Input'                        Creates the inputChange method, which
class App extends Component {                        takes inputValue as an argument
  constructor() {
    ...                                                    Logs out the inputValue value to
  }                                                         make sure the method is working
  inputChange(inputValue) {
    console.log(' Input Value: ' , inputValue)
    this.setState({ inputValue })
  }                                                      Sets the state with the new value—same as
  render() {                                              this.setState({inputValue: inputValue})
    const { inputValue } = this.state
    return (
      <View style={styles.container}>
        <ScrollView
          keyboardShouldPersistTaps='always'            Passes inputValue as a property
          style={styles.content}>                        to the Input component
          <Heading />
          <Input
            inputValue={inputValue}
            inputChange={(text) => this.inputChange(text)} />
        </ScrollView>                                  Passes inputChange as a property
      </View>                                            to the Input component
    )
  }
}}
```

inputChange takes one argument, the value of the TextInput, and updates the input-
Value in the state with the returned value from the TextInput.

Now, you need to wire up the function with the TextInput in the Input component.
Open app/Input.js, and update the TextInput component with the new inputChange
function and the inputValue property.

> **Listing 3.9   Adding inputChange and inputValue to the TextInput**

```
...
const Input = ({ inputValue, inputChange }) => (
  <View style={styles.inputContainer}>                  Destructures the inputValue
    <TextInput                                           and inputChange props
      value={inputValue}
      style={styles.input}
      placeholder='What needs to be done?'
      placeholderTextColor='#CACACA'
      selectionColor='#666666'                          Sets the onChangeText
      onChangeText={inputChange} />                      method to inputChange
  </View>
)
...
```

You destructure the props inputValue and inputChange in the creation of the stateless
component. When the value of the TextInput changes, the inputChange function is
called, and the value is passed to the parent component to set the state of inputValue.
You also set the value of the TextInput to be inputValue, so you can later control and
reset the TextInput. onChangeText is a method that will be called every time the value
of the TextInput component is changed and will be passed the value of the TextInput.

Run the project again and see how it looks (figure 3.13). You're logging the value of the input, so as you type you should see the value being logged out to the console (figure 3.14).

Figure 3.13 Updated view after adding the `TextInput`

```
⊙  ▽   chrome-extension://fm...gofadop ▾   ☐ Preserve log ☑ Show all messages

  Console was cleared                                                    debugger-ui:75
  Running application "TodoApp" with appParams: {"rootTag":1,"initialProps":{}}. __DEV__   infoLog.js:17
  === true, development-level warning are ON, performance optimizations are OFF
  Input Value:  H                                                        App.js:26
  Input Value:  He                                                       App.js:26
  Input Value:  Hel                                                      App.js:26
  Input Value:  Hell                                                     App.js:26
  Input Value:  Hello                                                    App.js:26
  Input Value:  Hello                                                    App.js:26
  Input Value:  Hello w                                                  App.js:26
  Input Value:  Hello wo                                                 App.js:26
  Input Value:  Hello wor                                                App.js:26
  Input Value:  Hello worl                                               App.js:26
  Input Value:  Hello world                                              App.js:26
> |
```

Figure 3.14 Logging out the `TextInput` value with the `inputChange` method

Now that the value of the `inputValue` is being stored in the state, you need to create a button to add the items to a list of todos. Before you do, create a function that you'll bind to the button to add the new todo to the array of todos defined in the constructor. Call this function `submitTodo`, and place it after the `inputChange` function and before the `render` function.

Listing 3.10   Adding the `submitTodo` function

If inputValue isn't empty, creates and assigns a todo variable an object with a title, a todoIndex, and a complete Boolean (you'll create the todoIndex shortly).

Checks whether inputValue is empty or only contains whitespace. If it's empty, returns without doing anything else.

```
...
submitTodo () {
  if (this.state.inputValue.match(/^\s*$/)) {
    return
  }
  const todo = {
    title: this.state.inputValue,
    todoIndex,
    complete: false
  }
  todoIndex++
  const todos = [...this.state.todos, todo]
  this.setState({ todos, inputValue: '' }, () => {
    console.log('State: ', this.state)
  })
}
...
```

Increments the todoIndex

Pushes the new todo to the existing array of todos

Once the state is set, you have the option to pass a callback function. Here, a callback function from setState logs out the state to make sure everything is working.

Sets the state of the todos to match the updated array of this.state.todos, and resets inputValue to an empty string

Next, create the `todoIndex` at the top of the App.js file, below the last `import` statement.

Listing 3.11   Creating the `todoIndex` variable

```
...
import Input from './Input'

let todoIndex = 0

class App extends Component {
...
```

Now that the `submitTodo` function has been created, create a file called Button.js and wire up the function to work with the button.

Listing 3.12   Creating the `Button` component

```
import React from 'react'
import { View, Text, StyleSheet, TouchableHighlight } from 'react-native'
```

```
const Button = ({ submitTodo }) => (
  <View style={styles.buttonContainer}>
    <TouchableHighlight
      underlayColor='#efefef'
      style={styles.button}
      onPress={submitTodo}>
      <Text style={styles.submit}>
        Submit
      </Text>
    </TouchableHighlight>
  </View>
)

const styles = StyleSheet.create({
  buttonContainer: {
    alignItems: 'flex-end'
  },
  button: {
    height: 50,
    paddingLeft: 20,
    paddingRight: 20,
    backgroundColor: '#ffffff',
    width: 200,
    marginRight: 20,
    marginTop: 15,
    borderWidth: 1,
    borderColor: 'rgba(0,0,0,.1)',
    justifyContent: 'center',
    alignItems: 'center'
  },
  submit: {
    color: '#666666',
    fontWeight: '600'
  }
})
```

Destructures the submitTodo function, which was passed as a prop to the component

Attaches submitTodo to the onPress function available to the TouchableHighlight component. This function will be called when the TouchableHighlight is touched or pressed.

```
export default Button
```

In this component, you use TouchableHighlight for the first time. TouchableHighlight is one of the ways you can create buttons in React Native and is fundamentally comparable to the HTML button element.

With TouchableHighlight, you can wrap views and make them respond properly to touch events. On press down, the default backgroundColor is replaced with a specified underlayColor property that you'll provide as a prop. Here you specify an underlayColor of '#efefef', which is a light gray; the background color is white. This will give the user a good sense of whether the touch event has registered. If no underlayColor is defined, it defaults to black.

TouchableHighlight supports only one main child component. Here, you pass in a Text component. If you want multiple components in a TouchableHighlight, wrap them in a single View, and pass this View as the child of the TouchableHighlight.

NOTE There's also quite a bit of styling going on in listing 3.12. Don't worry about styling specifics in this chapter: we cover them in depth in chapters 4 and 5. But do look at them, to get an idea how styling works in each component. This will help a lot in the in-depth later chapters, because you'll already have been exposed to some styling properties and how they work.

You've created the `Button` component and wired it up with the function defined in App.js. Now bring this component into the app (app/App.js) and see if it works!

Listing 3.13 Importing the `Button` component

```
...
import Button from './Button'              ◄── Imports the new Button component

let todoIndex = 0

...
constructor() {
    super()
    this.state = {
      inputValue: '',
      todos: [],                            Binds the method to the class in
      type: 'All'                           the constructor. Because you're
    }                                       using classes, functions won't be
    this.submitTodo = this.submitTodo.bind(this)  ◄── auto-bound to the class.
  }
...
render () {
    let { inputValue } = this.state
    return (
      <View style={styles.container}>
        <ScrollView
          keyboardShouldPersistTaps='always'   Place the Button below the
          style={styles.content}>              Input component, and pass in
          <Heading />                          submitTodo as a prop.
          <Input
            inputValue={inputValue}
            inputChange={(text) => this.inputChange(text)} />
          <Button submitTodo={this.submitTodo} />  ◄──
        </ScrollView>
      </View>
    )
  }
```

You import the `Button` component and place it under the `Input` component in the render function. `submitTodo` is passed in to the `Button` as a property called `this.submitTodo`.

Now, refresh the app. It should look like figure 3.15. When you add a todo, the `TextInput` should clear, and the app state should log to the console, showing an array of todos with the new todo in the array (figure 3.16).

Now that you're adding todos to the array of todos, you need to render them to the screen. To get started with this, you need to create two new components: `TodoList` and `Todo`. `TodoList` will render the list of `Todos` and will use the `Todo` component for each individual todo. Begin by creating a file named Todo.js in the app folder.

Figure 3.15   Updated app with the `Button` component

```
Elements  Sources  Network  Console  Timeline  Profiles  Application  Security  Audits  Redux                    :  ✕

⊘ ▽   chrome-extension://fm...gofadop ▼  ☐ Preserve log  ☑ Show all messages

Console was cleared                                                                                    debugger-ui:75
Running application "TodoApp" with appParams: {"rootTag":1,"initialProps":{}}. __DEV__ === true, development-level    infoLog.js:17
warning are ON, performance optimizations are OFF
State:  ▼ Object {inputValue: "", todos: Array[1], type: "All"} ⓘ                                       App.js:36
            inputValue: ""
          ▼ todos: Array[1]
            ▼ 0: Object
                complete: false
                title: "Todo 1"
                todoIndex: 0
              ▶ __proto__: Object
              length: 1
            ▶ __proto__: Array[0]
            type: "All"
          ▶ __proto__: Object
  ›
```

Figure 3.16   Logging the state

Listing 3.14 Creating the Todo component

```
import React from 'react'
import { View, Text, StyleSheet } from 'react-native'

const Todo = ({ todo }) => (
  <View style={styles.todoContainer}>
    <Text style={styles.todoText}>
      {todo.title}
    </Text>
  </View>
)

const styles = StyleSheet.create({
  todoContainer: {
    marginLeft: 20,
    marginRight: 20,
    backgroundColor: '#ffffff',
    borderTopWidth: 1,
    borderRightWidth: 1,
    borderLeftWidth: 1,
    borderColor: '#ededed',
    paddingLeft: 14,
    paddingTop: 7,
    paddingBottom: 7,
    shadowOpacity: 0.2,
    shadowRadius: 3,
    shadowColor: '#000000',
    shadowOffset: { width: 2, height: 2 },
    flexDirection: 'row',
    alignItems: 'center'
  },
  todoText: {
    fontSize: 17
  }
})

export default Todo
```

The Todo component takes one property for now—a todo—and renders the title in a Text component. You also add styling to the View and Text components.

Next, create the TodoList component (app/TodoList.js).

Listing 3.15 Creating the TodoList component

```
import React from 'react'
import { View } from 'react-native'
import Todo from './Todo'

const TodoList = ({ todos }) => {
  todos = todos.map((todo, i) => {
    return (
      <Todo
        key={todo.todoIndex}
        todo={todo} />
```

```
      )
    })
    return (
      <View>
        {todos}
      </View>
    )
}

export default TodoList
```

The TodoList component takes one property for now: an array of todos. You then map over these todos and create a new Todo component (imported at the top of the file) for each todo, passing in the todo as a property to the Todo component. You also specify a key and pass in the index of the todo item as a key to each component. The key property helps React identify the items that have changed when the diff with the virtual DOM is computed. React will give you a warning if you leave this out.

The last thing you need to do is import the TodoList component into the App.js file and pass in the todos as a property.

Listing 3.16 Importing the TodoList component

```
...
import TodoList from './TodoList'
...
render () {
    const { inputValue, todos } = this.state
    return (
      <View style={styles.container}>
        <ScrollView
          keyboardShouldPersistTaps='always'
          style={styles.content}>
          <Heading />
          <Input inputValue={inputValue} inputChange={(text) => this.
   inputChange(text)} />
          <TodoList todos={todos} />
          <Button submitTodo={this.submitTodo} />
        </ScrollView>
      </View>
    )
  }
...
```

Run the app. When you add a todo, you should see it pop up in the list of todos (figure 3.17).

The next steps are to mark a todo as complete, and to delete a todo. Open App.js, and create toggleComplete and deleteTodo functions below the submitTodo function. toggleComplete will toggle whether the todo is complete, and deleteTodo will delete the todo.

Figure 3.17   Updated app with the
TodoList component

Listing 3.17   Adding `toggleComplete` and `deleteTodo` functions

Binds the toggleComplete method
to the class in the constructor

Binds the deleteTodo method to
the class in the constructor

deleteTodo takes the todoIndex
as an argument, filters the todos
to return all but the todo with
the index that was passed in,
and then resets the state to the
remaining todos.

```
constructor () {
  ...
  this.toggleComplete = this.toggleComplete.bind(this)
  this.deleteTodo = this.deleteTodo.bind(this)
}
...
deleteTodo (todoIndex) {
  let { todos } = this.state
  todos = todos.filter((todo) => todo.todoIndex !== todoIndex)
  this.setState({ todos })
}
```

```
toggleComplete (todoIndex) {
  let todos = this.state.todos
  todos.forEach((todo) => {
    if (todo.todoIndex === todoIndex) {
      todo.complete = !todo.complete
    }
  })
  this.setState({ todos })
}
...
```

toggleComplete also takes the todoIndex as an argument, and loops through the todos until it finds the todo with the given index. It changes the complete Boolean to the opposite of complete's current setting, and then resets the state of the todos.

To hook in these functions, you need to create a button component to pass in to the todo. In the app folder, create a new file called TodoButton.js.

Listing 3.18   Creating TodoButton.js

```
import React from 'react'
import { Text, TouchableHighlight, StyleSheet } from 'react-native'

const TodoButton = ({ onPress, complete, name }) => (
  <TouchableHighlight
    onPress={onPress}
    underlayColor='#efefef'
    style={styles.button}>
    <Text style={[
      styles.text,
      complete ? styles.complete : null,
      name === 'Delete' ? styles.deleteButton : null ]}
    >
      {name}
    </Text>
  </TouchableHighlight>
)

const styles = StyleSheet.create({
  button: {
    alignSelf: 'flex-end',
    padding: 7,
    borderColor: '#ededed',
    borderWidth: 1,
    borderRadius: 4,
    marginRight: 5
  },
  text: {
    color: '#666666'
  },
  complete: {
    color: 'green',
    fontWeight: 'bold'
  },
  deleteButton: {
    color: 'rgba(175, 47, 47, 1)'
  }
})
export default TodoButtton
```

Takes onPress, complete, and name as props

Checks whether complete is true, and applies a style

Checks whether the name property equals "Delete" and, if so, applies a style

Now, pass the new functions as props to the TodoList component.

Listing 3.19   Passing `toggleComplete` and `deleteTodo` as props to `TodoList`

```
render () {
  ...
        <TodoList
          toggleComplete={this.toggleComplete}
          deleteTodo={this.deleteTodo}
          todos={todos} />
        <Button submitTodo={this.submitTodo} />
  ...
}
```

Next, pass toggleComplete and deleteTodo as props to the Todo component.

Listing 3.20   Passing `toggleComplete` and `deleteTodo` as props to `ToDo`

```
...
const TodoList = ({ todos, deleteTodo, toggleComplete }) => {
  todos = todos.map((todo, i) => {
    return (
      <Todo
        deleteTodo={deleteTodo}
        toggleComplete={toggleComplete}
        key={i}
        todo={todo} />
    )
  })
...
```

Finally, open Todo.js and update the Todo component to bring in the new TodoButton component and some styling for the button container.

Listing 3.21   Updating Todo.js to bring in `TodoButton` and functionality

```
import TodoButton from './TodoButton'
...
const Todo = ({ todo, toggleComplete, deleteTodo }) => (
  <View style={styles.todoContainer}>
    <Text style={styles.todoText}>
      {todo.title}
    </Text>
    <View style={styles.buttons}>
      <TodoButton
        name='Done'
        complete={todo.complete}
        onPress={() => toggleComplete(todo.todoIndex)} />
      <TodoButton
        name='Delete'
        onPress={() => deleteTodo(todo.todoIndex)} />
    </View>
  </View>
)
```

```
const styles = StyleSheet.create({
...
  buttons: {
    flex: 1,
    flexDirection: 'row',
    justifyContent: 'flex-end',
    alignItems: 'center'
  },
...
)}
```

You add two TodoButtons: one named Done, and one named Delete. You also pass toggleComplete and deleteTodo as functions to be called as the onPress you defined in TodoButton.js. If you refresh the app and add a todo, you should now see the new buttons (figure 3.18).

If you click Done, the button text should be bold and green. If you click Delete, the todo should disappear from the list of todos.

You're now almost done with the app. The final step is to build a tab bar filter that will show either all the todos, only the complete todos, or only the incomplete todos. To get this started, you'll create a new function that will set the type of todos to show.

Figure 3.18   App with TodoButtons displayed

In the constructor, you set a state type variable to 'All' when you first created the app. You'll now create a function named setType that will take a type as an argument and update the type in the state. Place this function below the toggleComplete function in App.js.

Listing 3.22 Adding the setType function

```
constructor () {
  ...
  this.setType = this.setType.bind(this)
}
...
setType (type) {
  this.setState({ type })
}
...
```

Next, you need to create the TabBar and TabBarItem components. First, create the TabBar component: add a file in the app folder named TabBar.js.

Listing 3.23 Creating the TabBar component

```
import React from 'react'
import { View, StyleSheet } from 'react-native'
import TabBarItem from './TabBarItem'

const TabBar = ({ setType, type }) => (
  <View style={styles.container}>
    <TabBarItem  type={type} title='All'
      setType={() => setType('All')} />
    <TabBarItem type={type} border title='Active'
      setType={() => setType('Active')} />
    <TabBarItem type={type} border title='Complete'
      setType={() => setType('Complete')} />
  </View>
)

const styles = StyleSheet.create({
  container: {
    height: 70,
    flexDirection: 'row',
    borderTopWidth: 1,
    borderTopColor: '#dddddd'
  }
})

export default TabBar
```

This component takes two props: setType and type. Both are passed down from the main App component.

You're importing the yet-to-be-defined `TabBarItem` component. Each `TabBarItem` component takes three props: `title`, `type`, and `setType`. Two of the components also take a `border` prop (Boolean), which if set will add a left border style.

Next, create a file in the app folder named TabBarItem.js.

Listing 3.24 Creating the `TabBarItem` component

```
import React from 'react'
import { Text, TouchableHighlight, StyleSheet } from 'react-native'

const TabBarItem = ({ border, title, selected, setType, type }) => (
  <TouchableHighlight
    underlayColor='#efefef'
    onPress={setType}
    style={[
      styles.item, selected ? styles.selected : null,
      border ? styles.border : null,
      type === title ? styles.selected : null ]}>
      <Text style={[ styles.itemText, type === title ? styles.bold : null ]}>
      {title}
      </Text>
  </TouchableHighlight>
)

const styles = StyleSheet.create({
  item: {
    flex: 1,
    justifyContent: 'center',
    alignItems: 'center'
  },
  border: {
    borderLeftWidth: 1,
    borderLeftColor: '#dddddd'
  },
  itemText: {
    color: '#777777',
    fontSize: 16
  },
  selected: {
    backgroundColor: '#ffffff'
  },
  bold: {
    fontWeight: 'bold'
  }
})

export default TabBarItem
```

In the `TouchableHighlight` component, you check a few props and set styles based on the prop. If `selected` is true, you give it the style `styles.selected`. If `border` is true, you give it the style `styles.border`. If `type` is equal to the `title`, you give it `styles.selected`.

In the `Text` component, you also check to see whether `type` is equal to `title`. If so, add a bold style to it.

To implement the `TabBar`, open app/App.js, bring in the `TabBar` component, and set it up. You'll also bring in type to the `render` function as part of destructuring `this.state`.

Listing 3.25   Implementing the `TabBar` component

```
...
import TabBar from './TabBar'
class App extends Component {
...
render () {
  const { todos, inputValue, type } = this.state
  return (
    <View style={styles.container}>
      <ScrollView
        keyboardShouldPersistTaps='always'
        style={styles.content}>
        <Heading />
        <Input inputValue={inputValue}
               inputChange={(text) => this.inputChange(text)} />
        <TodoList
          type={type}
          toggleComplete={this.toggleComplete}
          deleteTodo={this.deleteTodo}
          todos={todos} />
        <Button submitTodo={this.submitTodo} />
      </ScrollView>
      <TabBar type={type} setType={this.setType} />
    </View>
  )
}
}
...
```

Here, you bring in the `TabBar` component. You then destructure type from the state and *pass it not only to the new* TabBar *component, but also to the* TodoList *component;* you'll use this type variable in just a second when filtering the todos based on this type. You also pass the `setType` function as a prop to the `TabBar` component.

The last thing you need to do is open the `TodoList` component and add a filter to return only the todos of the type you currently want back, based on the tab that's selected. Open TodoList.js, destructure the type out of the props, and add the following `getVisibleTodos` function before the `return` statement.

Listing 3.26   Updating the `TodoList` component

```
...
const TodoList = ({ todos, deleteTodo, toggleComplete, type }) => {
  const getVisibleTodos = (todos, type) => {
    switch (type) {
      case 'All':
        return todos
      case 'Complete':
        return todos.filter((t) => t.complete)
      case 'Active':
```

```
        return todos.filter((t) => !t.complete)
  }
}

todos = getVisibleTodos(todos, type)
todos = todos.map((todo, i) => {
...
```

You use a switch statement to check which type is currently set. If 'All' is set, you return the entire list of todos. If 'Complete' is set, you filter the todos and only return the complete todos. If 'Active' is set, you filter the todos and only return the incomplete todos.

You then set the todos variable as the returned value of getVisibleTodos. Now you should be able to run the app and see the new TabBar (figure 3.19). The TabBar will filter based on which type is selected.

Figure 3.19   Final todo app

Summary

- `AppRegistry` is the JavaScript entry point to running all React Native apps.
- The React Native component `TextInput` is similar to an HTML `input`. You can specify several props, including a `placeholder` to show text before the user starts to type, a `placeholderTextColor` that styles the placeholder text, and a `selectionColor` that styles the cursor for the `TextInput`.
- `TouchableHighlight` is one way to create buttons in React Native; it's comparable to the HTML `button` element. You can use `TouchableHighlight` to wrap views and make them respond properly to touch events.
- You learned how to enable the developer tools in both iOS and Android emulators.
- Using the JavaScript console (available from the developer menu) is a good way to debug your app and log useful information.

Part 2

Developing applications in React Native

Wﬁith the basics covered, you can start adding features to your React Native app. The chapters in this part cover styling, navigation, animations, and elegant ways to handle data using data architectures (with a focus on Redux).

Chapters 4 and 5 teach how to apply styles either inline with components or in stylesheets that components can reference. And because React Native components are the main building blocks of your app's UI, chapter 4 spends some time teaching useful things you can do with the View component. Chapter 5 builds on the skills taught in chapter 4. It covers aspects of styling that are platform specific, as well as some advanced techniques, including using flexbox to make it easier to lay out an application.

Chapter 6 shows how to use the two most-recommended and most-used navigation libraries, React Navigation and React Native Navigation. We walk through creating the three main types of navigators—tabs, stack, and drawer—and how to control the navigation state.

Chapter 7 covers the four things you need to do to create animations, the four types of animatable components that ship with the Animated API, how to create custom animatable components, and several other useful skills.

In chapter 8, we explore handling data with data architectures. Because Redux is the most widely adopted method of handling data in the React ecosystem, you use it to build an app, meanwhile learning data-handling skills. We show how to use the Context API and how to implement Redux with a React Native app by using reducers to hold the Redux state and delete items from the example app. We also cover how to use providers to pass global state to the rest of the app, how to use the connect function to access the example app from a child component, and how to use actions to add functionality.

Introduction to styling

This chapter covers

- Styling using JavaScript
- Applying and organizing styles
- Applying styles to `View` components
- Applying styles to `Text` components

It takes talent to build mobile applications, but it takes *style* to make them great. If you're a graphic designer, you know this intuitively, deep in your bones. If you're a developer, you're probably groaning and rolling your eyes. In either case, understanding the fundamentals of styling Reactive Native components is critical to making an engaging application that others want to use.

In all likelihood, you have some experience with CSS, even if it's nothing more than seeing the syntax. You can easily understand what a CSS rule like `background-color: 'red'` is meant to do. As you begin reading this chapter, it may appear as though styling components in React Native is as simple as using camelCase names for CSS rules. For instance, setting the background color on a React Native component uses almost the same syntax, `backgroundColor: 'red'`—but be forewarned, this is where the similarities end.

Try not to hang on to how you did things in CSS. Embrace the React Native way, and you'll find that learning how to style components is a much more pleasant experience—even for a developer.

The first section of this chapter provides an overview of styling components. We'll make sure you understand the various ways to apply styles to components and discuss how to organize styles in an application. Forming good organizational habits now will make things easier to manage and will facilitate the use of more advanced techniques down the road.

Because React Native is styled using JavaScript, we'll talk about how to start thinking of styles as code and how to take advantage of JavaScript features like variables and functions. The final two sections explore styling `View` components and `Text` components. In some cases, we'll use short examples to explain a topic, but for the most part, we'll walk through styling something real. You'll take what you learn and apply it to the construction of a Profile Card.

For all the example code in this chapter, you can start with the default generated app and replace the contents of App.js with the code from the individual listings. Complete source files can be found at www.manning.com/books/react-native-in-action and in the book's Git repository at https://github.com/dabit3/react-native-in-action under chapter-4.

4.1   Applying and organizing styles in React Native

React Native comes with many built-in components, and the community has built many more you can include with your projects. Components support a specific set of styles. Those styles may or may not be applicable to other types of components. For example, the `Text` component supports the `fontWeight` property (`fontWeight` refers to the thickness of the font), but the `View` component doesn't. Conversely, the `View` component supports the `flex` property (`flex` refers to the layout of components within a view), but the `Text` component doesn't.

Some styling elements are similar between components but not the same. For example, the `View` component supports the `shadowColor` property, whereas the `Text` component supports the `textShadowColor` property. Some styles, like `ShadowPropTypesIOS`, only apply to a specific platform (in this case, to iOS).

Learning the various styles and how to manipulate them takes time. That's why it's important to start with fundamentals like how to apply and organize styles. This section will focus on teaching those styling fundamentals, so you'll have a good foundation from which to start exploring styles and building the example Profile Card component.

> **TIP**   For a solid reference on how to make mobile apps usable, see Matt Lacey's *Usability Matters* (Manning, 2018; www.manning.com/books/usability-matters).

4.1.1   Applying styles in applications

To compete in the marketplace, mobile applications must have a sense of style. You can develop a fully functional app, but if it looks terrible and isn't engaging, people aren't going to be interested. You don't have to build the hottest-looking app in the world, but you do have to commit to creating a polished product. A polished, sharp-looking app greatly influences people's perception of the app's quality.

You can apply styles to elements in React Native in a number of ways. In chapters 1 and 3, we went over inline styling (shown in the next listing) and styling using a StyleSheet (listing 4.2).

Listing 4.1 Using inline styles

```
import React, { Component } from 'react'
import { Text, View } from 'react-native'

export default class App extends Component {
  render () {
    return (
      <View style={{marginLeft: 20, marginTop: 20}}>       ◄──  Applies an inline style to a
                                                                  React Native component
        <Text style={{fontSize: 18,color: 'red'}}>Some Text</Text>   ◄──┐
      </View>                                                            │
    )                                        Applies multiple inline styles at once
  }
}
```

As you can see, it's possible to specify multiple styles at once by supplying an object to the styles property.

Listing 4.2 Referencing styles defined in a StyleSheet

```
import React, { Component } from 'react'
import { StyleSheet, Text, View } from 'react-native'

export default class App extends Component {
  render () {
    return (                                 References the container style
                                             defined in the styles stylesheet
      <View style={styles.container}>    ◄──
        <Text style={[styles.message,styles.warning]}>Some Text</Text>  ◄──┐
      </View>                                            Uses an array to reference
    )                                                    both the message and warning
  }                                                      styles from the stylesheet
}

const styles = StyleSheet.create({
  container: {           ◄──┐
    marginLeft: 20,         │
    marginTop: 20           │
  },                        │
  message: {             ◄──┼── Defines the styles using StyleSheet.create
    fontSize: 18            │
  },                        │
  warning: {             ◄──┘
    color: 'red'
  }
});
```

Functionally, there's no difference between using an inline style versus referencing a style defined in a `StyleSheet`. With `StyleSheet`, you create a `style` object and refer to each style individually. Separating the styles from the `render` method makes the code easier to understand and promotes reuse of styles across components.

When using a style name like `warning`, it's easy to recognize the intent of the message. But the inline style `color: 'red'` offers no insight into why the message is red. Having styles specified in one place rather than inline on many components makes it easier to apply changes across the entire application. Imagine you wanted to change warning messages to yellow. All you have to do is change the style definition once in the stylesheet, `color: 'yellow'`.

Listing 4.2 also shows how to specify multiple styles by supplying an array of style properties. Remember when doing this that the last style passed in will override the previous style if there's a duplicate property. For example, if an array of styles like this is supplied, the last value for `color` will override all the previous values:

```
style={[{color: 'black'},{color: 'yellow'},{color: 'red'}]}
```

In this example, the color will be red.

It's also possible to combine the two methodologies by specifying an array of styling properties using inline styles and references to stylesheets:

```
style={[{color: 'black'}, styles.message]}
```

React Native is very flexible in this regard, which can be both good and bad. Specifying inline styles when you're quickly trying to prototype something is extremely easy, but in the long haul, you'll want to be careful how you organize your styles; otherwise your application can quickly become a mess and difficult to manage. By organizing your styles, you'll make it easier to do the following:

- Maintain your application's codebase
- Reuse styles across components
- Experiment with styling changes during development

4.1.2   Organizing styles

As you might suspect from the previous section, using inline styles isn't the recommended way to go: stylesheets are a much more effective way to manage styles. But what does that mean in practice?

When styling websites, we use stylesheets all the time. Often we use tools like Sass, Less, and PostCSS to create monolithic stylesheets for the entire application. In the world of the web, styles are in essence global, but that isn't the React Native way.

React Native focuses on the component. The goal is to make components as reusable and standalone as possible. Having a component dependent on an application's stylesheet is the antithesis of modularity. In React Native, styles are scoped to the component—not to the application.

How to accomplish this encapsulation depends entirely on your team's preference. There's no right or wrong way, but in the React Native community, you'll find two common approaches:

- Declaring stylesheets in the same file as the component
- Declaring stylesheets in a separate file, outside of the component

DECLARING STYLESHEETS IN THE SAME FILE AS THE COMPONENT

As you've done so far in this book, a popular way to declare styles is within the component that will be using them. The major benefit of this approach is that the component and its styles are completely encapsulated in a single file. This component can then be moved or used anywhere in the app. This is a common approach to component design, one you'll see often in the React Native community.

When including the stylesheet definitions with the component, the typical convention is to specify the styles after the component. All the listings in this book have, so far, followed this convention.

DECLARING STYLESHEETS IN A SEPARATE FILE

If you're used to writing CSS, putting your styles into a separate file might seem like a better approach and feel more familiar. The stylesheet definitions are created in a separate file. You can name it whatever you want (styles.js is typical), but be sure the extension is .js; it's JavaScript, after all. The stylesheet file and component file are saved in the same folder.

A file structure like that shown in figure 4.1 retains the close relationship between components and styles and affords a bit of clarity by not mixing style definitions with the functional aspects of the components. Listing 4.3 corresponds to a styles.js file that would be used to style a component like ComponentA and ComponentB in the figure. Use meaningful names when defining your stylesheets, so it's clear what part of a component is being styled.

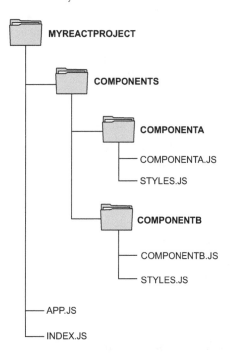

Figure 4.1 An example file structure with styles separated from components in a single folder instead of a single file

Listing 4.3   **Externalizing a component's stylesheets**

```
import { StyleSheet } from 'react-native'          Creates a stylesheet, and saves
                                                   it in the styles constant
const styles = StyleSheet.create({
  container: {                                  Defines a style for the container.
    marginTop: 150,                             It can be referenced by the
    backgroundColor: '#ededed',                 component as styles.container.
    flexWrap: 'wrap'
  }
})
                                                   Creates a second stylesheet, and
                                                   saves it in the buttons constant
const buttons = StyleSheet.create({
  primary: {                                    Defines a style for the primary button.
    flex: 1,                                    It can be referenced by the component
    height: 70,                                 as buttons.primary.
    backgroundColor: 'red',
    justifyContent: 'center',
    alignItems: 'center',
    marginLeft: 20,
    marginRight: 20
  }                                             Exports both the styles and buttons
})                                              stylesheets so the component will have
                                                access to the constants
export { styles, buttons }
```

The component imports the external stylesheets and can reference any styles defined
within them.

Listing 4.4   **Importing external stylesheets**

```
import { styles, buttons } from './component/styles'    Imports multiple stylesheets
                                                        exported from styles.js
<View style={styles.container}>
  <TouchableHighlight style={buttons.primary} />        Reference to the buttons.primary
    ...                                                 style created in styles.js
  </TouchableHighlight>
</View>
```

Reference
to the styles.
container
style created
in styles.js

4.1.3   *Styles are code*

You've already seen how JavaScript is used to define styles in React Native. Despite having a full scripting language with variables and functions, your styles have been rather static, but they certainly don't have to be!

Web developers have fought with CSS for years. New technologies like Sass, Less, and PostCSS were created to work around the many limitations of cascading stylesheets. Even a simple thing like defining a variable to store the primary color of a site was impossible without CSS preprocessors. The CSS Custom Properties for Cascading Variables Module Level 1 candidate recommendation in December 2015 introduced the concept of custom properties, which are akin to variables; but at the time of writing, fewer than 80% of browsers in use support this functionality.

Let's take advantage of the fact that we're using JavaScript and start thinking of styles as code. You'll build a simple application that gives the user a button to change the theme from light to dark. But before you start coding, let's walk through what you're trying to build.

The application has a single button on the screen. That button is enclosed by a small square box. When the button is pressed, the themes will toggle. When the light theme is selected, the button label will say White, the background will be white, and the box around the button will be black. When the dark theme is selected, the button label will say Black, the background will be black, and the box around the button will be white. Figure 4.2 shows what the screen should look like when the themes are selected.

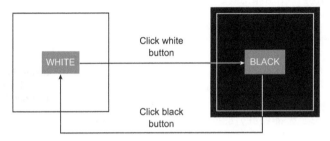

Figure 4.2 A simple application that supports two themes, white and black. Users can press the button to toggle between a white background and a black background.

For this example, organize the styles in a separate file, styles.js. Then, create some constants to hold the color values, and create two stylesheets for the light and dark themes.

Listing 4.5 Dynamic stylesheets extracted from the main component file

```
import {StyleSheet} from 'react-native';

export const Colors = {
    dark: 'black',
    light: 'white'
};

const baseContainerStyles = {
    flex: 1,
    justifyContent: 'center',
    alignItems: 'center'
};

const baseBoxStyles = {
    justifyContent: 'center',
    alignItems: 'center',
    borderWidth: 2,
    height: 150,
    width: 150
};

const lightStyleSheet = StyleSheet.create({
```

Constant defining the colors that will correspond to the light and dark themes

JavaScript object to hold the base container styles

JavaScript object to hold the base box styles

Creates the stylesheet for the light theme

```
        container: {
            ...baseContainerStyles,
            backgroundColor: Colors.light
        },
        box: {
            ...baseBoxStyles,
            borderColor: Colors.dark
        }
    });
    const darkStyleSheet = StyleSheet.create({          ◄──── Creates the stylesheet
        container: {                                          for the dark theme
            ...baseContainerStyles,
            backgroundColor: Colors.dark
        },
        box: {
            ...baseBoxStyles,
            borderColor: Colors.light
        }
    });
    export default function getStyleSheet(useDarkTheme){
        return useDarkTheme ? darkStyleSheet : lightStyleSheet;    ◄────
    }
```

Function that will return the appropriate theme based on a Boolean value (points to `export default function getStyleSheet(useDarkTheme)`)

Returns the dark theme if useDarkTheme is true; otherwise returns the light theme (points to `return useDarkTheme ? darkStyleSheet : lightStyleSheet;`)

Once the styles have been configured, you can start building the component app in App. js. Because you only have light and dark themes, create a utility function, getStyleSheet, which takes a Boolean value. If true is supplied, the dark theme will be returned; otherwise the light theme will be returned.

Listing 4.6   Application that toggles between light and dark themes

```
import React, { Component } from 'react';
import { Button, StyleSheet, View } from 'react-native';
import getStyleSheet from './styles';          ◄────

export default class App extends Component {

    constructor(props) {
        super(props);
        this.state = {
            darkTheme: false                ◄────
        };
        this.toggleTheme = this.toggleTheme.bind(this);    ◄────
    }

    toggleTheme() {
        this.setState({darkTheme: !this.state.darkTheme})
    };

    render() {

        const styles = getStyleSheet(this.state.darkTheme);    ◄────
        const backgroundColor =
```

Imports the getStyleSheet function from the externalized styles (points to `import getStyleSheet from './styles';`)

Initializes the component's state to show the light theme by default (points to `darkTheme: false`)

Toggles the theme value in state whenever the function is called (points to `toggleTheme()` block)

To avoid exceptions, the toggleTheme function must be bound to the component. (points to `this.toggleTheme = this.toggleTheme.bind(this);`)

Uses the imported getStyleSheet function to get the appropriate stylesheet for whichever theme should be displayed (points to `const styles = getStyleSheet(this.state.darkTheme);`)

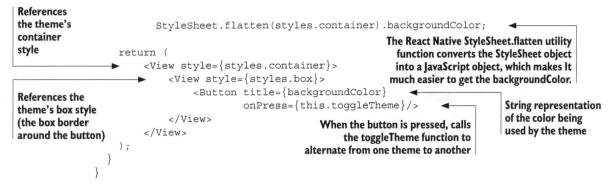

The application toggles themes: feel free to experiment and take it a bit further. Try changing the light theme to a different color. Notice how easy it is, because the colors are defined as constants in one place. Try changing the button label in the dark theme to be the same color as the background instead of always white. Try creating an entirely new theme, or modify the code to support many different themes instead of just two—have fun!

4.2 Styling view components

Now that you've had a proper overview of styling in React Native, let's talk more about individual styles. This chapter covers many of the basic properties you'll use all the time. In chapter 5, we'll go into more depth and introduce styles you won't see every day and styles that are platform specific. But for now, let's focus on the basics: in this section, that's the `View` components. The `View` component is the main building block of a UI and is one of the most important components to understand to get your styling right. Remember, a `View` element is similar to an HTML `div` tag in the sense that you can use it to wrap other elements and build blocks of UI code in it.

As you progress through the chapter, you'll use what you've learned to build a real component: a Profile Card. Building the Profile Card will show how to put everything together. Figure 4.3 shows what the component will look like at the end of this section. In the process of creating this component, you'll learn how to do the following:

- Create a border around the profile container using `borderWidth`
- Round the corners of that border with `borderRadius`
- Create a border that looks like a circle by using a `borderRadius` half the size of the component's width
- Position everything using margin and padding properties

The next few sections will teach the styling techniques you'll need to know to create the Profile Card component. We'll start easy by talking about how to set a component's background color. You'll be able to use that same technique to set the background color of the Profile Card.

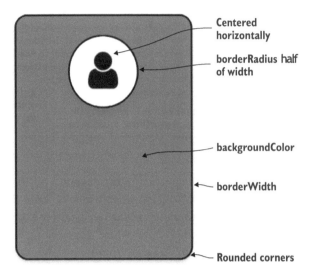

Figure 4.3   The Profile Card component after the structural `View` **components have been styled. The Profile Card is a rectangle with rounded corners and a circular section for a profile image.**

4.2.1   Setting the background color

Without a splash of color, a user interface (UI) looks boring and dull. You don't need an explosion of color to make things look interesting, but you do need a bit. The `backgroundColor` property sets the background color of an element. This property takes a string of one of the properties shown in table 4.1. The same colors are available when rendering text to the screen as well.

Table 4.1   Supported color formats

Supported color format	Example
`#rgb`	`'#06f'`
`#rgba`	`'#06fc'`
`#rrggbb`	`'#0066ff'`
`#rrggbbaa`	`'#ff00ff00'`
`rgb(number, number, number)`	`'rgb(0, 102, 255)'`
`rgb(number, number, number, alpha)`	`'rgba(0, 102, 255, .5)'`
`hsl(hue, saturation, lightness)`	`'hsl(216, 100%, 50%)'`
`hsla(hue, saturation, lightness, alpha)`	`'hsla(216, 100%, 50%, .5)'`
Transparent background	`'transparent'`
Any CSS3-specified named color (black, red, blue, and so on)	`'dodgerblue'`

Fortunately, the supported color formats are the same ones supported by CSS. We won't go into great detail, but because this may be the first time you've seen some of these formats, here's a quick explanation:

- rgb stands for red, green, and blue. You can specify the values for red, green, and blue using a scale from 0–255 (or in hexadecimal 00–ff). Higher numbers mean more of each color.
- alpha is similar to opacity (0 is transparent, 1 is solid).
- hue represents 1 degree on a 360-degree color wheel, where 0 is red, 120 is green, and 240 is blue.
- saturation is the intensity of the color from a 0% shade of gray to 100% full color.
- lightness is a percentage between 0% and 100%. 0% is darker (closer to black), and 100% is light (closer to white).

You've seen backgroundColor applied in previous examples, so let's take things a step further in the next example. To use your new skills to create something real, let's start building the Profile Card. Right now, it won't look like much, as you can see in figure 4.4—it's just a 300 × 400 colored rectangle.

Figure 4.4   A simple 300 × 400 colored rectangle that forms the base of the Profile Card component

The following listing shows the initial code. Don't worry about the fact that most of it has nothing to do with styling. We'll walk through each piece, but you need a foundation from which to start.

Listing 4.7 Initial framework for the Profile Card component

```
import React, { Component } from 'react';
import { StyleSheet, View} from 'react-native';

export default class App extends Component<{}> {
    render() {
        return (
            <View style={styles.container}>
                <View style={styles.cardContainer}/>
            </View>
        );
    }
}

const profileCardColor = 'dodgerblue';

const styles = StyleSheet.create({
    container: {
        flex: 1,
        justifyContent: 'center',
        alignItems: 'center'
    },
    cardContainer: {
        backgroundColor: profileCardColor,
        width: 300,
        height: 400
    }
});
```

The outermost View element references the container style that centers the child View component.

The inner View element will become the Profile Card component.

Defines the color for the Profile Card in a variable in case you need to use it in more than one place

Style definition for the outermost container

Style definition for the Profile Card container

Sets the Profile Card backgroundColor to the constant set earlier

The first View component is the outermost element. It acts as a container around everything else. Its sole purpose is to center child components on the device's display. The second View component will be the container for the Profile Card. For now, it's a 300 × 400 colored rectangle.

4.2.2 Setting border properties

Applying a background color to a component definitely makes it stand out, but without a crisp border line delineating the edge of the component, it looks like the component is floating in space. A clear delineation between components will help users understand how to interact with your mobile application.

Adding a border around a component is the best way to give screen elements a concrete, real feeling. There are quite a few border properties, but conceptually there are only four: borderColor, borderRadius, borderStyle, and borderWidth. These properties apply to the component as a whole.

For the color and width, there are individual properties for each side of the border: borderTopColor, borderRightColor, borderBottomColor, borderLeftColor, borderTopWidth, borderRightWidth, borderBottomWidth, and borderLeftWidth. For the border radius, there are properties for each corner: borderTopRightRadius, borderBottomRightRadius, borderBottomLeftRadius, and borderTopLeftRadius. But there's only one borderStyle.

CREATING BORDERS WITH THE COLOR, WIDTH AND STYLE PROPERTIES

To set a border, you must first set borderWidth. borderWidth is the size of the border, and it's always a number. You can either set a borderWidth that applies to the entire component or choose which borderWidth you want to set specifically (top, right, bottom, or left). You can combine these properties in many different ways to get the effect you like. See figure 4.5 for some examples.

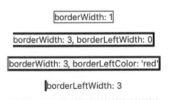

Figure 4.5 Examples of various combinations of border style settings

As you can see, you can combine border styles to create combinations of border effects. The next listing shows how easy this is to do.

Listing 4.8 Setting various border combinations

```
import React, { Component } from 'react';
import { StyleSheet, Text, View} from 'react-native';

export default class App extends Component<{}> {
    render() {
      return (
        <View style={styles.container}>
          <Example style={{borderWidth: 1}}>
              <Text>borderWidth: 1</Text>
          </Example>
          <Example style={{borderWidth: 3, borderLeftWidth: 0}}>
              <Text>borderWidth: 3, borderLeftWidth: 0</Text>
          </Example>
          <Example style={{borderWidth: 3, borderLeftColor: 'red'}}>
              <Text>borderWidth: 3, borderLeftColor: 'red'</Text>
          </Example>
          <Example style={{borderLeftWidth: 3}}>
              <Text>borderLeftWidth: 3</Text>
          </Example>
          <Example style={{borderWidth: 1, borderStyle: 'dashed'}}>
              <Text>borderWidth: 1, borderStyle: 'dashed'</Text>
          </Example>
        </View>
      );
    }
}

const Example = (props) => (
    <View style={ [styles.example,props.style] }>
        {props.children}
    </View>
);
```

Sets borderWidth to 1

Increases borderWidth to 3, removes the left border, and sets borderLeftWidth to 0

Sets borderWidth to 3, adds back the left border, and sets the color to red

Sets only a left border, with borderLeftWidth set to 3

Changes borderStyle from the default solid to dashed

Reusable Example component with a default set of styles that can easily be overridden by passing in style properties

```
const styles = StyleSheet.create({
    container: {
        flex: 1,
        justifyContent: 'center',
        alignItems: 'center'
    },
    example: {
        marginBottom: 15
    }
});
```

When only `borderWidth` is specified, `borderColor` defaults to `'black'` and `borderStyle` defaults to `'solid'`. If `borderWidth` or `borderColor` is set at the component level, those properties can be overridden by using a more specific property like `borderWidthLeft`; specificity takes precedence over generality.

> **NOTE** `borderStyle` is a bit buggy, and I suggest sticking with the default, solid border. If you try to change the border width of any side and have `borderStyle` set to `'dotted'` or `'dashed'`, you'll get an error. This will probably be fixed at some point, but for now don't spend too much time scratching your head if `borderStyle` doesn't work the way you expect. File that away in your brain, and let's move along.

USING BORDER RADIUS TO CREATE SHAPES

Another border property that can be used to great effect is `borderRadius`. A lot of objects in the real world have straight edges, but seldom does a straight line convey any sense of style. You wouldn't buy an automobile that looked like a box. You want your car to have nice curved lines that look sleek. Using the `borderRadius` style gives you the ability to add a bit of style to your applications. You can make many different, interesting shapes by adding curves in the right spots.

With `borderRadius`, you can define how rounded border corners appear on elements. As you may suspect, `borderRadius` applies to the entire component. If you set `borderRadius` and don't set one of the more specific values, like `borderTopLeftRadius`, all four corners will be rounded. Look at figure 4.6 to see how to round different borders to create cool effects.

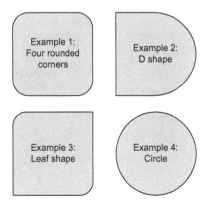

Figure 4.6   **Examples of various border radius combinations. Example 1: a square with four rounded corners. Example 2: a square with the right two corners rounded, making a D shape. Example 3: a square with the opposite corners rounded, which looks like a leaf. Example 4: a square with a border radius equal to half the length of a side, which results in a circle.**

Creating the shapes in figure 4.6 is relatively simple, as shown in listing 4.9. Honestly, the trickiest part about this code is making sure you don't make the text too big or too long. I'll show you what I mean shortly, in listing 4.10.

Listing 4.9 Setting various border radius combinations

```
import React, { Component } from 'react';
import { StyleSheet, Text, View} from 'react-native';

export default class App extends Component<{}> {
    render() {
        return (
            <View style={styles.container}>
                <Example style={{borderRadius: 20}}>
                    <CenteredText>
                        Example 1:{"\n"}4 Rounded Corners
                    </CenteredText>
                </Example>
                <Example style={{borderTopRightRadius: 60,
                            borderBottomRightRadius: 60}}>
                    <CenteredText>
                        Example 2:{"\n"}D Shape
                    </CenteredText>
                </Example>
                <Example style={{borderTopLeftRadius: 30,
                            borderBottomRightRadius: 30}}>
                    <CenteredText>
                        Example 3:{"\n"}Leaf Shape
                    </CenteredText>
                </Example>
                <Example style={{borderRadius: 60}}>
                    <CenteredText>
                        Example 4:{"\n"}Circle
                    </CenteredText>
                </Example>
            </View>
        );
    }
}

const Example = (props) => (
    <View style={[styles.example,props.style]}>
        {props.children}
    </View>
);

const CenteredText = (props) => (
    <Text style={[styles.centeredText, props.style]}>
        {props.children}
    </Text>
);

const styles = StyleSheet.create({
    container: {
        flex: 1,
        flexDirection: 'row',
        flexWrap: 'wrap',
```

Example 1: a square with four rounded corners

This is JavaScript, so you can specify a hard return inline with the text by using {"\n"}.

Example 2: a square with the right two corners rounded

Example 3: a square with the opposite corners rounded

Example 4: a square with a border radius equal to half the length of a side

Reusable component for rendering the centered text elements

React Native uses flexbox to control layout.

```
        marginTop: 75
    },
    example: {
        width: 120,
        height: 120,
        marginLeft: 20,
        marginBottom: 20,
        backgroundColor: 'grey',
        borderWidth: 2,
        justifyContent: 'center'
    },
    centeredText: {   ◄─────────────
        textAlign: 'center',
        margin: 10
    }
});
```

Style that centers the text
within the text components

Pay particular attention to the style that centers the text. You got lucky by using `margin: 10`. If you used `padding: 10`, the background of the text component would occlude the underlying border stroke of the `View` component (see figure 4.7).

By default, a `Text` component inherits the background color of its parent component. Because the bounding box of the `Text` component is a rectangle, the background overlaps the nice rounded corners. Obviously, using the `margin` property solves the problem, but it's also possible to remedy the situation another way. You could add `backgroundColor: 'transparent'` to the `centeredText` style. Making the text component's background transparent allows the underlying border to show through and look normal again, as in figure 4.6.

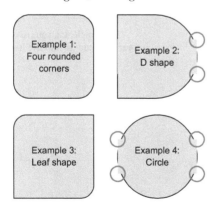

Figure 4.7 This is what figure 4.6 would look like if the `centeredText` style used `padding: 10` instead of `margin: 10` to position the text. The small circles highlight the points at which the bounding box of the `Text` component overlaps the border of the `View` component.

ADDING BORDERS TO YOUR PROFILE CARD COMPONENT

With your newfound knowledge of border properties, you can almost complete the initial layout of the Profile Card component. Using only the border properties from the last section, you can transform the 300 × 400 colored rectangle into something that more closely resembles what you want. Figure 4.8 shows how far you can get with an image and the techniques you've learned so far. It includes an image to use as a placeholder for a person's photo; you'll find it in the source code. But the circle is created by manipulating the border radius as described in the previous examples.

Figure 4.8 Incorporating border properties into the Profile Card component transforms the 300 × 400 colored rectangle into something more akin to what you want for the final Profile Card component.

Clearly there are some layout issues with the Profile Card, but you're almost there. We'll discuss how to use the margin and padding styles in the next section to get everything aligned correctly.

Listing 4.10 Incorporating border properties into the Profile Card

```
import React, { Component } from 'react';
import { Image, StyleSheet, View} from 'react-native';         ◄──── Imports the Image
                                                                     component from
export default class App extends Component<{}> {                     react-native
    render() {
        return (
            <View style={styles.container}>
                <View style={styles.cardContainer}>
                    <View style={styles.cardImageContainer}>
                        <Image style={styles.cardImage
                                source={require('./user.png')}/>      ◄──── user.png is located in the same
                    </View>                                                 directory as the application code.
                </View>
            </View>
        );
    }
}


const profileCardColor = 'dodgerblue';

const styles = StyleSheet.create({
    container: {
        flex: 1,
        justifyContent: 'center',
        alignItems: 'center'
    },
    cardContainer: {
        borderColor: 'black',      ◄──── Adds the border properties
        borderWidth: 3,                   to the Profile Card
        borderStyle: 'solid',
```

```
        borderRadius: 20,
        backgroundColor: profileCardColor,
        width: 300,
        height: 400
    },
    cardImageContainer: {
        backgroundColor: 'white',
        borderWidth: 3,
        borderColor: 'black',
        width: 120,
        height: 120,
        borderRadius: 60,
    },
    cardImage: {
        width: 80,
        height: 80
    }
});
```

> The image container is a 120 × 120 square with a borderRadius of 60 (half of 120), which results in a circle.

> Styles for the actual image

The differences between listing 4.10 and the previous Profile Card code (listing 4.7) have been bolded to highlight the incremental changes.

4.2.3   *Specifying margins and padding*

You could explicitly position every component on the screen and lay it out exactly like you want, but that would be extremely tedious if the layout needed to be responsive to user actions. It makes more sense to position items relative to one another, so if you move one component, the other components can move in response based on their relative positions.

The margin style allows you to define this relationship between components. The padding style lets you define the relative position of a component to its border. Using these properties together provides a great deal of flexibility when laying out components. You'll use these properties every day, so it's important to understand what they mean and do.

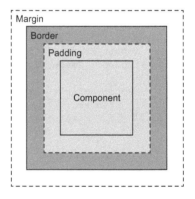

Figure 4.9   A common depiction of how margins, padding, and borders interrelate

Conceptually, margins and padding work exactly the same as they do in CSS. The customary depiction of how margins and padding relate to borders and the content area still applies (see figure 4.9).

Functionally, you're likely to run into bugs when dealing with margins and padding. You might be tempted to call them "quirks," but either way they're a pain. For the most part, margins on `View` components behave reasonably well and work across iOS and Android. Padding tends to work a little differently between OSs. At the time of writing, padding text components in an Android environment doesn't work at all; I suspect that will change in an upcoming release.

USING THE MARGIN PROPERTY

When laying out components, one of the first problems to solve is how far the components are from one another. To avoid specifying a distance for each component, you need a way to specify a relative position. The margin property allows you to define the perimeter of the component, which determines how far an element is from the previous or parent component. Articulating the layout this way allows the container to figure out where the components should be positioned with respect to one another rather than you having to calculate the position of every single component.

The available margin properties are margin, marginTop, marginRight, margin-Bottom, and marginLeft. If only the general margin property is set, without another, more-specific value such as marginLeft or marginTop, then that value applies to all sides of the component (top, right, bottom, and left). If both margin and a more-specific margin property are specified (for example, marginLeft), then the more-specific margin property takes precedence. It works exactly the same as the border properties. Let's apply some of these styles: see figure 4.10.

The margins all position the components as expected, but notice how the Android device clips the component when negative margins are applied. If you plan to support both iOS and Android, test on each device from the beginning of your project. Don't develop on iOS and think everything you styled will behave the same on Android. Listing 4.11 shows the code for the examples in figure 4.10.

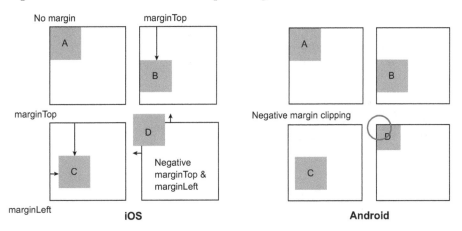

Figure 4.10   Examples of applying margins to components. In iOS, example A has no margins applied. Example B has a top margin applied. Example C has top and left margins. Example D has both negative top and negative left margins. In Android, negative margins behave a bit differently: the component is clipped by the parent container.

Listing 4.11   Applying various margins to components

```
import React, { Component } from 'react';
import { StyleSheet, Text, View} from 'react-native';

export default class App extends Component<{}> {
```

```
    render() {
        return (
            <View style={styles.container}>
                <View style={styles.exampleContainer}>
                    <Example>
                        <CenteredText>A</CenteredText>
                    </Example>
                </View>
                <View style={styles.exampleContainer}>
                    <Example style={{marginTop: 50}}>
                        <CenteredText>B</CenteredText>
                    </Example>
                </View>
                <View style={styles.exampleContainer}>
                    <Example style={{marginTop: 50, marginLeft: 10}}>
                        <CenteredText>C</CenteredText>
                    </Example>
                </View>
                <View style={styles.exampleContainer}>
                    <Example style={{marginLeft: -10, marginTop: -10}}>
                        <CenteredText>D</CenteredText>
                    </Example>
                </View>
            </View>
        );
    }
}

const Example = (props) => (
    <View style={[styles.example,props.style]}>
        {props.children}
    </View>
);

const CenteredText = (props) => (
    <Text style={[styles.centeredText, props.style]}>
        {props.children}
    </Text>
);

const styles = StyleSheet.create({
    container: {
        alignItems: 'center',
        flex: 1,
        flexDirection: 'row',
        flexWrap: 'wrap',
        justifyContent: 'center',
        marginTop: 75
    },
    exampleContainer: {
        borderWidth: 1,
        width: 120,
        height: 120,
        marginLeft: 20,
        marginBottom: 20,
```

Base example with no margins applied → (points to `<Example>`)

marginTop of 50 → (points to `<Example style={{marginTop: 50}}>`)

marginTop of 50 and marginLeft of 10 → (points to `<Example style={{marginTop: 50, marginLeft: 10}}>`)

Applies negative margins to marginTop and marginLeft → (points to `<Example style={{marginLeft: -10, marginTop: -10}}>`)

```
    },
    example: {
        width: 50,
        height: 50,
        backgroundColor: 'grey',
        borderWidth: 1,
        justifyContent: 'center'
    },
    centeredText: {
        textAlign: 'center',
        margin: 10
    }
});
```

USING THE PADDING PROPERTY

You can think of margins as the distance between elements, but padding represents the space between the content of the element and the border of the same element. When padding is specified, it allows the content of the component to not be flush against the border. In figure 4.9, the backgroundColor property bleeds through the component's edges up to the border, which is the space defined by padding. The available properties available for padding are padding, paddingLeft, paddingRight, paddingTop, and paddingBottom. If only the main padding property is set without another, more-specific value such as paddingLeft or paddingTop, then that value is passed to all sides of the component (top, right, bottom, and left). If both padding and a more-specific padding property are specified, such as paddingLeft, then the more-specific padding property takes precedence. This behavior is exactly like borders and margins.

Rather than create a new example to show how padding is different than margins, let's reuse the code from listing 4.11 and make a few tweaks. Change the margin styles on the example components to padding styles, and add a border around the Text components and change their background color. Figure 4.11 shows what you'll end up with.

Listing 4.12   Modifying listing 4.11 to replace margins with padding

```
import React, { Component } from 'react';

...

        <View style={styles.container}>
          <View style={styles.exampleContainer}>        Example A: unchanged, with
            <Example style={{}}>              ◀——      no margins or padding
                <CenteredText>A</CenteredText>
            </Example>
          </View>
          <View style={styles.exampleContainer}>        Example B: marginTop
            <Example style={{paddingTop: 50}}>    ◀——    changed to paddingTop
                <CenteredText>B</CenteredText>
            </Example>                       Example C: marginTop and marginLeft changed
          </View>                            to paddingTop and paddingLeft, respectively
          <View style={styles.exampleContainer}>
            <Example style={{paddingTop: 50, paddingLeft: 10}}>    ◀——
                <CenteredText>C</CenteredText>
```

```
            </Example>
        </View>
        <View style={styles.exampleContainer}>
            <Example style={{paddingLeft: -10, paddingTop: -10}}>    ◄────────┐
                <CenteredText>D</CenteredText>
            </Example>                                        Example D: marginLeft and marginTop
        </View>                                               changed to paddingLeft and marginTop,
    </View>                                                   respectively. The negative values remain.

...


    },
    centeredText: {
        textAlign: 'center',        ┌─────────────────────────────
        margin: 10,                 │ Adds a border and background
        borderWidth: 1,   ◄─────────┘ color to the Text component
        backgroundColor: 'lightgrey'
    }
});
```

Unlike margins, which specify the space between the component and its parent component, padding applies from the border of the component to its children. In example B, padding is calculated from the top border, which *pushes* the Text component B down from the top border. Example C adds a paddingLeft value, which also *pushes* the Text component C inward from the left border. Example D applies negative padding values to paddingTop and paddingLeft.

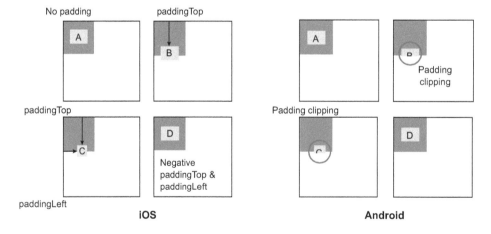

Figure 4.11   Changing the margin styles from the previous example to padding styles. Example A, with no padding, looks the same as when no margins are applied. Example B shows the component with paddingTop applied. Example C is the same, but it also applies paddingLeft. Example D applies negative padding values to paddingTop and paddingLeft, which are ignored.

A few interesting observations can be made. Example B and example C are both clipped on the Android device. Example C's Text component's width is compressed, and the negative values for `padding` are ignored in example D.

4.2.4   *Using position to place components*

So far, everything we've looked at has been positioned relative to another component, which is the default layout position. Sometimes it's beneficial to take advantage of absolute positioning and place a component exactly where you want it. The implementation of the `position` style in React Native is similar to CSS, but there aren't as many options. By default, all elements are laid out relative to one another. If `position` is set to `absolute`, then the element is laid out relative to its parent. The available properties for `position` are `relative` (the default position) and `absolute`.

CSS has other values, but those are the only two in React Native. When using `absolute` positioning, the following properties are also available: `top`, `right`, `bottom`, and `left`.

Let's look at a simple example to demonstrate the difference between relative and absolute positioning. In CSS, positioning can get much more confusing, but in React Native the "everything has relative positioning by default" makes it much easier to position items. In figure 4.12, blocks A, B, and C are laid out relative to one another in a row. Without any margin or padding, they're lined up one after another. Block D is a sibling to the ABC row of blocks, meaning the main container is the parent container for the ABC row and block D.

Block D is set to {`position: 'absolute', right: 0, bottom: 0`}, so it's positioned in the lower-right corner of its container. Block E is also set to {`position: 'absolute', right: 0, bottom: 0`}, but its parent container is block B, which means block E is positioned absolutely but with respect to block B. Block E appears in the lower-right corner of block B, instead. Listing 4.13 shows the code for this example.

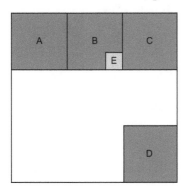

Figure 4.12   An example showing blocks A, B, and C laid out relative to one another. Block D has an absolute position of right: 0 and bottom: 0. Block E also has an absolute position of right: 0 and bottom: 0, but its parent is block B and not the main container, whereas D's parent was the main container.

Listing 4.13   Relative and absolute positioning comparison

```
import React, { Component } from 'react';
import { StyleSheet, Text, View} from 'react-native';

export default class App extends Component<{}> {
    render() {
        return (
            <View style={styles.container}>              Row containing blocks A, B, and C
                <View style={styles.row}>
                    <Example>
                        <CenteredText>A</CenteredText>       Block E is absolutely
                    </Example>                               positioned in the
                    <Example>                                lower-right corner
                        <CenteredText>B</CenteredText>       of its parent
                        <View style={[styles.tinyExample,    container, block B.
                                    {position: 'absolute',
                                     right: 0,
                                     bottom: 0}]}>
                            <CenteredText>E</CenteredText>
                        </View>
                    </Example>
                    <Example>
                        <CenteredText>C</CenteredText>       Block D is absolutely
                    </Example>                               positioned in the
                </View>                                      lower-right corner of
                <Example style={{position: 'absolute',       its parent container.
                            right: 0, bottom: 0}}>
                    <CenteredText>D</CenteredText>
                </Example>
            </View>
        );
    }
}

const Example = (props) => (
    <View style={[styles.example,props.style]}>
        {props.children}
    </View>
);

const CenteredText = (props) => (
    <Text style={[styles.centeredText, props.style]}>
        {props.children}
    </Text>
);

const styles = StyleSheet.create({
    container: {
        width: 300,
        height: 300,
        margin: 40,
        marginTop: 100,
        borderWidth: 1
    },
    row: {              The flexbox direction is specified as row, so
                        the blocks are in a row across the screen.
```

```
        flex: 1,
        flexDirection: 'row'
    },
    example: {
        width: 100,
        height: 100,
        backgroundColor: 'grey',
        borderWidth: 1,
        justifyContent: 'center'
    },
    tinyExample: {
        width: 30,
        height: 30,
        borderWidth: 1,
        justifyContent: 'center',
        backgroundColor: 'lightgrey'
    },
    centeredText: {
        textAlign: 'center',
        margin: 10
    }
});
```

NOTE In listing 4.13, the `flexDirection` property is specified as `'row'`, so the blocks are in a row across the screen. React Native uses an open source, cross-platform layout library called Yoga (https://yogalayout.com). Yoga implements the flexbox layout mode, which you often see in CSS and is used frequently in React Native. We'll spend a lot of time in the next chapter talking about flexbox. Margins, padding, and position are all great layout tools, but flexbox is the tool you'll use most often.

We're finished with the fundamentals of styling `View` components. You've learned about some layout techniques: margins, padding, and position. Let's revisit the Profile Card component and fix the pieces that aren't yet laid out properly.

4.2.5 Profile Card positioning

The following listing has the code changes that need to be made to listing 4.10 to space the circle and user image properly and center everything. Figure 4.13 shows the result.

> **Listing 4.14 Modifying Profile Card styles to fix the layout**

```
...
    cardContainer: {
        alignItems: 'center',        ◄─── Aligns the circle in the horizontal
        borderColor: 'black',              center of the Profile Card
        borderWidth: 3,
        borderStyle: 'solid',
        borderRadius: 20,
        backgroundColor: profileCardColor,
        width: 300,
        height: 400
```

```
},
cardImageContainer: {
    alignItems: 'center',
    backgroundColor: 'white',
    borderWidth: 3,
    borderColor: 'black',
    width: 120,
    height: 120,
    borderRadius: 60,
    marginTop: 30,
    paddingTop: 15
},
...
```

Aligns the user image in the horizontal center of the circle →

Provides padding between the inner part of the circle and the contained image →

Provides space between the top of the circle and the top of the Profile Card →

Figure 4.13   The Profile Card component after all the `View` components have been lined up properly

Now, the major `View` components for the Profile Card are in place. By using the techniques discussed so far, you've built a nice-looking foundation for the component, but you're not finished. You need to add information about the person: name, occupation, and a brief profile description. All that information is text based, so the next thing you'll learn is how to style `Text` components.

4.3   *Styling Text components*

In this section, we'll discuss how to style `Text` components. After you have a working knowledge of how to make text look great, we'll take another look at the Profile Card and add some information about the user. Figure 4.14 is the finished Profile Card component with the user's name and occupation and a brief profile description. But before we revisit the Profile Card, let's look at the styling techniques that will enable you to finish building it.

4.3.1   *Text components vs. View components*

With the exception of flex properties, which we have yet to cover, most of the styles applicable to `View` elements will also work as expected with `Text` elements. Text

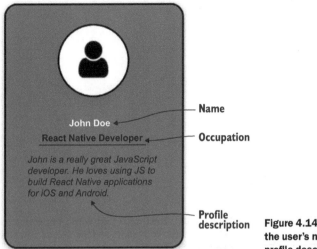

Figure 4.14 The completed Profile Card with the user's name and occupation and a brief profile description

elements can have borders and backgrounds and are affected by layout properties like `margin`, `padding`, and `position`.

The reverse can't be said. Most of the styles `Text` elements can use won't work for `View` elements, which makes perfect sense. If you've ever used a word processor, you know you can use different fonts for text and change the font color; that you can resize, bold, and italicize the text; and that you can apply decorations like underlines.

Before we get into text-specific styling, let's talk about color, a style common to both `Text` and `View` components. Then you'll use color along with everything you've learned thus far to start adding text to the Profile Card.

COLORING TEXT

The `color` property applies to `Text` components in exactly the same way as it does to `View` components. As expected, this property specifies the color of the text in a `Text` element. All the color formats listed in table 4.1 still apply—even `transparent`, although I can't imagine how that's of benefit. By default, the text color is black.

Figure 4.14 showed three `Text` elements in the Profile Card:

- Name
- Occupation
- Profile description

Using what you've already learned, you can center and position the text, change the color of the name from black to white, and add a simple border to separate the occupation from the description. Figure 4.15 shows what you'll end up with by applying techniques in your arsenal.

By this point, you should be able to follow along with listing 4.15 and understand everything that's going on. Don't feel bad if you don't—if necessary, go back and re-read the appropriate sections.

Figure 4.15   The Profile Card with `Text` **elements added using text styling defaults and the** `color` **property for the name set to white**

Listing 4.15   Adding text to the Profile Card

```
import React, { Component } from 'react';
import { Image, StyleSheet, Text, View} from 'react-native';

export default class App extends Component<{}> {
  render() {
    return (
      <View style={styles.container}>
        <View style={styles.cardContainer}>
          <View style={styles.cardImageContainer}>
            <Image style={styles.cardImage}
                   source={require('./user.png')}/>
          </View>
          <View>
            <Text style={styles.cardName}>
              John Doe
            </Text>
          </View>
          <View style={styles.cardOccupationContainer}>
            <Text style={styles.cardOccupation}>
              React Native Developer
            </Text>
          </View>
          <View>
            <Text style={styles.cardDescription}>
              John is a really great JavaScript developer. He
              loves using JS to build React Native applications
              for iOS and Android.
            </Text>
          </View>
        </View>
      </View>
    );
```

Imports the Text component from react-native

Text component that renders the person's name

Container around the occupation text that sets a bottom border separating the occupation from the description

Text component that renders the occupation

Text component that renders the profile description

```
        }
    }

const profileCardColor = 'dodgerblue';

const styles = StyleSheet.create({
    container: {
        flex: 1,
        justifyContent: 'center',
        alignItems: 'center'
    },
    cardContainer: {
        alignItems: 'center',
        borderColor: 'black',
        borderWidth: 3,
        borderStyle: 'solid',
        borderRadius: 20,
        backgroundColor: profileCardColor,
        width: 300,
        height: 400
    },
    cardImageContainer: {
        alignItems: 'center',
        backgroundColor: 'white',
        borderWidth: 3,
        borderColor: 'black',
        width: 120,
        height: 120,
        borderRadius: 60,
        marginTop: 30,
        paddingTop: 15
    },
    cardImage: {
        width: 80,
        height: 80
    },
    cardName: {                         Styles for the name Text component;
        color: 'white',          ◀──   the color is 'white'.
        marginTop: 30,
    },
    cardOccupationContainer: {   ◀──┤ Styles for the occupation container
        borderColor: 'black',
        borderBottomWidth: 3
    },                                  Styles for the occupation text (currently
    cardOccupation: {            ◀──┤  only positional styling)
        marginTop: 10,
        marginBottom: 10,
    },
    cardDescription: {   ◀────  Styles for the profile description
        marginTop: 10,
        marginRight: 40,
        marginLeft: 40,
        marginBottom: 10
    }
});
```

At this point, you have all the content for the Profile Card, but it's pretty plain. In the next couple of sections, we'll talk about how to set font properties and add decorative styles to text.

4.3.2 Font styles

If you've ever used a word processor or written an email with rich text capabilities, you've been able to change fonts, increase or decrease the font size, bold or italicize the text, and so on. These are the same styles you'll learn how to change in this section. By adjusting these styles, you can make text more compelling and attractive to the end user. We'll discuss these properties: `fontFamily`, `fontSize`, `fontStyle`, and `fontWeight`.

SPECIFYING A FONT FAMILY

The `fontFamily` property is deceptively simple. If you stick with the defaults, it's easy; but if you want to use a specific font, you can run into trouble quickly. Both iOS and Android come with a default set of fonts. For iOS, a large number of available fonts can be implemented out of the box. For Android, there's Roboto, a monospace font, and some simple serif and sans serif variants. For a full list of Android and iOS fonts available out of the box in React Native, go to https://github.com/dabit3/react-native-fonts.

If you wanted to use a monospaced font in an application, you couldn't specify either of the following:

- `fontFamily: 'monospace'`—The `'monospace'` option isn't supported on iOS, so on that platform you'll get the error "Unrecognized font family `'monospace'`." But on Android, the font will render correctly without any problems. Unlike CSS, you can't supply multiple fonts to the `fontFamily` property.
- `fontFamily: 'American Typewriter, monospace'`—You'll again get an error on iOS, "Unrecognized font family `'American Typewriter, monospace'`." But on Android, when you supply a font it doesn't support, it falls back to the default. That might not be true in every version of Android, but suffice it to say neither approach will work.

If you want to use different fonts, you'll have to use React Native's `Platform` component. Well discuss `Platform` in more detail in chapter 10, but I want to introduce it, so you can see how to work around this dilemma. Figure 4.16 shows the American Typewriter font rendered on iOS and the generic monospace font used on Android.

The following listing shows the code that produced this example. Pay attention to how the `fontFamily` is set using `Platform.select`.

Figure 4.16   An example of rendering monospaced fonts on both iOS and Android

Listing 4.16 Displaying monospaced fonts on iOS and Android

```
import React, { Component } from 'react';
import { Platform, StyleSheet, Text, View} from 'react-native';
```
Imports the Platform component from react-native

```
export default class App extends Component<{}> {
    render() {
        return (
            <View style={styles.container}>
                <View style={styles.row}>
                    <CenteredText>
                        I am a monospaced font on both platforms
                    </CenteredText>
                    <BottomText>
                        {Platform.OS}
                    </BottomText>
                </View>
            </View>
        );
    }
}
```
Platform.OS can also tell you what OS the code is running on.

```
const CenteredText = (props) => (
    <Text style={[styles.centeredText, props.style]}>
        {props.children}
    </Text>
);
```
Takes advantage of your absolute positioning knowledge

```
const BottomText = (props) => (
    <CenteredText style={[{position: 'absolute', bottom: 0},
                         props.style]}>
        {props.children}
    </CenteredText>
);

const styles = StyleSheet.create({
    container: {
        width: 300,
        height: 300,
        margin: 40,
        marginTop: 100,
        borderWidth: 1
    },
    row: {
        alignItems: 'center',
        flex: 1,
        flexDirection: 'row',
        justifyContent: 'center'
    },
    centeredText: {
        textAlign: 'center',
        margin: 10,
        fontSize: 24,
        ...Platform.select({
            ios: {
```
Uses Platform.select to pick the styles for the appropriate platform

```
                fontFamily: 'American Typewriter'
            },
            android: {
                fontFamily: 'monospace'
            }
        })
    }
});
```

This example shows how to select fonts based on the OS, but the set of fonts at your disposal is still limited to what comes with React Native out of the box. You can add custom fonts to a project using font files (TTF, OTF, and so on) and linking them to your application as assets. In theory the process is simple, but success varies greatly depending on the OS and the font files being used. I want you to know it's possible to do, but if you want to give it try, break out your search engine of choice and look into `react-native link`.

ADJUSTING TEXT SIZE WITH FONTSIZE

`fontSize` is pretty simple: it adjusts the size of the text in a `Text` element. You've used this quite a bit already, so we won't go into much detail other than the fact that the default `fontSize` is 14.

CHANGING FONT STYLES

You can use `fontStyle` to change the font style to italic. The default is `'normal'`. The only two options at this moment are `'normal'` and `'italic'`.

SPECIFYING FONT WEIGHTS

`fontWeight` refers to the thickness of the font. The default is `'normal'` or `'400'`. The options for `fontWeight` are `'normal'`, `'bold'`, `'100'`, `'200'`, `'300'`, `'400'`, `'500'`, `'600'`, `'700'`, `'800'`, and `'900'`. The smaller the value, the lighter/thinner the text. The larger the value, the thicker/bolder the text.

Now that you know how to change the font styles, you can almost finish the Profile Card component. Let's change some font styles and see how close you can get to the final product, as shown in figure 4.17. The next listing shows how to change the styles from listing 4.16 to achieve this look.

Listing 4.17   Setting font styles for Text elements in the Profile Card

```
...
cardName: {
    color: 'white',
    fontWeight: 'bold',          ◀──────  Changes the font weight
    fontSize: 24,       ◀                 of the name text to bold
    marginTop: 30,
},                                Changes the font size
...                               of the name text to 24
cardOccupation: {
    fontWeight: 'bold',    ◀───────  Bolds the occupation text
    marginTop: 10,
    marginBottom: 10,
},
cardDescription: {
```

```
        fontStyle: 'italic',          ◄─────┤ Italicizes the description text
        marginTop: 10,
        marginRight: 40,
        marginLeft: 40,
        marginBottom: 10
    }
    ...
```

Figure 4.17   The Profile Card with font styles applied to the Name, Occupation, and Description texts

Modifying the font styles for the name, occupation, and description text helps differentiate each of the sections, but the name still doesn't stand out much. The next section covers some decorative ways to style text and how to use those techniques to make the name stand out in the Profile Card.

4.3.3 *Using decorative text styles*

In this section, you'll go beyond the basics of changing font styles and start applying decorative styles to text. I'll show you how to do things like underline and strikethrough text and add drop shadows. These techniques can add a lot of visual variety to applications and help text elements stand out from one another.

Here are the properties we'll cover in this section:

- *iOS and Android*—lineHeight, textAlign, textDecorationLine, textShadowColor, textShadowOffset, and textShadowRadius
- *Android only*—textAlignVertical
- *iOS only*—letterSpacing, textDecorationColor, textDecorationStyle, and writingDirection.

Notice that some of the properties only apply to one OS or another. Some values that can be assigned to the properties are also OS-specific. It's important to keep this in mind, especially if you're relying on a specific style to highlight a particular element of text on the screen.

lineHeight specifies the height of the Text element. Figure 4.18 and listing 4.18 show an example of how this behaves differently on iOS versus Android. A lineHeight of 100 is applied to the Text B element: the height of that line is significantly greater than the others. Also notice how iOS and Android position the text within the line differently. On Android, the text is positioned at the bottom of the line.

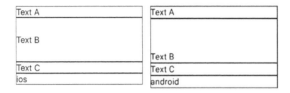

Figure 4.18   Example of using lineHeight **on iOS and Android.**

Listing 4.18   Applying lineHeight **to a** Text **element in iOS and Android**

```
import React, { Component } from 'react';
import { Platform, StyleSheet, Text, View} from 'react-native';

export default class App extends Component<{}> {
    render() {
        return (
            <View style={styles.container}>
                <TextContainer>
                    <LeftText>Text A</LeftText>
                </TextContainer>
                <TextContainer>
                    <LeftText style={{lineHeight: 100}}>      ◀── Sets lineHeight to 100
                        Text B
                    </LeftText>
                </TextContainer>
                <TextContainer>
                    <LeftText>Text C</LeftText>
                </TextContainer>
                <TextContainer>
                    <LeftText>{Platform.OS}</LeftText>
                </TextContainer>
            </View>
        );
    }
}

const LeftText = (props) => (
    <Text style={[styles.leftText, props.style]}>
        {props.children}
    </Text>
);

const TextContainer = (props) => (
    <View style={[styles.textContainer, props.style]}>
        {props.children}
```

```
      </View>
);

const styles = StyleSheet.create({
    container: {
        width: 300,
        height: 300,
        margin: 40,
        marginTop: 100
    },
    textContainer: {
        borderWidth: 1        ◄─────┐  Setting a border lets you easily
    },                              │  see the height of the line.
    leftText: {
        fontSize: 20
    }
});
```

ALIGNING TEXT HORIZONTALLY

textAlign refers to how the text in the element will be horizontally aligned. The options for textAlign are 'auto', 'center', 'right', 'left', and 'justify' ('justify' is iOS only).

UNDERLINING TEXT OR ADDING LINES THROUGH TEXT

Use the textDecorationLine property to add either an underline or a line through the given text. The options for textDecorationLine are 'none', 'underline', 'line-through', and 'underline line-through'. The default value is 'none'. When you specify 'underline line-through', a single space separates the values in quotes.

TEXT-DECORATION STYLES (IOS ONLY)

iOS supports several text-decoration styles that Android doesn't. The first is text-DecorationColor, which allows you to set a color for textDecorationLine. iOS also supports styling the line itself. On Android, the line is always solid, but on iOS tex-tDecorationStyle lets you specify 'solid', 'double', 'dotted', and 'dashed'. Android will ignore these additional styles.

To use the additional iOS decoration styles, specify them in conjunction with the primary textDecorationLine style. For example:

```
{
  textDecorationLine: 'underline',
  textDecorationColor: 'red',
  textDecorationStyle: 'double'
}
```

ADDING SHADOWS TO TEXT

You can use the textShadowColor, textShadowOffset, and textShadowRadius properties to add a shadow to a Text element. To create a shadow, you need to specify three things:

- The color
- The offset
- The radius

The offset specifies the position of the shadow relative to the component casting the shadow. The radius basically defines how blurry the shadow appears. You can specify a text shadow like this:

```
{
  textShadowColor: 'red',
  textShadowOffset: {width: -2, height: -2},
  textShadowRadius: 4
}
```

CONTROLLING LETTER SPACING (IOS ONLY)

`letterSpacing` specifies the spacing between text characters. It's not something you'll use every day, but it can produce some interesting visual effects. Keep in mind that it's iOS only, so use it if you need it.

EXAMPLES OF TEXT STYLES

We've gone through a lot of different styles in this section. Figure 4.19 shows various styles applied to `Text` components.

Here's a quick rundown of the styles being used for each example in figure 4.19:

- A is italic text using `{fontStyle: 'italic'}`.
- B shows text decoration with an underline and a line through the text. The style for this is `{textDecorationLine: 'underline line-through'}`.
- C expands on example B by also applying some iOS-only text styles, `{textDecorationColor: 'red', textDecorationStyle: 'dotted'}`. Notice how these styles have no effect in Android.
- D applies a shadow using `{textShadowColor: 'red', textShadowOffset: {width: -2, height: -2}, textShadowRadius: 4}`.
- E uses the iOS-only `{letterSpacing: 5}`, which doesn't affect Android.
- The text *ios* and *android* is styled using `{textAlign: 'center', fontWeight: 'bold'}`.

Use listing 4.19 as a starting point, and see how modifying the styles affects the result.

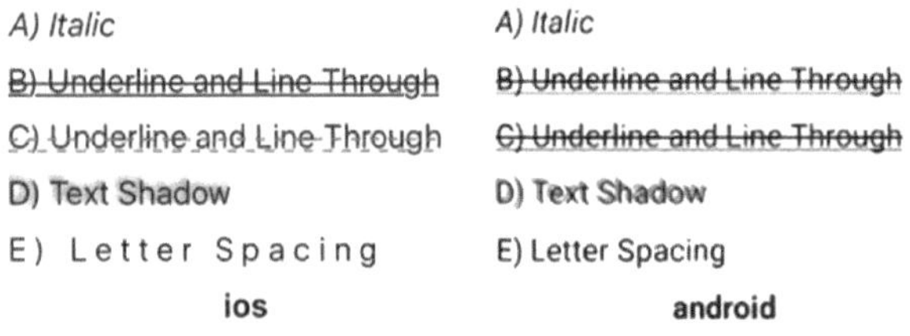

A) Italic	A) Italic
B) Underline and Line Through	B) Underline and Line Through
C) Underline and Line Through	C) Underline and Line Through
D) Text Shadow	D) Text Shadow
E) L e t t e r S p a c i n g	E) Letter Spacing
ios	**android**

Figure 4.19   Various examples of styling text components

Listing 4.19 Examples of styling `Text` components

```
import React, { Component } from 'react';
import { Platform, StyleSheet, Text, View} from 'react-native';

export default class App extends Component<{}> {
  render() {
    return (
      <View style={styles.container}>
        <LeftText style={{fontStyle: 'italic'}}>
          A) Italic
        </LeftText>
        <LeftText style={{textDecorationLine: 'underline line-through'}}>
          B) Underline and Line Through
        </LeftText>
        <LeftText style={{textDecorationLine: 'underline line-through',
                         textDecorationColor: 'red',
                         textDecorationStyle: 'dotted'}}>
          C) Underline and Line Through
        </LeftText>
        <LeftText style={{textShadowColor: 'red',
                         textShadowOffset: {width: -2, height: -2},
                         textShadowRadius: 4}}>
          D) Text Shadow
        </LeftText>
        <LeftText style={{letterSpacing: 5}}>
          E) Letter Spacing
        </LeftText>
        <LeftText style={{textAlign: 'center', fontWeight: 'bold'}}>
          {Platform.OS}
        </LeftText>
      </View>
    );
  }
}

const LeftText = (props) => (
    <Text style={[styles.leftText, props.style]}>
        {props.children}
    </Text>
);

const styles = StyleSheet.create({
    container: {
        width: 300,
        height: 300,
        margin: 40,
        marginTop: 100
    },
    leftText: {
        fontSize: 20,
        paddingBottom: 10
    }
});
```

Figure 4.20   The completed Profile Card example. Textual information has been added about the person using the text styling techniques covered in this section.

Now that you know how to create a shadow effect, let's add a shadow to the person's name so it stands out from the other text. Figure 4.20 shows the desired result.

The completed code for the Profile Card is provided next. You only have to add a tiny snippet to set the text shadow for the name.

Listing 4.20   Completed Profile Card example

```
import React, { Component } from 'react';
import { Image, StyleSheet, Text, View} from 'react-native';

export default class App extends Component<{}> {
    render() {
        return (
            <View style={styles.container}>
                <View style={styles.cardContainer}>
                    <View style={styles.cardImageContainer}>
                        <Image style={styles.cardImage
                                source={require('./user.png')}/>
                    </View>
                    <View>
                        <Text style={styles.cardName}>
                            John Doe
                        </Text>
                    </View>
                    <View style={styles.cardOccupationContainer}>
                        <Text style={styles.cardOccupation}>
                            React Native Developer
                        </Text>
                    </View>
                    <View>
                        <Text style={styles.cardDescription}>
                            John is a really great JavaScript developer.
                            He loves using JS to build React Native
                            applications for iOS and Android.
```

```
                              </Text>
                          </View>
                      </View>
                  </View>
              );
          }
      }

      const profileCardColor = 'dodgerblue';

      const styles = StyleSheet.create({
          container: {
              flex: 1,
              justifyContent: 'center',
              alignItems: 'center'
          },
          cardContainer: {
              alignItems: 'center',
              borderColor: 'black',
              borderWidth: 3,
              borderStyle: 'solid',
              borderRadius: 20,
              backgroundColor: profileCardColor,
              width: 300,
              height: 400
          },
          cardImageContainer: {
              alignItems: 'center',
              backgroundColor: 'white',
              borderWidth: 3,
              borderColor: 'black',
              width: 120,
              height: 120,
              borderRadius: 60,
              marginTop: 30,
              paddingTop: 15
          },
          cardImage: {
              width: 80,
              height: 80
          },
          cardName: {
              color: 'white',
              fontWeight: 'bold',
              fontSize: 24,
              marginTop: 30,
              textShadowColor: 'black',         ◄─── Sets the shadow color to black
                                                     on the Title text component
              textShadowOffset: {      ◄───
                  height: 2,                  Sets the shadow offset to
                  width: 2                    be down and to the right
              },
              textShadowRadius: 3      ◄────── Sets the shadow radius
          },
          cardOccupationContainer: {
              borderColor: 'black',
              borderBottomWidth: 3
```

```
    },
    cardOccupation: {
        fontWeight: 'bold',
        marginTop: 10,
        marginBottom: 10,
    },
    cardDescription: {
        fontStyle: 'italic',
        marginTop: 10,
        marginRight: 40,
        marginLeft: 40,
        marginBottom: 10
    }
});
```

There's a lot you could do to this basic example to make it even better, but the goal was to show how beneficial it is to understand styling concepts. You don't have to be a fantastic graphic designer to make a nice-looking component—a few simple techniques can make your application look great.

We covered a lot of ground in this chapter, but believe it or not, this has been a short introduction! We'll explore some additional advanced topics in chapter 5.

Summary

- Styles can be applied inline with components or by creating stylesheets that can be referenced by components.
- Styles should be organized in the same file as the component after the component definition or externalized into a separate styles.js file.
- Styles are code. The fact that JavaScript is a complete language with variables and functions affords many advantages over traditional CSS.
- View components are the main building blocks of a UI, and they have many styling properties.
- You can use borders in many ways to enhance the look of components. You can even use borders to create shapes, such as circles.
- You can use margins and padding to position components relative to one another.
- Absolute positioning lets you place a component anywhere within the parent container.
- Clipping can occur on Android devices, depending on how you set borders, margins, and padding.
- Specifying fonts other than the defaults can be tricky. Use the Platform component to select the appropriate font for the OS.
- Use general font styles like color, size, and weight to change the size and appearance of Text components.
- There are rendering differences between OSs, such as how the line height behaves differently between iOS and Android.
- Text-decorating styles can add underlines or drop shadows to text. The set of available styles differs from one OS to another.

Styling in depth

This chapter covers

- Platform-specific sizes and styles

- Adding drop shadows to components

- Moving and rotating components on the x- and y-axes

- Scaling and skewing components

- Using flexbox for layout

Chapter 4 introduced styling React Native components. It showed how to style `View` and `Text` components, styles you'll likely use every day and that mostly affect the look of a component. This chapter continues the discussion and goes into more depth with platform-specific styles; drop shadows; manipulating components with transformations such as translation, rotation, scaling, and skewing; and dynamically laying out components with flexbox.

Some of these topics may feel familiar. You used platform-specific styles and flexbox in several of the examples in chapter 4. We didn't cover them in detail, but you saw them in a few code listings.

This chapter expands on those topics. Transformations give you the power to manipulate components in two or three dimensions. You can translate components from one position to another, rotate components, scale components to different sizes, and skew components. Transforms are useful in their own right, but they will play a much bigger role in chapter 7, which discusses animation in detail.

We'll continue talking about some of the differences between platforms and look more deeply at flexbox. Because flexbox is a fundamental concept, it's important to properly understand it so you can create layouts and UIs in React Native. You'll probably use flexbox in every application you create. You'll use some of your new styling techniques to continue building new features into the `ProfileCard` example from the previous chapter.

5.1   Platform-specific sizes and styles

You've seen how to use the `Platform.select` utility function to choose fonts available only on iOS or Android. You used `Platform.select` to choose a monospaced font supported by each platform. You might not have thought much of that at the time, but it's important to keep in mind that you're developing for two different platforms. The styles you apply to a component may look or behave differently between the two OSs or even between different versions of iOS and Android.

You aren't coding for a single device; you're not even coding for a single OS. The beauty of React Native is that you're using JavaScript to create applications that can run on both iOS and Android. If you look through the React Native documentation, you'll see many components suffixed with IOS or Android, such as `ProgressBarAndroid`, `ProgressViewIOS`, and `ToolbarAndroid`, so it should come as no surprise that styles can be platform specific too.

You may not have noticed that you've never specified a size in pixels for anything, like `width: 300` vs `width: '300px'`. That's because even the concept of size is different between the iOS and Android operating systems.

5.1.1   Pixels, points, and DPs

Size can be a confusing topic, but it's important to keep in mind if you need to be absolutely precise when positioning components on the screen. Even if you're not trying to produce a high-fidelity layout, it will be useful to understand the concepts in case you encounter small discrepancies in your layouts from one device to another.

Let's start from the beginning and define a pixel. A *pixel* is the smallest unit of programmable color on a display. A pixel is typically made up of red, green, and blue (RGB) color components. By manipulating the intensity of each RGB value, the pixel emits a color you see. A pixel doesn't tell you anything until you start looking at the physical properties of the display: screen size, resolution, and dots per inch.

The *screen size* is the diagonal measurement of the screen, from one corner to another. For example, the original screen size of the iPhone was 3.5 inches, while the screen size of the iPhone X is 5.8 inches. Although the iPhone X is considerably bigger, the size doesn't mean anything until you understand how many pixels fit within that screen size.

Resolution is the number of pixels in the display, which is most typically expressed as the number of pixels along the width and height of the device. The original iPhone was 320 × 480, while the iPhone X is 1125 × 2436.

Screen size and resolution can then be used to calculate the pixel density: *pixels per inch* (PPI). You'll often see this expressed as *dots per inch* (DPI), which is a holdover term from the printing world, where a dot of color was printed on the page. PPI and DPI are often used interchangeably even though that's not exactly correct, so if you see DPI used in reference to a screen, know that PPI is what's truly being discussed.

The PPI gives you a measure of image sharpness. Imagine if two screens had the same resolution, 320 × 480 (half VGA). What would the same image look like on the 3.5-inch iPhone display versus a 17-inch HVGA monitor display? The same image would look much sharper on the iPhone, because it has 163 PPI versus the CRT monitor, which has 34 PPI. You can fit nearly five times as much information in the same physical space on the original iPhone. Table 5.1 compares the diagonal size, resolution, and PPI of the two devices.

Table 5.1   Comparison of a 17-inch HVGA monitor's PPI vs. the original iPhone's PPI

	HVGA monitor	Original iPhone
Diagonal size	17 inches	3.5 inches
Resolution	320 × 480	320 × 480
PPI	34	163

Why does this matter? Because neither iOS nor Android uses the actual physical measurements to render content to a device's screen. iOS uses an abstract measurement of points, and Android uses a similar abstract measurement of density-independent pixels.

When the iPhone 4 came on the scene, it had the same physical size as its predecessors; but it had a fancy new Retina screen with a resolution of 640 × 960, quadrupling the resolution of the original device. If the iPhone had rendered images from existing apps at a 1:1 scale, everything would be drawn at a quarter size on the new Retina display. It would have been an insane proposition for Apple to make such a change and break all the existing apps.

Instead, Apple introduced the logical concept of a *point.* A point is a unit of distance that can be scaled independently of a device's resolution, so a 320 × 480 image that took up the entire screen on an original iPhone could be scaled up 2x to fully fit within the Retina display. Figure 5.1 provides a visualization of pixel density for several iPhone models.

The original iPhone's 163 PPI is the basis for the iOS point. An iOS point is 1/163 of an inch. Without going into more detail, Android uses a similar measure called a *device-independent pixel* (DIP, often abbreviated DP). An Android DP is 1/160 of an inch.

When defining styles in React Native, you use the logical concept of a pixel, a point on iOS, and a DP on Android. When working at the native level, you occasionally may need to work with device pixels by multiplying the logical pixels by the screen scale (for example, 2x, 3x).

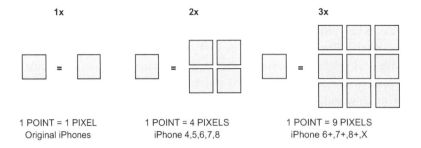

Figure 5.1   A visualization of points compared to pixel density for iPhones. The original iPhone had a resolution of 320 × 480. The iPhone 4 had a resolution of 640 × 960, quadruple the resolution of the original device. The iPhone 4 has twice the PPI (326 vs. 163), so images are said to be scaled up 2x.

5.1.2   Creating drop shadows with ShadowPropTypesIOS and Elevation

In chapter 4, you used the text shadow properties to add a drop shadow to the `ProfileCard` title. Both iOS and Android support adding a drop shadow to a `Text` component. It would be nice to spruce up more of the `ProfileCard` by adding drop shadows to the card and circular image container, but there isn't a common style property for `View` components to use between the two platforms.

That doesn't mean all is lost. The `ShadowPropTypesIOS` style can be used to add a drop shadow on iOS devices; it doesn't affect the z-order of the component. On Android, you can use the `Elevation` style to simulate a drop shadow, but it *does* affect the z-order of the component.

CREATING DROP SHADOWS IN IOS WITH SHADOWPROPTYPESIOS

Let's look at how to use `ShadowPropTypesIOS` styles to add drop shadows to a few view components. Figure 5.2 shows various shadow effects that can be achieved. Table 5.2 lists the specific settings used to achieve each shadow effect. The important takeaways are as follows:

- If you don't supply a value for `shadowOpacity`, you won't see a shadow.
- Shadows offsets are expressed in terms of width and height, but you can think of this as moving the shadow in the x and y directions. You can even specify negative values for width and height.
- A `shadowOpacity` of 1 is completely solid, whereas a value of 0.2 is more transparent.
- A value for `shadowRadius` effectively blurs the edges of the shadow. The shadow is more diffuse.

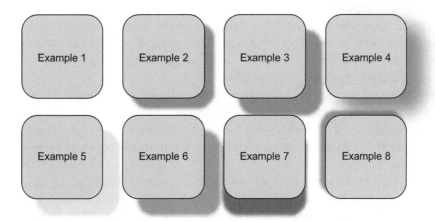

Figure 5.2 iOS-specific examples of how to apply `ShadowPropTypesIOS` **styles to** `View` **components. Example 1 has a shadow applied but no opacity set, which causes the drop shadow to not be displayed. Example 2 has the same shadow effect but with opacity set to 1. Example 3 has a slightly larger shadow, and example 4 has the same size shadow with a shadow radius. Example 5 has the same shadow size, but opacity is changed from 1 to 0.2. Example 6 changes the color of the shadow. Example 7 shows the shadow applied in only one direction, and example 8 shows the shadow applied in the opposite direction.**

Table 5.2 Shadow properties used to create the examples in figure 5.2

		shadowOffset			
Example	shadowColor	width (x)	height (y)	shadowOpacity	shadowRadius
1	Black	10	10		
2	Black	10	10	1	
3	Black	20	20	1	
4	Black	20	20	1	20
5	Black	20	20	0.2	
6	Red	20	20	1	
7	Black		20	1	
8	Black	-5	-5	1	

The code for this figure can be found in the git repository under chapter5/figures/ Figure-5.2-ShadowPropTypesIOS. If you run the code for this example, remember to run it in the iOS simulator. On an Android device, you'll just see eight boring squares with rounded corners. ShadowPropTypesIOS styles are ignored on Android.

APPROXIMATING DROP SHADOWS ON ANDROID DEVICES WITH ELEVATION

How do you get the same effect on Android devices? The truth is, you can't. You *can* use Android's elevation style to affect the z-order of components. If two or more components occupy the same space, you can decide which one should be in front by giving it the larger elevation and therefore the larger z-index, which will create a small drop shadow, but it isn't nearly as striking as the shadow effects you can achieve on iOS. Note that this only applies to Android, because iOS doesn't support the `elevation` style and will gladly ignore it if it's specified.

Nevertheless, let's see `elevation` in action. To do so, you'll create a `View` component with three boxes, each of which is positioned absolutely. You'll give them three different elevations—1, 2, and 3—and then you'll reverse the assignment of the elevations and see how that affects the layout. Figure 5.3 shows the results of these elevation adjustments.

Table 5.3 shows the absolute positions and elevations used for each group of boxes. Notice that nothing has changed except the `elevation` assigned to each of the boxes. iOS ignores the style and always renders box C on top of box B, and box B on top of box A. But Android respects the style and flips the order in which it renders the boxes, so box A is now on top of box B, and box B is on top of box C.

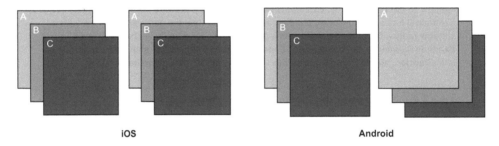

iOS   Android

Figure 5.3   Examples of using the `elevation` style on iOS and Android. On iOS, elevation is ignored; all components retain the same z-order, so whatever component is last in the layout is on top. On Android, elevation is used, and the z-order is changed; in the second example, where the elevation assignments are reversed, A is on top.

Table 5.3   Elevation settings for figure 5.3

Example	color	top	left	elevation
A	Red	0	0	1
B	Orange	20	20	2
C	Blue	40	40	3
A	Red	0	0	3
B	Orange	20	20	2
C	Blue	40	40	1

5.1.3 Putting it into practice: drop shadows in the ProfileCard

Let's go back to the `ProfileCard` example from the last chapter and add some drop shadows that will look great on iOS and not so great on Android. You'll add a drop shadow to the entire `ProfileCard` container and to the circular image container. Figure 5.4 shows what you're shooting for on iOS and what you'll get on Android.

Notice that even with `elevation` applied on Android, you don't see much of a shadow. The reality is, on Android you'll never get close to the shadow effects that can be produced on iOS with React Native out of the box. If you really must have drop shadows on Android, then I suggest looking for a component on npm or yarn that does what you need. Experiment with different components, and see if you can get the Android version looking as sharp as the iOS version. I don't have any recommendations; I stay away from drop shadows or accept the differences.

The code in this chapter begins with listing 4.20: the completed `ProfileCard` example from chapter 4. Listing 5.1 only shows the changes needed to apply the drop shadows to the component. You don't need to add a lot of code to get the drop shadows on iOS. Look at the listing on an Android device, and see how the `elevation` setting causes the faintest of shadows.

Figure 5.4 The `ProfileCard` on iOS and Android after drop shadows have been added to the card container and the circular image container. The drop shadows on iOS are created using the iOS-specific shadow properties: `shadowColor`, `shadowOffset`, and `shadowOpacity`. On Android, the `elevation` property is used to try to create depth. It produces only a minor shadow effect, far inferior to the shadows produced on iOS.

Listing 5.1   Adding drop shadows to the `ProfileCard`

```
import React, { Component } from 'react';
import { Image, Platform, StyleSheet, Text, View} from 'react-native';
...
cardContainer: {
...
  height: 400,
  ...Platform.select({
    ios: {
      shadowColor: 'black',
      shadowOffset: {
        height: 10
      },
      shadowOpacity: 1
    },
    android: {
      elevation: 15
    }
  })
},
cardImageContainer: {
...
  paddingTop: 15,
  ...Platform.select({
    ios: {
      shadowColor: 'black',
      shadowOffset: {
        height: 10,
      },
      shadowOpacity: 1
    },
    android: {
      borderWidth: 3,
      borderColor: 'black',
      elevation: 15
    }
  })
},
...
```

Imports the Platform utility component to programmatically select styles based on the platform

Adds a drop shadow to the card container based on the platform

Adds a drop shadow to the circular image container

Just as with font selection in chapter 4, you use the `Platform.select` function to apply different styles to components based on the platform: iOS or Android. In some cases, like the drop shadow, one platform may perform much better than the other; but in most cases the styles will behave the same on both platforms, which is an amazing benefit of React Native.

5.2   Using transformations to move, rotate, scale, and skew components

Up to this point, the styles we've discussed have mostly affected the appearance of components. You learned how to set properties like the style, weight, size, and color of borders and fonts. You applied background colors and shadow effects, and you saw how to manipulate the appearance of components relative to one another by using margins and padding. But we haven't explored how to manipulate a component's position or orientation on the screen independent of everything else. How do you move a component on the screen, or rotate a component in a circle?

The answer is *transformations*. React Native provides a number of useful transforms that allow you to modify the shape and position of a component in 3D space. You can move components from one position to another, rotate components about all three axes, and scale and skew components in the x and y directions. Alone, transformations can produce some interesting effects, but their true power comes from sequencing them together to form animations.

This section will give you a firm understanding of transforms and how they affect the components to which they're applied. If you clearly understand what they do, you'll be better able to link them together to create meaningful animations later.

The `transform` style takes an array of transform properties that define how to apply a transformation to a component. For example, to rotate a component 90 degrees and shrink it by 50%, apply this transform to the component:

```
transform: [{rotate: '90deg', scale: .5}]
```

The `transform` style supports the following properties:

- `perspective`
- `translateX` and `translateY`
- `rotateX`, `rotateY`, and `rotateZ` (`rotate`)
- `scale`, `scaleX`, and `scaleY`
- `skewX` and `skewY`

5.2.1   *3D effects with perspective*

`perspective` gives an element 3D space by affecting the distance between the z plane and the user. This is used with other properties to give a 3D effect. The larger the `perspective` value, the greater the z-index of a component, which makes it appear closer to the user. If the z-index is negative, the farther away the component appears.

5.2.2   *Moving elements along the x- and y-axes with translateX and translateY*

The translation properties move an element along the x (`translateX`) or y (`translateY`) axis from the current position. This isn't very useful in normal development because you already have `margin`, `padding`, and other position properties available. But this becomes useful for animations, to move a component across the screen from one position to another.

Let's look at how to move a square using the `translateX` and `translateY` style properties. In figure 5.5, a square is placed in the center of the display and then moved in each of the four cardinal and four ordinal directions: NW (upper left), N (top), NE (upper right), W (left), E (right), SW (bottom left), S (bottom), and SE (bottom right). In each case, the center of the square is moved by 1.5 times the square's size in the x or y direction or in both directions.

When studying geometry, you typically see the positive y-axis drawn going up instead of down. But on mobile devices, the convention is to have the positive y-axis go down the screen, which reflects the most common interaction of scrolling down the screen to view more content. Coupled with that bit of knowledge, it's pretty easy to see how moving the center square in figure 5.5 in the positive x direction and in the positive y direction results in the square ending up in the bottom right corner. By combining `translateX` and `translateY`, you can move components in any direction in the Cartesian plane (x-y plane).

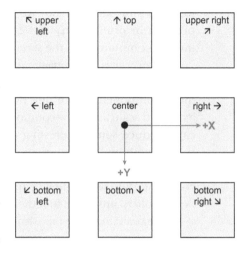

Figure 5.5   A depiction of a center square being moved in each of the four cardinal and four ordinal directions: NW (upper left), N (top), NE (upper right), W (left), E (right), SW (bottom left), S (bottom), and SE (bottom right)

There's no corresponding translation for movement in the z plane. The z-axis is perpendicular to the face of the device, which means you're looking straight at it. Moving a component forward or backward would be imperceptible without some corresponding size change. The `perspective` transform is intended to handle this type of visual effect.

In the next section, we'll use the same example and focus on the center row, where the center square was translated to the left and to the right. You'll see what happens when you rotate components along each of the three axes.

5.2.3   *Rotating elements with rotateX, rotateY, and rotateZ (rotate)*

The rotation properties do exactly what it sounds like they would: they rotate elements. Rotation occurs along an axis: x, y, or z. The origin of the rotation is the center point of the element before any transformations are applied, so if you use `translateX` or `translateY`, keep in mind that the rotation will be around the axis at the original location. The amount of rotation can be specified in either degrees (deg) or radians (rad). The examples use degrees:

```
transform: [{ rotate:   '45deg' }]
transform: [{ rotate:   '0.785398rad' }]
```

Figure 5.6 shows the positive and negative direction of rotation for each axis. The `rotate` transform does the same thing as the `rotateZ` transform.

Let's rotate a 100 × 100 square about the x-axis in increments of 35°, as shown in figure 5.7. A center line is drawn through each square, so it's easier to see how the squares are rotating. You can visualize rotation about the x-axis in the positive direction as the square rotating from the top into the page. The bottom is coming closer to you as the top moves further away.

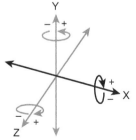

Figure 5.6   The positive and negative direction of rotation for each axis

RotateX

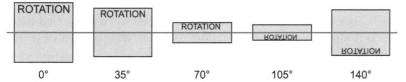

Figure 5.7   Rotating a 100 × 100 square about the x-axis in increments of 35°.
After 90°, the "ROTATION" label can be seen through the element, upside down.

At 90°, you're looking at the square on its edge (because it doesn't have any thickness, you don't see a thing). After the square has rotated past the 90° mark, you start to see the back of the square. If you look closely in figure 5.7, you can see the "ROTATION" label is upside down, because you're looking through what was the back of the square.

The next example will rotate the same 100 × 100 square about the y-axis, instead continuing to use increments of 35° to demonstrate the rotation (see figure 5.8). Picture the right side of the square moving away from you, into the page. After the square has rotated beyond the 90° mark, you can see the "ROTATION" label through the component. Because you're looking through the back of the component, the text appears backward.

Compare figure 5.8 to figure 5.7. Fundamentally, rotation about the y-axis is no different than rotation about the x-axis. I aligned the squares in figure 5.8 vertically so you can easily see the axis of rotation. I like to visualize rotation in the y-axis by picturing a book opening and closing: if you're opening a book, the cover is rotating in the negative direction. If you're closing the book, then you're rotating the cover in the positive direction.

Rotation about the z-axis is the easiest to visualize. Rotation in the positive direction spins the object in a clockwise fashion, and rotation in the negative direction spins the square in a counterclockwise fashion. For this example, shown in figure 5.9, the axis of rotation is

RotateY

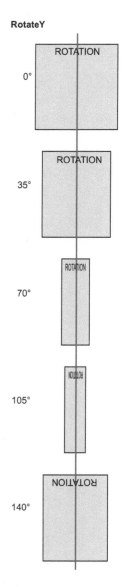

Figure 5.8   Rotating a 100 × 100 square about the y-axis in increments of 35°. After 90°, the "ROTATION" label can be seen through the element, backward.

RotateZ

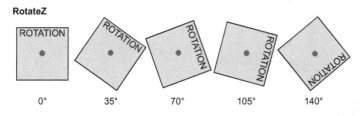

Figure 5.9   Rotating a 100 × 100 square about the z-axis in increments of 35°. The positive rotation is clockwise, and the negative rotation is counterclockwise.

represented as a dot in the center of the square, because the z-axis is, basically, your line of sight; it goes straight into the screen.

Hopefully, it's fairly obvious now how the rotation transforms work. Understanding the direction in which positive and negative rotations affect an object is probably the most complex part. But when you start combining other transforms in conjunction with rotation, you may be surprised by the results. Remember that the transform property is an array of transforms, so multiple transforms can be supplied at once, and order matters! Specifying a transform and switching the order of the elements in the array will yield different results.

Let's investigate how altering the order in which the transforms are specified affects the final layout. Let's apply three different transforms to a square: translate in the y direction 50 points, translate in the x direction 150 points, and rotate the square 45°. Figure 5.10 specifies the transform in the order just described. The original/previous position of the square has a dotted border and the new position of the square has a solid outline, so you can see how the transformation affects the position and orientation of the original square.

The result in figure 5.10 is pretty much as expected, but what will happen if you apply the rotation after moving the square in the y direction? Look at figure 5.11 and find out.

Whoa, what happened? The square is completely off the screen after the transformations are applied! It might not be immediately obvious what happened, which is why figure 5.11 is annotated with the new axis orientation.

After the rotation, the +x- and +y-axes are no longer oriented vertically and horizontally on the screen: they're rotated by 45°. When the `translateX` transform is applied, the square is moved 150 points in the +x direction, but the +x direction is now at a 45° angle from the original x-axis.

The next section shows another interesting aspect of rotational transforms.

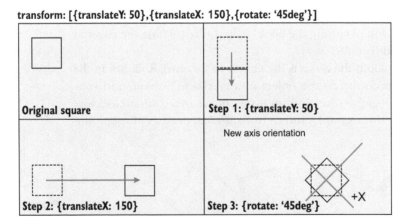

Figure 5.10 Applying `transform: [{translateY: 50},{translateX: 150},{rotate: '45deg'}]` to the original square

transform: [{translateY: 50},{rotate: '45deg'},{translateX: 150}]

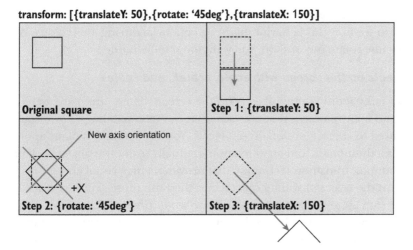

Figure 5.11   Applying `transform: [{translateY: 50},{rotate: '45deg'},{translateX: 150}]` to the original square. Rotating the square changes the orientation of the x- and y-axes, so when the square is translated 150 points in the +x direction, it's moved diagonally down and out of the viewport.

5.2.4   Setting visibility when rotating an element more than 90°

If you look back at figures 5.7 and 5.8, when you rotate the square about the x- or y-axis and go beyond the 90° point, you can still see the text that was on the front face of the square. The `backfaceVisibility` property dictates whether an element is visible when the element is rotated more than 90°. This property can be set to either `'visible'` or `'hidden'`. This property isn't a transform, but it gives you the ability to hide or show elements when viewing the back face of an object.

The `backfaceVisibility` property defaults to `'visible'`, but if you changed `backfaceVisibility` to `'hidden'`, you wouldn't see the element at all once the component rotated more than 90° in either the x or y direction. In figures 5.7 and 5.8, the squares corresponding to the 105° and 140° rotations would disappear. If that sounds confusing, look at figure 5.12.

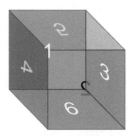

Cube: backfaceVisibility: 'visible'

Cube: backfaceVisibility: 'hidden'

Figure 5.12   A demonstration of how setting the `backfaceVisibility` property to `'hidden'` hides elements that have rotated beyond 90°. The cube on the left shows faces 2, 4, and 5, all of which have rotated 180°. The cube on the right has hidden those faces.

In the figure, you can easily see the effect of setting `backfaceVisibility` to `'hidden'`. It's also easy to see how this behavior might be beneficial during animations. When the faces of the cube rotate out of sight, you want them to be hidden.

5.2.5   *Scaling objects on the screen with scale, scaleX, and scaleY*

This section talks about scaling objects on the screen. There are many practical uses for scaling and many patterns that take advantage of its capabilities. For instance, scaling can be used to create thumbnails of objects. You've seen this in many applications; the user taps a thumbnail, and an animation gradually scales the object back up to full size. It's a common transition technique that provides a nice visual effect.

You'll learn the basics of scaling objects and then use those skills to create a thumbnail of the `ProfileCard` that opens to full size when pressed. Later, this chapter discusses flexbox and how it can be used to manage a bunch of `ProfileCard` thumbnails in a gallery interface, from which you can press profiles to view them in more detail.

`scale` multiplies the size of the element by the number passed to it, the default being 1. To make an element appear larger, pass a value larger than 1; to make it appear smaller, pass a value smaller than 1.

The element can also be scaled along a single axis using `scaleX` or `scaleY`. `scaleX` stretches the element horizontally along the x-axis, and `scaleY` stretches the element vertically along the y-axis. Let's create a few squares to show the effects of scaling: see figure 5.13.

Nothing unusual happens; scaling an object is pretty straightforward. Listing 5.2 shows how simple it is.

Figure 5.13   Examples of how scaling transforms the original square. All the squares start the same size and shape as A, which has the default scale of 1. B scales the square by 0.5, shrinking it. C scales the square by 2, enlarging it. D uses `scaleX`, transforming the square along the x-axis by 3x. E uses `scaleY`, transforming the square along the y-axis by 1.5x.

Listing 5.2   Scaling squares using `scale`, `scaleX`, and `scaleY`

```
import React, { Component } from 'react';
import { StyleSheet, Text, View} from 'react-native';
```

Scales the default square only in the x direction, stretching it horizontally

Scales the default square only in the y direction, stretching it vertically

Default 50 × 50 square with no scaling applied

Scales the default square by 0.5, shrinking it

Scales the default square by 2, making it larger

```
export default class App extends Component<{}> {
    render() {
        return (
            <View style={styles.container}>
                <Example style={{}}>A,1</Example>
                <Example style={{transform: [{scale: 0.5}]}}>B,0.5</Example>
                <Example style={{transform: [{scale: 2}]}}>C,2</Example>
                <Example style={{transform: [{scaleX: 3}]}}>D,X3</Example>
                <Example style={{transform: [{scaleY: 1.5}]}}>E,Y1.5</Example>
            </View>
        );
    }
}

const Example = (props) => (
    <View style={[styles.example,props.style]}>
        <Text>
            {props.children}
        </Text>
    </View>
);

const styles = StyleSheet.create({
    container: {
        marginTop: 75,
        alignItems: 'center',
        flex: 1
    },
    example: {
        width: 50,
        height: 50,
        borderWidth: 2,
        margin: 15,
        alignItems: 'center',
        justifyContent: 'center'
    },
});
```

5.2.6 *Using the scale transform to create a thumbnail of the ProfileCard*

Now that you've seen scaling in action, let's use this technique to create a thumbnail of the ProfileCard. Normally you'd animate what I'm about to show you, to avoid flickering, but let's see how to use scaling in a practical way. Figure 5.14 shows a small, scaled-down version of the ProfileCard component—a thumbnail. If you press the thumbnail, the component will return to full size. If you press the full-size component, it will collapse back down into a thumbnail view.

Begin with the code from listing 5.1. As far as styles go, you only need to add one new style to do the scaling transform from full size to thumbnail. The remainder of the code reorganizes the component's pieces into a more reusable structure and provides the touch capabilities to handle the onPress events.

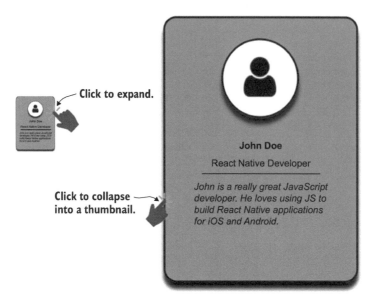

Figure 5.14   Scaling the full-sized `ProfileCard` down 80% into a
thumbnail image. Pressing the thumbnail restores the `ProfileCard` to its
original size, and pressing the full-sized component collapses the component
into a thumbnail.

Listing 5.3   Scaling `ProfileCard` from full size to thumbnail

```
import React, { Component } from 'react';
import PropTypes from 'prop-types';
import update from 'immutability-helper';
import { Image, Platform, StyleSheet, Text,
         TouchableHighlight, View} from 'react-native';

const userImage = require('./user.png');

const data = [{
    image: userImage,
    name: 'John Doe',
    occupation: 'React Native Developer',
    description: 'John is a really great Javascript developer. ' +
'He loves using JS to build React Native applications ' +
'for iOS and Android',
    showThumbnail: true
  }
];

const ProfileCard = (props) => {

  const { image, name, occupation,
          description, onPress, showThumbnail } = props;
  let containerStyles = [styles.cardContainer];
```

PropTypes lets you specify what properties the ProfileCard component can accept.

The TouchableHighlight component enables touch processing.

The immutability helper function update lets you update a specific piece of the component's state.

Data elements have been extracted to generalize the component.

The ProfileCard component is now separated from the App code.

```
  if (showThumbnail) {
    containerStyles.push(styles.cardThumbnail);
  }

  return (
    <TouchableHighlight onPress={onPress}>
      <View style={[containerStyles]}>
        <View style={styles.cardImageContainer}>
          <Image style={styles.cardImage} source={image}/>
        </View>
        <View>
          <Text style={styles.cardName}>
            {name}
          </Text>
        </View>
        <View style={styles.cardOccupationContainer}>
          <Text style={styles.cardOccupation}>
            {occupation}
          </Text>
        </View>
        <View>
          <Text style={styles.cardDescription}>
            {description}
          </Text>
        </View>
      </View>
    </TouchableHighlight>
  )
};

ProfileCard.propTypes = {
  image: PropTypes.number.isRequired,
  name: PropTypes.string.isRequired,
  occupation: PropTypes.string.isRequired,
  description: PropTypes.string.isRequired,
  showThumbnail: PropTypes.bool.isRequired,
  onPress: PropTypes.func.isRequired
};

export default class App extends Component<{}> {

  constructor(props, context) {
    super(props, context);
    this.state = {
      data: data
    }
  }
  handleProfileCardPress = (index) => {
    const showThumbnail = !this.state.data[index].showThumbnail;
    this.setState({
      data: update(this.state.data,
                   {[index]: {showThumbnail: {$set: showThumbnail}}})
    });
  };
  render() {
    const list = this.state.data.map(function(item, index) {
```

If showThumbnail is true, the component is scaled down by 80%.

Processes presses to minimize and maximize the component

Component state is maintained in the higher-order App component.

Handler function to process onPress events

List (array) of ProfileCard components

```
        const { image, name, occupation, description, showThumbnail } = item;
        return <ProfileCard key={'card-' + index}
                    image={image}
                    name={name}
                    occupation={occupation}
                    description={description}
                    onPress={this.handleProfileCardPress.bind(this, index)}
                    showThumbnail={showThumbnail}/>
      }, this);

      return (
        <View style={styles.container}>
          {list}    ◄────────┐
        </View>             │   Renders the list in the overall container
      );
    }
  }
                          ┌────────────────────────────────┐
...                       │ The cardThumbnail style reduces │
  cardThumbnail: {    ◄───┤ the component's size by 80%.    │
    transform: [{scale: 0.2}]
  },
...
```

By reorganizing the structure of the component, you can better handle adding more `ProfileCard` components to the application. In section 5.3, you'll add more Profile-Cards and see how to organize them into a gallery layout.

5.2.7   *Skewing elements along the x- and y-axes with skewX and skewY*

Before we leave transforms and talk about layout, let's look at the skewX and skewY transformations. In the source code that produced the cubes for the backfaceVisibility example shown in figure 5.12 (github chapter5/figures/Figure-5.12-BackfaceVisibility), you can see that skewing the squares was essential to producing the three-dimensional affect for the cube faces. Let's discuss what skewX and skewY do, so when you explore the source code in detail, you'll understand what you're seeing.

The skewX property skews an element along the x-axis. Similarly, the skewY property skews an element along the y-axis. Figure 5.15 shows the results of skewing a square as follows:

- Square A has no transformation applied to it.
- Square B is skewed along the x-axis by 45°.
- Square C is skewed along the x-axis by –45°.
- Square D is skewed along the y-axis by 45°.
- Square E is skewed along the y-axis by –45°.

As with scaling, skewing an element is relatively simple: provide an angle, and specify the axis. The next listing gives all the details.

> **NOTE**   At the time of writing, the skewX transform doesn't work correctly on Android.

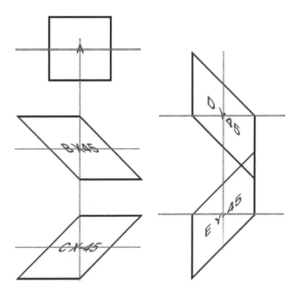

Figure 5.15 Examples of skewing a square along the x-and y-axes on iOS. Square A has no transformation applied. Square B is skewed along the x-axis by 45°. Square C is skewed along the x-axis by –45°. Square D is skewed along the y-axis by 45°, and square E is skewed along the y-axis by –45°.

Listing 5.4   Examples showing how skewing transforms a square

```
import React, { Component } from 'react';
import { StyleSheet, Text, View} from 'react-native';

export default class App extends Component<{}> {
  render() {
    return (
    <View style={styles.container}>
      <Example style={{}}>A</Example>
      <Example style={{transform: [{skewX: '45deg'}]}}>
        B X45
      </Example>
      <Example style={{transform: [{skewX: '-45deg'}]}}>
        C X-45
      </Example>
      <Example style={{transform: [{skewY: '45deg'}]}}>
        D Y45
      </Example>
      <Example style={{transform: [{skewY: '-45deg'}]}}>
        E Y-45
      </Example>
    </View>
    );
```

Skews the square 45° along the x-axis

Skews the square –45° along the x-axis

Skews the square 45° along the y-axis

Skews the square –45° along the y-axis

```
    }
}

const Example = (props) => (
    <View style={[styles.example,props.style]}>
        <Text>
            {props.children}
        </Text>
    </View>
);

const styles = StyleSheet.create({
    container: {
        marginTop: 50,
        alignItems: 'center',
        flex: 1
    },
    example: {
        width: 75,
        height: 75,
        borderWidth: 2,
        margin: 20,
        alignItems: 'center',
        justifyContent: 'center'
    },
});
```

5.2.8   *Transformation key points*

We've covered a lot of transformative ideas in this section! Some of them were relatively simple, while others may have been hard to visualize at first. I didn't show many examples that combine transforms, so you could focus on what individual transforms do. I encourage you to take any of the examples and include additional transformations, to experiment and see what happens.

   In chapter 7, when we discuss animation, you'll see how transformations can make things come alive. For now, take away these key points:

- The origin of the x- and y-axes is at upper left, meaning the positive direction for y is down the screen. You saw this with absolute positioning in the previous chapter, but it's likely the opposite of what you're used to, which can make it hard to reason about what a transformation will do.
- The origin for rotations and translations is always at the element's original location. You can't translate an object in the x or y direction and then rotate it about a new center point.

Transformations are a great way to move components around the screen, but you won't use them on an everyday basis. Most often, you'll use Yoga, a layout engine that implements much of the W3C's flexbox web specification. In the next section, we'll discuss Yoga's flexbox implementation in detail.

5.3 *Using flexbox to lay out components*

Flexbox is a layout implementation that React Native uses to provide an efficient way for users to create UIs and control positioning. The React Native flexbox implementation is based on the W3C flexbox web specification but doesn't share 100% of the API. It aims to give you an easy way to reason about, align, and distribute space among items in a layout, even when their size isn't known or is dynamic.

NOTE Flexbox layout is only available for use on `View` components.

You've already seen flexbox used in many of the examples. It's powerful and makes laying out items so much easier than alternative methods that it's difficult *not* to use it. You'll benefit greatly by taking time to understand the material in this section. Here are the alignment properties used to control the flexbox layout: `flex`, `flexDirection`, `justifyContent`, `alignItems`, `alignSelf`, and `flexWrap`.

5.3.1 *Altering a component's dimensions with flex*

The `flex` property specifies the ability of a component to alter its dimensions to fill the space of the container it's in. This value is relative to the `flex` properties specified for the rest of the items in the same container.

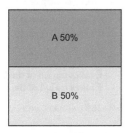

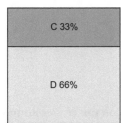

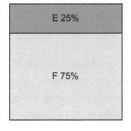

Figure 5.16   Three examples of layouts using the `flex` property. The top example is 1:1, with A = {`flex: 1`} and B = {`flex: 1`}, resulting in each taking up 50% of the space. The middle example is 1:2, with C = {`flex: 1`} and D = {`flex: 2`}, resulting in C taking up 33% of the space and D taking up 66%. The bottom example is 1:3, with E = {`flex: 1`} and F = {`flex: 3`}, resulting in E taking up 25% of the space and F taking up 75% of the space.

If you have a `View` element with a height of 300 and a width of 300, and a child `View` element with a property of `flex: 1`, then the child view will completely fill the parent view. If you decide to add another child element with a `flex` property of `flex: 1`, each view will take up equal space in the parent container. The `flex` number is only important relative to the other `flex` items occupying the same space.

Another way to look at this is to think of the `flex` properties as being percentages. For example, if you want the child components to take up 66.6% and 33.3%, respectively, you can use `flex:66` and `flex:33`. Rather than `flex:66` and `flex:33`, you can specify `flex:2` and `flex:1` and achieve the same layout effect.

To better understand how this works, let's look at a few examples shown in figure 5.16. These are easily achieved by setting the appropriate `flex` value on the individual elements. The following listing shows the steps necessary to create such a layout.

Listing 5.5   Flex views with 1:1 ratio, 1:2, and 1:3 ratios

```
...
render() {
  return (
    <View style={styles.container}>
      <View style={[styles.flexContainer]}>
        <Example style={[{flex: 1},styles.darkgrey]}>A 50%</Example>
        <Example style={[{flex: 1}]}>B 50%</Example>
      </View>
      <View style={[styles.flexContainer]}>
        <Example style={[{flex: 1},styles.darkgrey]}>C 33%</Example>
        <Example style={{flex: 2}}>D 66%</Example>
      </View>
      <View style={[styles.flexContainer]}>
        <Example style={[{flex: 1},styles.darkgrey]}>E 25%</Example>
        <Example style={{flex: 3}}>F 75%</Example>
      </View>
    </View>
  );
}
...
```

> The items have the same flex value, so they take up the same amount of space in their parent container.

> C takes up 1/3 of the total space, and D takes up 2/3 of the total space.

> E takes up 1/4 of the total space, and F takes up 3/4 of the total space.

5.3.2   Specifying the direction of the flex with flexDirection

In the previous examples, the items in flex containers are laid out in a column (y-axis), meaning top to bottom. A is stacked on B, C is stacked on D, and E is stacked on F. Using the `flexDirection` property, you can change the primary axis of the layout, and therefore change the direction of the layout. `flexDirection` is applied to the parent view that contains

All that's needed to achieve the layout in figure 5.17 is to add a single line of code to the `flexContainer` style, which is the parent container for each of the example components. Changing `flexDirection` on this container affects the layout of all its flex children. Add `flexDirection: 'row'` to the style, and see how it changes the layout.

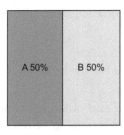 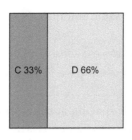 

Figure 5.17 **The same example as in figure 5.16, but with `flexDirection` set to `'row'`. Now the items take up space horizontally within the row rather than vertically within the column.**

Listing 5.6 **Adding `flexDirection: 'row'` to the parent container**

```
flexContainer: {
    width: 150,              flexContainer is the parent
    height: 150,             container of each example.
    borderWidth: 1,
    margin: 10,              Causes the children to
    flexDirection: 'row'     be laid out horizontally
},
```

The child elements now appear left to right. There are two options for `flexDirection`: `'row'` and `'column'`. The default setting is `'column'`. If you don't specify a `flexDirection` property, content will be laid out in a column. This property is something you'll use a lot when developing apps in React Native, so it's important to grasp it and understand how it works.

5.3.3 Defining how space is used around a component with justifyContent

Using the `flex` property, you can specify how much space each component takes up in its parent container; but what if you're not trying to take up the entire space? How can you use flexbox to lay out components using their original size?

`justifyContent` defines how space is distributed between and around flex items along the primary axis of the container (the flex direction). `justifyContent` is declared on the parent container. Five options are available:

- `center` causes the children to be centered within the parent container. The free space is distributed on both sides of the clustered group of children.
- `flex-start` groups the components at the beginning of the flex column or row, depending on what value is assigned to `flexDirection`. `flex-start` is the default value for `justifyContent`.
- `flex-end` acts in the opposite manner: it groups items together at the end of the container.
- `space-around` attempts to evenly distribute space around each element. Don't confuse this with distributing the elements evenly in the container; the space is distributed around the elements. If it were based on the elements, you'd expect
  space – element – space – element – space

Instead, flexbox allocates the same amount of space on each side of the element, yielding

space – element – space – space – element – space

In both cases, the amount of whitespace is the same; but in the latter, the space between elements is greater.

- `space-between` doesn't apply spacing at the start or end of the container. The space between any two consecutive elements is the same as the space between any other two consecutive elements.

Figure 5.18 demonstrates how each of the `justifyContent` properties distributes space between and around the flex elements. Every example uses two elements to help depict what is happening.

Listing 5.7 shows the code used to generate figure 5.18. Look at it carefully, to understand how it works, and then try to do the following: add more elements to each example to see what happens as the number of items increases; and set `flexDirection` to `row` to see what happens when the items are laid out horizontally instead of vertically.

Listing 5.7   Examples showing the `justifyContent` options

```
...
render() {
  return (
    <View style={styles.container}>                          Uses the justifyContent: 'center' option
      <FlexContainer style={[{justifyContent: 'center'}]}>  ◀───
        <Example>center</Example>
        <Example>center</Example>                             Uses the justifyContent: 'flex-start' option
      </FlexContainer>
      <FlexContainer style={[{justifyContent: 'flex-start'}]}>  ◀───
        <Example>flex-start</Example>
        <Example>flex-start</Example>                        Uses the justifyContent: 'flex-end' option
      </FlexContainer>
      <FlexContainer style={[{justifyContent: 'flex-end'}]}>  ◀───
        <Example>flex-end</Example>
        <Example>flex-end</Example>
      </FlexContainer>
      <FlexContainer style={[{justifyContent: 'space-around'}]}>  ◀───
        <Example>space-around</Example>
        <Example>space-around</Example>                      Uses the justifyContent: 'space-around' option
      </FlexContainer>
      <FlexContainer style={[{justifyContent: 'space-between'}]}>  ◀───
        <Example>space-between</Example>
        <Example>space-between</Example>                      Uses the justifyContent:
      </FlexContainer>                                        'space-between' option
    </View>
  );
}
...
```

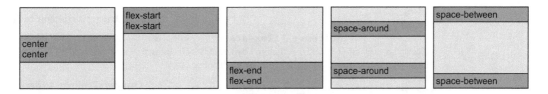

Figure 5.18 Examples of how `justifyContent` affects the distribution of space between flexible child elements for each of the supported options: `center`, `flex-start`, `flex-end`, `space-around`, and `space-between`.

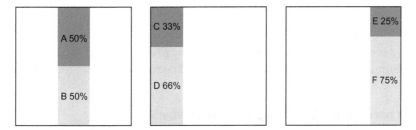

Figure 5.19 Modified examples from figure 5.16, using the non-default `alignItems` properties: `center`, `flex-start`, and `flex-end`

5.3.4 Aligning children in a container with alignItems

`alignItems` defines how to align children along the secondary axis of their container. This property is declared on the parent view and affects its flex children just as `flex-Direction` did. There are four possible values for `alignItems`: `stretch`, `center`, `flex-start`, and `flex-end`.

`stretch` is the default, used in figures 5.17 and 5.18. Each example component is stretched to fill its parent container. Figure 5.19 revisits figure 5.16 and shows what happens with the other options: `center`, `flex-start`, and `flex-end`. Because a precise width isn't specified for the example components, they only take up as much space horizontally as is necessary to render their contents rather than stretching to fill the space. In the first case, `alignItems` is set to `'center'`. In the second case, `alignItems` is set to `'flex-start'`. And last `alignItems` is set to `'flex-end'`. Use listing 5.8 to change the alignments on each of the examples from listing 5.5.

Listing 5.8 Using non-default `alignItems` properties

```
render() {
  return (
    <View style={styles.container}>
      <View style={{[styles.flexContainer,
                  {alignItems: 'center'}]}>           ◄——————  Changes the alignItems
        <Example style={{[styles.darkgrey]}}>A 50%</Example>      property to center
        <Example>B 50%</Example>
```

```
      </View>
      <View style={[styles.flexContainer,              Changes alignItems to flex-start
                  {alignItems: 'flex-start'}]}>  ◄─┐
        <Example style={[styles.darkgrey]}>C 33%</Example>
        <Example style={{flex: 2}}>D 66%</Example>
      </View>
      <View style={[styles.flexContainer,              Changes alignItems to flex-end
                  {alignItems: 'flex-end'}]}>    ◄─┐
        <Example style={[styles.darkgrey]}>E 25%</Example>
        <Example style={{flex: 3}}>F 75%</Example>
      </View>
    </View>
  );
}
```

Now that you've seen how to use the other `alignItems` properties and their effects on the default column layout, why don't you set `flexDirection` to `'row'` and see what happens?

5.3.5   *Overriding the parent container's alignment with alignSelf*

So far, all the flex properties have been applied to the parent container. `alignSelf` is applied directly to an individual flex child.

With `alignSelf`, you can access the `alignItems` property for individual elements within the container. In essence, `alignSelf` gives you the ability to override whatever alignment was set on the parent container, so a child object can be aligned independently of its peers. The available options are `auto`, `stretch`, `center`, `flex-start`, and `flex-end`. The default value is `auto`, which takes the value from the parent container's `alignItems` setting. The remaining properties affect the layout in the same way as their corresponding properties on `alignItems`.

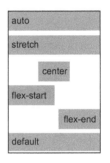

In figure 5.20, the parent container doesn't have `alignItems` set, so it defaults to `stretch`. In the first example, the `auto` value inherits `stretch` from its parent container. The next four examples lay out exactly as you'd expect. The final example has no `alignSelf` property set, so it defaults to `auto` and is laid out the same as the first example.

Figure 5.20   How each `alignSelf` property affects the layout when its parent container's `alignItems` property is set to the default value of `stretch`

Listing 5.9 does something a little different. Rather than supply the style directly to the `Example` element, you create a new component property: `align`. It's passed down to the `Example` component and used to set `alignSelf`. Otherwise, the example is the same as many others in this chapter; it explores the effects of each value applied to the style.

```
import React, { Component } from 'react';
import { StyleSheet, Text, View} from 'react-native';
```

Sets alignSelf explicitly to stretch

Sets alignSelf to flex-start

Sets alignSelf to auto, which picks up the parent container's value of stretch

Sets alignSelf to center

Sets alignSelf to flex-end

The default value for alignSelf is auto.

Uses the align property to set the Example component's alignItems style

```
export default class App extends Component<{}> {
    render() {
        return (
            <View style={styles.container}>
                <FlexContainer style={[]}>
                    <Example align='auto'>auto</Example>
                    <Example align='stretch'>stretch</Example>
                    <Example align='center'>center</Example>
                    <Example align='flex-start'>flex-start</Example>
                    <Example align='flex-end'>flex-end</Example>
                    <Example>default</Example>
                </FlexContainer>
            </View>
        );
    }
}

const FlexContainer = (props) => (
    <View style={[styles.flexContainer,props.style]}>
        {props.children}
    </View>
);

const Example = (props) => (
    <View style={[styles.example,
                  styles.lightgrey,
                  {alignSelf: props.align || 'auto'},
                  props.style
    ]}>
        <Text>
            {props.children}
        </Text>
    </View>
);

const styles = StyleSheet.create({
    container: {
        marginTop: 50,
        alignItems: 'center',
        flex: 1
    },
    flexContainer: {
        backgroundColor: '#ededed',
        width: 120,
        height: 180,
        borderWidth: 1,
        margin: 10
    },
    example: {
        height: 25,
        marginBottom: 5,
        backgroundColor: '#666666'
    },
});
```

5.3.6   *Preventing clipped items with flexWrap*

You learned earlier in this section that the flexDirection property takes two values: column (the default) and row. column lays out items vertically, and row lays out items horizontally. What you haven't seen is a situation in which items flow off the screen because they don't fit.

flexWrap takes two values: nowrap and wrap. The default value is nowrap, meaning items will flow off the screen if they don't fit. The items are clipped, and the user can't see them. To work around this problem, use the wrap value.

In figure 5.21, the first example uses nowrap, and the squares flow off the screen. The row of squares is chopped off at the right edge. The second example uses wrap, and the squares wrap around and start a new row. Listing 5.10 shows the code.

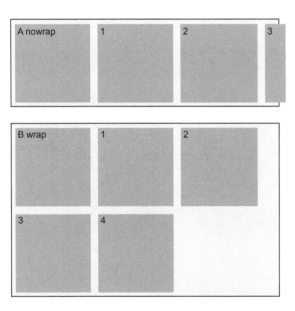

Figure 5.21   An example of two overflowing containers: one with flexWrap set to nowrap and the other with flexWrap set to wrap

Listing 5.10   Example of how flexWrap values affect layout

```
import React, { Component } from 'react';
import { StyleSheet, Text, View} from 'react-native';

export default class App extends Component<{}> {
    render() {
        return (
            <View style={styles.container}>
                <NoWrapContainer>        ◄──  flexWrap is set to nowrap: the
                    <Example>A nowrap</Example>    squares overflow off the screen.
```

```
                        <Example>1</Example>
                        <Example>2</Example>
                        <Example>3</Example>        flexWrap is set to wrap:
                        <Example>4</Example>        the row of squares wraps
                    </NoWrapContainer>              around to start a new line.
                    <WrapContainer>      ◄────────
                        <Example>B wrap</Example>
                        <Example>1</Example>
                        <Example>2</Example>
                        <Example>3</Example>
                        <Example>4</Example>
                    </WrapContainer>
                </View>
            );
        }
}                                                    Uses the noWrapContainer
                                                     style for the first example
const NoWrapContainer = (props) => (
    <View style={[styles.noWrapContainer,props.style]}>   ◄────────
        {props.children}
    </View>
);                                          Uses the wrapContainer
                                            style for the second example
const WrapContainer = (props) => (
    <View style={[styles.wrapContainer,props.style]}>   ◄────────
        {props.children}
    </View>
);

const Example = (props) => (
    <View style={[styles.example,props.style]}>
        <Text>
            {props.children}
        </Text>
    </View>
);

const styles = StyleSheet.create({
    container: {
        marginTop: 150,
        flex: 1
    },
    noWrapContainer: {                      Sets flexDirection to row
        backgroundColor: '#ededed',         and flexWrap to nowrap
        flexDirection: 'row',      ◄────────
        flexWrap: 'nowrap',
        borderWidth: 1,
        margin: 10
    },
    wrapContainer: {
        backgroundColor: '#ededed',
        flexDirection: 'row',      ◄────────
        flexWrap: 'wrap',
        borderWidth: 1,                     Sets flexDirection to row
        margin: 10                          and flexWrap to wrap
    },
```

```
    example: {
        width: 100,
        height: 100,
        margin: 5,
        backgroundColor: '#666666'
    },
});
```

It's easy to see which behavior is preferable when laying out tiles, but you may come across a situation in which nowrap will serve you better. Either way, you should now have a clear understanding of flexbox and the many ways it can help you build responsive layouts in React Native.

Summary

- When sizing items for display, iOS uses points and Android uses density-independent pixels. The systems of measurement are different but should have little impact on development unless you need pixel-perfect graphics.
- Some styles are only available on one platform or another. ShadowPropTypeIOS is only available on iOS, and elevation is only recognized on Android.
- Components can be moved in the x and y directions using the translateX and translateY transforms.
- Components can be rotated about the x-, y-, and z-axes using rotateX, rotateY, and rotateZ. The point of rotation is the original location of the object before any transforms have been applied.
- Components can be scaled in the x and y directions to make the components grow or shrink.
- Components can also be skewed in the x and y directions.
- Several transformations can be applied at the same time, but the order in which they're specified matters. Rotating a component changes the orientation of the component for subsequent transformations.
- The flexDirection property defines the primary axis, the default being column (y-axis).
- The justifyContent property defines how items should be laid out along the primary axis.
- The alignItems property defines how items should be laid out along the secondary axis.
- The alignSelf property can be used to override the alignItems property specified by a parent container.
- The flexWrap property tells flexbox how to handle items that would typically overflow off the screen.

Navigation

One of the core pieces of functionality in any mobile application is navigation. Before building an application, I recommend that you spend some time strategizing how you want the app to handle navigation and routing. This chapter covers the three main types of navigation typical to mobile applications: tab-based, stack-based, and drawer-based navigation.

Tab-based navigation typically has tabs either at the top or bottom of the screen; pressing a tab takes you to the screen that correlates with the tab. Many popular apps like Twitter, Instagram, and Facebook implement this type of navigation on their main screens.

Stack-based navigation transitions from one screen to another, replacing the current screen, and usually implements some sort of animated transition. You can then go backward or continue moving forward in the stack. You can think of stack-based navigation like an array of components: pushing a new component into the array takes you to the screen of the new component. To go back, you pop the last screen from the stack and are navigated to the previous screen. Most navigation libraries handle this popping and pushing for you.

Drawer-based navigation is typically a side menu that pops out from either the left or right side of the screen and shows a list of options. When you press an option, the drawer closes, and you're taken to the new screen.

The React Native framework doesn't include a navigation library. When building navigation in a React Native app, you have to go with a third-party navigation library. A few good navigation libraries are available, but in this chapter, I use React Navigation as the navigation library of choice to build out the demo app. The React Navigation library is recommended by the React Native team and is maintained by many people in the React and React Native community.

React Navigation is a JavaScript-based navigation implementation. All the transitions and controls are handled by JavaScript. Some teams prefer a native solution for many reasons: for instance, they may be adding React Native to an existing native app and want navigation to be consistent throughout the app. If you're interested in a native navigation solution, check out React Native Navigation, an open source React Native navigation library built and maintained by the engineers at Wix.

6.1   *React Native navigation vs. web navigation*

Because the paradigm of navigation on the web is much different than that of React Native, navigation is a stumbling block for many developers new to React Native. On the web, we're used to working with URLs. There are many ways to navigate to a new route, depending on the framework or environment, but typically you want to send the user to a new URL and maybe add some URL parameters if needed.

In React Native, routes are based around components. You load or show a component using the navigator you're working with. Depending on whether it's tab based, stack based, drawer based, or a combination of these, the routing will also differ. We'll walk through all this when you build the demo app in the next section.

You also need to keep up with the data and state throughout the routes and possibly access methods defined elsewhere in the app, so having a strategy around data and method sharing is important. You can manage data and methods either at the top level, where the navigation is defined, or using a state-management library such as Redux or MobX. In the example, you'll manage data and methods in the class at the top level of the app.

6.2   *Building a navigation-based app*

In this chapter, you'll learn how to implement navigation by building out an app that uses both tab-based and stack-based navigation. The app you'll create is called Cities; it's shown in figure 6.1. It's a travel app that lets you keep up with all the cities you visit or want to visit. You can also add locations in each city you want to visit.

The main navigation is tab based, and one of the tabs includes a stack-based navigation. The left tab shows the list of cities you've created, and the right tab contains a form to create new cities. On the left tab, you can press an individual city to view it as well as view and create locations in the city.

Figure 6.1 Completed Cities app with screens for adding a city, listing cities, viewing city details, and viewing locations within the city

To get started, create a new React Native application. In your terminal, navigate to an empty directory, and install the new React Native application using the React Native CLI:

```
react-native init CitiesApp
```

Next, navigate into the new directory, and install two dependencies: React Navigation and uuid. React Navigation is the navigation library, and uuid will be used to create unique IDs for cities in order to identify them uniquely:

```
cd CitiesApp
npm install react-navigation uuid
```

Now, let's get to work creating components! Create a new main directory called src in the root of the application. This directory will hold most of the new code for the app. In this new directory, add three main subdirectories: Cities, AddCity, and components.

Because the main navigation is tab based, you'll separate the main application into two main components (`Cities` and `AddCity`), each having its own tab. The AddCity folder will only contain a single component, AddCity.js. The Cities folder will contain two components: Cities.js to view the list of cities, and City.js to view an individual city. The components folder will hold any reusable components; in this case, it will hold a single component.

You'll also have src/index.js and src/theme.js files. src/index.js will hold all the navigation configuration, and theme.js will be where you keep themeable configuration—in this case, a primary color configuration. Figure 6.2 shows the project's complete folder structure.

Now that you've created the folder structure and installed the necessary dependencies, let's write some code. The first file you'll work with is src/theme.js. Here, you'll set the primary color and make it exportable for use in the app. The theme color I've chosen for the app is blue, but feel free to use any color you want; the app will work the same if you change the color value in this file.

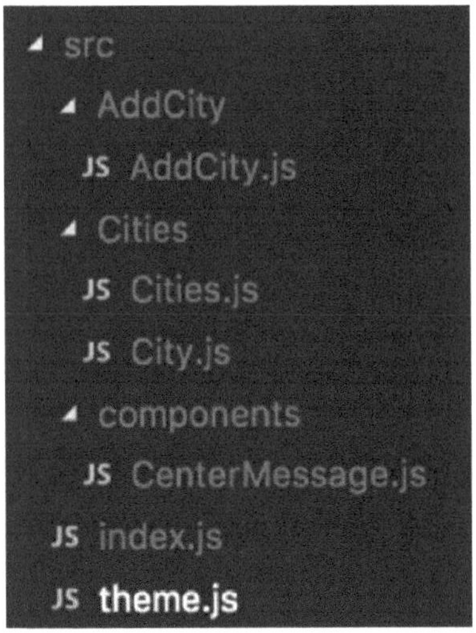

Figure 6.2   The complete src folder structure

Listing 6.1   Creating a theme file with a primary color

```
const colors = {
  primary: '#1976D2'
}

export {
  colors
}
```

You can import this primary color throughout the application if you wish, and change it in one place if you choose to do so.

Next, edit src/index.js to create the main navigation configuration. You'll create both navigation instances here: the tab-based navigation and the stack-based navigation.

Listing 6.2   Creating the navigation configuration

```
import React from 'react'

import Cities from './Cities/Cities'        ◁── Imports the three components
import City from './Cities/City'                 to have in the scope of the file
import AddCity from './AddCity/AddCity'

import { colors } from './theme'    ◁── Imports colors from the theme

import { createBottomTabNavigator,           Imports the two
        createStackNavigator } from 'react-navigation'   ◁── navigators to access
                                                             from React Navigation
const options = {    ◁── Creates an options object to hold
  navigationOptions: {    configuration for the stack navigator
    headerStyle: {
      backgroundColor: colors.primary
    },
```

```
      headerTintColor: '#fff'
  }
}

const CitiesNav = createStackNavigator({        ◄──────┤ Creates the first navigation instance
  Cities: { screen: Cities },
  City: { screen: City }
}, options)
                                                      ┌ Creates the tab navigator using
                                                      │ the CitiesNav stack navigator
const Tabs = createBottomTabNavigator({    ◄──────┤ for one tab and the AddCity
  Cities: { screen: CitiesNav },                     │ component for the second tab
  AddCity: { screen: AddCity }
})

export default Tabs
```

When you create the `options` object, the stack navigator automatically places a header at the top of each route. The header is usually where you'll have the title of the current route as well as buttons like a Back button. The `options` object also defines the background color and the tint color of the header.

For the first navigation instance, `createStackNavigator` takes two arguments: the route configuration and any configuration regarding things like styling to apply to the navigation. You pass in two routes as the first argument, and the `options` object as the second argument.

Next, update App.js to include the new navigation and render it as the main entry point. In addition to rendering the navigation component, App.js will contain and control any methods and data to be made available to the application.

Listing 6.3   Updating App.js to use the navigation configuration

```
import React, { Component } from 'react';
import {
  Platform,
  StyleSheet,
  Text,
  View
} from 'react-native';

import Tabs from './src'    ◄──────┤ Imports the navigation from src/index.js

export default class App extends Component {
  state = {                     ◄──────┐
    cities: []                         │ Creates an initial state
                                       │ of cities, an empty array
                                                          ┌ Adds a new city to the existing list
  }                                                       │ of cities stored in the state
  addCity = (city) => {    ◄──────────────────────────┤
    const cities = this.state.cities
    cities.push(city)
    this.setState({ cities })
                                           ┌ Adds a location to the array
  }                                        │ of locations in a chosen city
  addLocation = (location, city) => {    ◄──────┤
    const index = this.state.cities.findIndex(item => {
      return item.id === city.id
    })
```

```
    const chosenCity = this.state.cities[index]
    chosenCity.locations.push(location)
    const cities = [
      ...this.state.cities.slice(0, index),
      chosenCity,
      ...this.state.cities.slice(index + 1)
    ]
    this.setState({
      cities
    })
  }
  render() {
    return (
      <Tabs   ◄──────
        screenProps={{
          cities: this.state.cities,
          addCity: this.addCity,
          addLocation: this.addLocation
        }}
      />
    )
  }
}
```

> Returns the Tabs component and passes
> in a screenProps object containing the
> cities array, the addCity method, and
> the addLocation method

App.js has three main pieces of functionality. It creates the initial state of the app: an empty array called `cities`. Each city will be an object and will have a name, country, ID, and array of locations. The `addCity` method lets you add new cities to the `cities` array stored in the state. The `addLocation` method identifies the city you want to add a location to, updates the city, and resets the state with the new data.

React Navigation has a way to pass these methods and the state down to all the routes being used by the navigator. To do this, pass a prop called `screenProps` containing whatever you want access to. Then, from within any route, `this.props.screenProps` gives access to the data or methods.

Next, you'll create a reusable component called `CenterMessage`, which is used in Cities.js and City.js (src/components/CenterMessage.js). It displays a message when the array is empty. For example, when the app first starts, it won't have any cities to list; you can display a message as shown in figure 6.3, instead of just showing a blank screen.

Listing 6.4   `CenterMessage` **component**

```
import React from 'react'
import {
  Text,
  View,
  StyleSheet
} from 'react-native'

import { colors } from '../theme'

const CenterMessage = ({ message }) => (
  <View style={styles.emptyContainer}>
```

```
        <Text style={styles.message}>{message}</Text>
      </View>
  )

  const styles = StyleSheet.create({
    emptyContainer: {
      padding: 10,
      borderBottomWidth: 2,
      borderBottomColor: colors.primary
    },
    message: {
      alignSelf: 'center',
      fontSize: 20
    }
  })
```

```
export default CenterMessage
```

This component is straightforward. It's a stateless component that receives only a message as a prop and displays the message along with some styling.

Next, in src/AddCity/AddCity.js, create the AddCity component that will allow you to add new cities to the cities array (see figure 6.4). This component will contain a

Figure 6.3 The reusable CenterMessage component displays a message centered within the display.

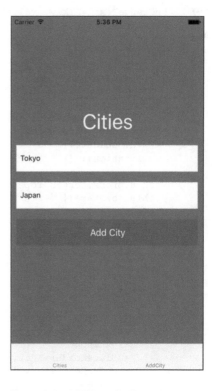

Figure 6.4 AddCity tab allows the user to enter a new city name and the country name.

form with two text inputs: one to hold the city name and one to hold the country name. In addition, a button will call the addCity method from App.js.

```
import React from 'react'
import {
  View,
  Text,
  StyleSheet,
  TextInput,
  TouchableOpacity
} from 'react-native'

import uuidV4 from 'uuid/v4'

import { colors } from '../theme'

export default class AddCity extends React.Component {
  state = {
    city: '',
    country: '',
  }
  onChangeText = (key, value) => {
    this.setState({ [key]: value })
  }
  submit = () => {
    if (this.state.city === '' || this.state.country === '') {
      alert('please complete form')
    }
    const city = {
      city: this.state.city,
      country: this.state.country,
      id: uuidV4(),
      locations: []
    }
    this.props.screenProps.addCity(city)
    this.setState({
      city: '',
      country: ''
    }, () => {
      this.props.navigation.navigate('Cities')
    })
  }
  render() {
    return (
      <View style={styles.container}>
        <Text style={styles.heading}>Cities</Text>
        <TextInput
          placeholder='City name'
          onChangeText={val => this.onChangeText('city', val)}
          style={styles.input}
          value={this.state.city}
```

The initial state holds a city name and a country name, both initially set as empty strings.

Holds much of the functionality for this component

Updates the state with either the city or name value. This will be attached to the TextInput and will fire whenever the input value changes.

```
            />
            <TextInput
              placeholder='Country name'
              onChangeText={val => this.onChangeText('country', val)}
              style={styles.input}
              value={this.state.country}
            />
            <TouchableOpacity onPress={this.submit}>
              <View style={styles.button}>
                <Text style={styles.buttonText}>Add City</Text>
              </View>
            </TouchableOpacity>
          </View>
        )
      }
    }
```

First, you check to make sure neither the city nor the country is an empty string. If either or both are empty, you return, because you don't want to store the data unless both fields are filled out. Next, you create an object to hold the city being adding to the cities array. Take the existing city and country values stored on the state, and add an ID value using the uuidV4 method and an empty locations array. Call this.props. screenProps.addCity, passing in the new city. Next, reset the state to clear out any values stored in the state. Finally, navigate the user to the Cities tab to show them their list of cities with the new city added, by calling this.props.navigation.navigate and passing in the string of the route to navigate to—in this case, 'Cities'.

Every component that's a screen in a navigator automatically has access to two props: screenProps and navigation. In listing 6.3, when you created the navigation component, you passed in three screenProps. In the submit method, you called this.props. screenProps.addCity, accessing and invoking this screenProps method. You also access the navigation prop by calling this.props.navigation.navigate. navigate is what you use to navigate between routes in React Navigation.

Next, add the styles for this component. This code goes below the class definition in src/AddCity/AddCity.js.

Listing 6.6   AddCity tab (styling)

```
const styles = StyleSheet.create({
  button: {
    height: 50,
    backgroundColor: '#666',
    justifyContent: 'center',
    alignItems: 'center',
    margin: 10
  },
  buttonText: {
    color: 'white',
    fontSize: 18
  },
```

```
  heading: {
    color: 'white',
    fontSize: 40,
    marginBottom: 10,
    alignSelf: 'center'
  },
  container: {
    backgroundColor: colors.primary,
    flex: 1,
    justifyContent: 'center'
  },
  input: {
    margin: 10,
    backgroundColor: 'white',
    paddingHorizontal: 8,
    height: 50
  }
})
```

Now, create src/Cities/Cities.js to list all the cities the app is storing and allow the user to navigate to an individual city (see figure 6.5). The functionality is shown in the following listing, and the styling is in listing 6.8.

Figure 6.5   Cities.js displays a list of cities that have been added to the application.

Listing 6.7 Cities route (functionality)

```
import React from 'react'
import {
  View,
  Text,
  StyleSheet,
  TouchableWithoutFeedback,
  ScrollView
} from 'react-native'

import CenterMessage from '../components/CenterMessage'

import { colors } from '../theme'

export default class Cities extends React.Component {
  static navigationOptions = {
    title: 'Cities',
    headerTitleStyle: {
      color: 'white',
      fontSize: 20,
      fontWeight: '400'
    }
  }
  navigate = (item) => {
    this.props.navigation.navigate('City', { city: item })
  }
  render() {
    const { screenProps: { cities } } = this.props
    return (
      <ScrollView  contentContainerStyle={[!cities.length && { flex: 1 }]}>
        <View style={[!cities.length &&
                       { justifyContent: 'center', flex: 1 }]}>
        {
          !cities.length && <CenterMessage message='No saved cities!'/>
        }
        {
          cities.map((item, index) => (
            <TouchableWithoutFeedback
              onPress={() => this.navigate(item)} key={index} >
              <View style={styles.cityContainer}>
                <Text style={styles.city}>{item.city}</Text>
                <Text style={styles.country}>{item.country}</Text>
              </View>
            </TouchableWithoutFeedback>
          ))
        }
        </View>
      </ScrollView>
    )
  }
}
```

Imports the CenterMessage component created in listing 6.4

Declares a static navigationOptions property on the class and declares the configuration for this route

Passes in the city as the second argument to this.props.navigation.navigate

Accesses and destructures the cities array from the screenProps prop available in the component

Checks if the cities array is empty. If so, shows the user a message that there are no cities currently in the app.

Maps over all the cities in the array, displaying the city name and country name. Also attaches the navigate method to the TouchableWithoutFeedback component.

In this listing, you first import the CenterMessage component. React Navigation has a way to control certain options around the navigation within a route. To do so, you can declare a static navigationOptions property on the class and declare the configuration for a route. In this case, you want to set a title and style the title, so give the configuration a `title` and `headerTitleStyle` property.

The `navigate` method calls `this.props.navigation.navigate` and passes in the route name as well as the city to access to in the `City` route. Pass in the city as the second argument; in the `City` route, you'll have access to this property in `props.navigation.state.params`. The render method accesses and destructures the `cities` array. It also includes logic to check whether the `cities` array is empty; if it is, show the user an appropriate message. You map over all the cities in the array, displaying the city name and country name. Attaching the `navigate` method to the `TouchableWithoutFeedback` component lets users navigate to the city by pressing anywhere on the city.

Listing 6.8 Cities route (styling)

```
const styles = StyleSheet.create({
  cityContainer: {
    padding: 10,
    borderBottomWidth: 2,
    borderBottomColor: colors.primary
  },
  city: {
    fontSize: 20,
  },
  country: {
    color: 'rgba(0, 0, 0, .5)'
  },
})
```

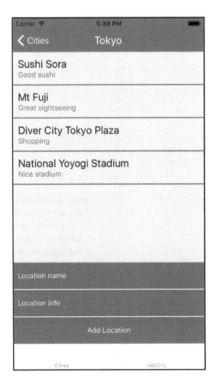

Figure 6.6 City.js shows locations within the city.

Next, create the `City` component (src/Cities/City.js) to hold the locations for each city as well as a form that lets users create a new location in a city; see figure 6.6. This component will access the cities from `screenProps` and will also use the `addLocation` method from `screenProps` to add a location to the city.

Listing 6.9 City route (functionality)

```
import React from 'react'
import {
  View,
  Text,
  StyleSheet,
  ScrollView,
  TouchableWithoutFeedback,
  TextInput,
  TouchableOpacity
} from 'react-native'

import CenterMessage from '../components/CenterMessage'
import { colors } from '../theme'

class City extends React.Component {
  static navigationOptions = (props) => {          ◄──────  Creates the static navigationOptions
    const { city } = props.navigation.state.params          property as in Cities.js
    return {
      title: city.city,
      headerTitleStyle: {
        color: 'white',
        fontSize: 20,
        fontWeight: '400'
      }
    }
  }
  state = {
    name: '',
    info: ''
  }
  onChangeText = (key, value) => {                 Destructures the city object,
    this.setState({                                creates a location object, and
      [key]: value                                 calls this.props.screenProps.
    })                                             addLocation to add the location
  }                                                and reset the state
  addLocation = () => {         ◄──────────────────┘
    if (this.state.name === '' || this.state.info === '') return
    const { city } = this.props.navigation.state.params
    const location = {
      name: this.state.name,
      info: this.state.info
    }
    this.props.screenProps.addLocation(location, city)
    this.setState({ name: '', info: '' })
  }
  render() {                                            ─┐  Destructures city
    const { city } = this.props.navigation.state.params  │ ◄──
    return (
      <View style={{ flex: 1 }}>
```

```
<ScrollView
  contentContainerStyle={
    [!city.locations.length && { flex: 1 }]
  }>
  <View style={[
      styles.locationsContainer,
      !city.locations.length && { flex: 1,
                                  justifyContent: 'center' }
  ]}>
    {
      !city.locations.length &&
      <CenterMessage message='No locations for this city!' />
    }
    {
      city.locations.map((location, index) => (      ◄─────────────────┐
        <View key={index} style={styles.locationContainer}>           │
          <Text style={styles.locationName}>{location.name}</Text>    │
          <Text style={styles.locationInfo}>{location.info}</Text>    │
        </View>                                                       │
      ))                                                              │
    }                                          Maps over the cities in the
  </View>                                      cities array, and returns a
</ScrollView>      Creates the form            component that displays the
<TextInput  ◄────────────┐                    city's name and information
  onChangeText={val => this.onChangeText('name', val)}
  placeholder='Location name'
  value={this.state.name}
  style={styles.input}
  placeholderTextColor='white'
/>
<TextInput
  onChangeText={val => this.onChangeText('info', val)}
  placeholder='Location info'
  value={this.state.info}
  style={[styles.input, styles.input2]}
  placeholderTextColor='white'
/>
<View style={styles.buttonContainer}>
  <TouchableOpacity onPress={this.addLocation}>
    <View style={styles.button}>
      <Text style={styles.buttonText}>Add Location</Text>
    </View>
  </TouchableOpacity>
</View>
      </View>
    )
  }
}
```

This code first creates the navigationOptions property. You use a callback function to return an object instead of just declaring an object, because you need access to the props in order to have access to the city information passed down by the navigation. You need to know the city title for use as the route title instead of a hard-coded string.

The addLocation method destructures the city object available from this.props. navigation.state.params for use later in the function. You then create a location object holding the location name and info. Calling `this.props.screenProps.addLoca-tion` adds the location to the city you're currently viewing and then resets the state. Again, destructure `city` from the navigation state. You need `city` in order to map over the locations in the city and also to use as an argument when creating a new location, to identify the city you're referencing. Finally, you map over the cities, returning a component that displays both the city name and city information, and create the form with two text inputs and a button.

6.3 Persisting data

You're finished and should be able to run the app. Play around with the app, add cities and locations, and then refresh it. Notice that all the cities disappear when you refresh. This is because you're only storing the data in memory. Let's use `AsyncStorage` to persist the state, so if the user closes or refreshes the app, their data remains available.

To do so, you'll work in the `App` component in App.js and do the following:

- Store the cities array in `AsyncStorage` every time a new city is added.
- Store the cities array in `AsyncStorage` every time a new location is added to a city.
- When the user opens the app, check `AsyncStorage` to see whether any cities are stored there. If so, update the state with those cities.
- `AsyncStorage` only accepts strings for stored values. So, when storing a value, call `JSON.stringify` on the value if it isn't already a string, and `JSON.parse` if you want to parse the stored value before using it.

Open App.js and make the changes:

1 Import `AsyncStorage`, and create a key variable.

```
import {
    #omitting previous imports
  AsyncStorage
} from 'react-native';

const key = 'state'

export default class App extends Component {
    #omitting class definition
```

2 Create a `componentDidMount` function that will check for `AsyncStorage` and get any item stored there with the key value you set:

```
async componentDidMount() {
  try {
    let cities = await AsyncStorage.getItem(key)
    cities = JSON.parse(cities)
    this.setState({ cities })
  } catch (e) {
    console.log('error from AsyncStorage: ', e)
  }
}
```

3   In the `addCity` method, store the `cities` array in `AsyncStorage` after the new cities array has been created:

```
addCity = (city) => {
  const cities = this.state.cities
  cities.push(city)
  this.setState({ cities })
  AsyncStorage.setItem(key, JSON.stringify(cities))
    .then(() => console.log('storage updated!'))
    .catch(e => console.log('e: ', e))
}
```

4   Update the `addLocation` method to store the city array after `setState` has been called.

```
addLocation = (location, city) => {
    #previous code omitted
  this.setState({
    cities
  }, () => {
    AsyncStorage.setItem(key, JSON.stringify(cities))
      .then(() => console.log('storage updated!'))
      .catch(e => console.log('e: ', e))
  })
}
```

Now, when the user opens the app after closing it, their data will still be available.

6.4   *Using DrawerNavigator to create drawer-based navigation*

We've gone over how to create stack-based and tab-based navigation. Let's look at the API for creating drawer-based navigation.

The drawer navigator has an API very similar to that of the stack and tab navigators. You'll use the `createDrawerNavigator` function from React Navigation to create a drawer-based navigation. First define the routes to use:

```
import Page1 from './routeToPage1'
import Page2 from './routeToPoage2'
```

Next, define the screens you want used in the navigator:

```
const screens = {
  Page1: { screen: Page1 },
  Page2: { screen: Page2 }
}
```

Now you can define the navigator using the screen configuration and use it in the app:

```
const DrawerNav = createDrawerNavigator(screens)

// somewhere in our app

<DrawerNav />
```

Summary

- Before building an application, spend time strategizing how you want it to handle navigation and routing.

- Many navigation libraries are available for React Native, but the two most recommended are React Navigation and React Native Navigation. React Navigation is a JavaScript-based navigation library, and React Native Navigation is a native implementation.

- There are three main types of navigators:
    - Tab-based navigation typically has tabs either at the top or bottom of the screen. When you press a tab, you're taken to the screen that correlates with that tab. For example, `createBottomTabNavigator` creates tabs at the bottom of the screen.
    - Stack-based navigation transitions from one screen to another, replacing the current screen. You can go backward or continue moving forward in the stack. Stack-based navigation usually implements some sort of animated transition. You create stack-based navigation using the `createStackNavigator` function.
    - Drawer-based navigation is typically a menu that pops out from either the left or right side of the screen and shows a list of options. When you press an option, the drawer closes and you're taken to the new screen. You create drawer-based navigation using the `createDrawerNavigator` function.

- Depending on which kind of navigation you use—tab-based, stack-based, drawer-based, or a combination of these—the routing will also differ. Every route or screen managed by the React Navigation library has a `navigation` prop you can use to control the navigation state.

- Use `AsyncStorage` to persist state so if the user closes or refreshes the app, their data is still available.

Animations

This chapter covers

- Creating basic animations using `Animated.timing`
- Using interpolation with animated values
- Creating animations and in parallel
- Staggering animations using `Animated.stagger`
- Using the native driver to offload animations to the native UI thread

One of the great things about React Native is the ability to easily create animations using the Animated API. This is one of the more stable and easy to use React Native APIs, and it's one of the few places in the React Native ecosystem where, unlike areas such as navigation and state management, there's almost 100% agreement on how a problem should be solved.

Animations are usually used to enhance the UI of an application and bring more life to the existing design. Sometimes, the difference between an average and above-average user experience can be attributed to using the right animations at the right time, thus setting an app apart from other, similar apps.

Real-world use cases that we cover in this chapter include the following:

- Expanding user inputs that animate when focused
- Animated welcome screens that have more life than a basic static welcome screen
- A custom animated loading indicator

In this chapter, we dive deeply into how to create animations. We'll cover everything you need to know to take full advantage of the Animated API.

7.1 Introducing the Animated API

The Animated API ships with React Native, so to use it, all you have to do is import it as you would any other React Native API or component. When creating an animation, you always need to do the following four things:

1. Import Animated from React Native.
2. Create an animatable value using the Animated API.
3. Attach the value to a component as a style.
4. Animate the animatable value using a function.

Out of the box, four types of animatable components ship with the Animated API:

- `View`
- `ScrollView`
- `Text`
- `Image`

The examples in this chapter work exactly the same across any of these components. In section 7.5, we also cover how to create a custom animated component using any element or component with `createAnimatedComponent`.

Let's take a quick look at what a basic animation might look like using Animated. In the example, you'll animate the top margin of a box (see figure 7.1).

Listing 7.1 Using Animated and updating the `marginTop` property

```
import React, { Component } from 'react';
import {
  StyleSheet,
  View,              Imports the Animated API
  Animated,   ◄───── from React Native
  Button
} from 'react-native';

export default class RNAnimations extends Component {
  marginTop = new Animated.Value(20);   ◄─────
  animate = () => {   ◄─────
    Animated.timing(
      this.marginTop,        Creates a function that will animate the value
      {
        toValue: 200,
        duration: 500,
```

Creates a class property called marginTop and assigns it to an animated value, passing in the starting value (20 in this case)

```
      }
    ).start();
  }
  render() {
    return (
      <View style={styles.container}>
        <Button
          title='Animate Box'
          onPress={this.animate}
        />
        <Animated.View
          style={[styles.box, { marginTop: this.marginTop } ]} />
      </View>
    );
  }
}

const styles = StyleSheet.create({
  container: {
    flex: 1,
    padding: 10,
    paddingTop: 50,
  },
  box: {
    width: 150,
    height: 150,
    backgroundColor: 'red'
  }
});
```

Attach the animate method to an onPress handler so you can call it

Use the Animated.View component instead of the regular View component

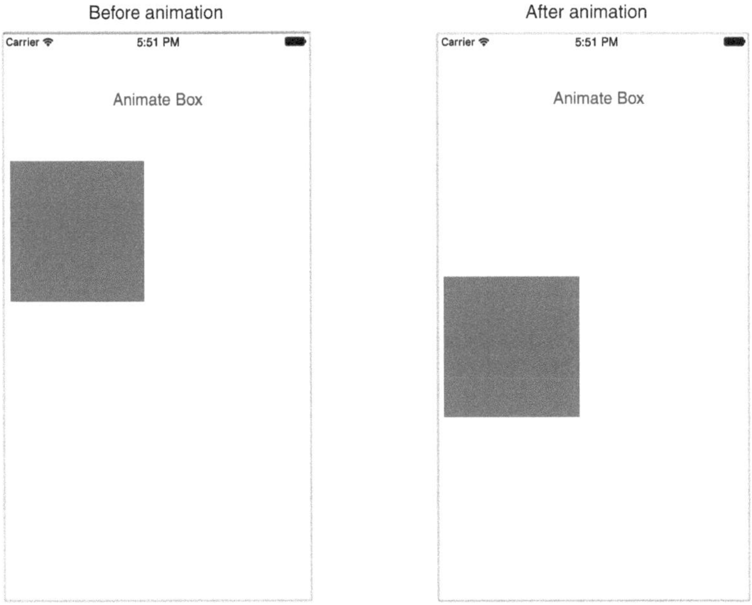

Before animation

Carrier 📶   5:51 PM

Animate Box

After animation

Carrier 📶   5:51 PM

Animate Box

Figure 7.1   Animating the top margin of a square box using Animated

This example uses the `timing` function to animate a value. The `timing` function takes two arguments: a starting value and a configuration object. The configuration object is passed a `toValue` to set the value the animation should animate to, and a duration in milliseconds to set the length of the animation.

Rather than a `View` component, you use an `Animated.View`. Animated has four components that can be animated out of the box: `View`, `Image`, `ScrollView`, and `Text`. In the styling of the `Animated.View`, you pass in an array of styles consisting of a base style (`styles.box`) and an animated style (`marginTop`).

Now that you've created a basic animated component, you'll create a few more animations using real-world use cases that may come in handy.

7.2 Animating a form input to expand on focus

In this example, you'll create a basic form input that expands when the user focuses it, and contracts when the input is blurred. This is a popular UI pattern.

Along with the props that you've used with the `TextInput` component so far in this book, such as `value`, `placeholder`, and `onChangeText`, you can also use `onFocus` and `onBlur` to call functions when the inputs are focused and blurred. That's how you'll achieve this animation (shown in figure 7.2).

Listing 7.2   Animating a `TextInput` to expand when the input is focused

```
import React, { Component } from 'react';
import {
  StyleSheet,
  View,
  Animated,
  Button,
  TextInput,
  Text,                          Creates an initial value for the
} from 'react-native';          animation, calling it animatedWidth

export default class RNAnimations extends Component {
  animatedWidth = new Animated.Value(200);
  animate = (value) => {
    Animated.timing(
      this.animatedWidth,        Creates an animate function that will animate
      {                          the animated value of animatedWidth
        toValue: value,
        duration: 750,
      }
    ).start()
  }
  render() {                     Attach the animatedWidth value to the style of
    return (                     the container View holding the Input component.
      <View style={styles.container}>
        <Animated.View style={{ width: this.animatedWidth }}>
          <TextInput
            style={[styles.input]}         Attach the animate method to the onBlur
            onBlur={() => this.animate(200)}     and onFocus handlers, passing in the desired
            onFocus={() => this.animate(325)}    width for when each event is fired.
```

```
            ref={input => this.input = input}
          />
        </Animated.View>
        <Button
          title='Submit'
          onPress={() => this.input.blur()}
        />
      </View>
    );
  }
}

const styles = StyleSheet.create({
  container: {
    flex: 1,
    padding: 10,
    paddingTop: 50,
  },
  input: {
    height: 50,
    marginHorizontal: 15,
    backgroundColor: '#ededed',
    marginTop: 10,
    paddingHorizontal: 9,
  },
});
```

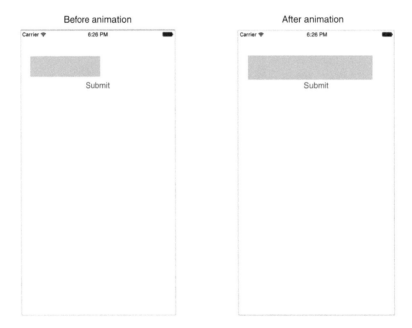

Figure 7.2   Animating a `TextInput` component when the input is focused

7.3   *Creating a custom loading animation using interpolation*

Many times, you need to create animations that are infinite loops, such as loading indicators and activity indicators. One easy way to create such animations is to use the `Animated.loop` function. In this section, you use `Animated.loop` along with the Easing module to create a loading indicator, spinning an image in an infinite loop!

So far, we've only looked at calling an animation using `Animated.timing`. In this example, you want the animation to run continuously without stopping. To do this, you'll use a new static method called `loop`. `Animated.loop` runs a given animation continuously: each time it reaches the end, it resets to the beginning and starts again.

You'll also deal with styling a little differently than in the past. In listings 7.1 and 7.2, you used the animated value directly in the `style` prop of the component. In subsequent examples, you'll store these animation values in variables and interpolate the values before using the new interpolated variables in the `style` prop. Because you're creating a spinning effect, you'll use strings instead of numbers: for example, you'll reference a value such as `360deg` for `style`.

Animated has a class method called `interpolate` that you can use to manipulate animated values, changing them into other values that you can also use. The `interpolate` method takes a configuration object with two keys: `inputRange` (array) and `outputRange` (also an array). `inputRange` is the original animated values you work with in a class, and `outputRange` specifies the values the original values should be changed to.

Finally, you'll change the easing value of the animation. *Easing* basically allows you to control the animation's motion. In this example, you want a smooth, even motion for the spin effect, so you'll use a linear easing function.

React Native has a built-in way to implement common easing functions. Just as you've imported other APIs and components, you can import the Easing module and use it along with Animated. Easing can be configured in the configuration object where you set values like `toValue` and `duration`, in the second argument of `Animated.timing`. Let's look at an example with an animated value called `animatedMargin`. Setting `animatedMargin` to 0 and animating the value to 200 would normally achieve the easing effect by directly animating the value between 0 and 200 in the timing function. Using interpolation, you can instead animate a value between 0 and 1 in the timing function and later interpolate the value by using the Animated `interpolate` class method, saving the value into another variable, and then referencing *that* variable in the style, usually in the render method:

```
const marginTop = animatedMargin.interpolate({
  inputRange: [0, 1],
  outputRange: [0, 200],
});
```

Now, use interpolation to create the loading indicator. You'll show the indicator when the application loads; in `componentDidMount`, you'll call `setTimeout`, which cancels the loading state after 2,000 milliseconds (see figure 7.3). The icon used here is located at https://github.com/dabit3/react-native-in-action/blob/chapter7/assets/35633-200.png; feel free to use it or any other image you want.

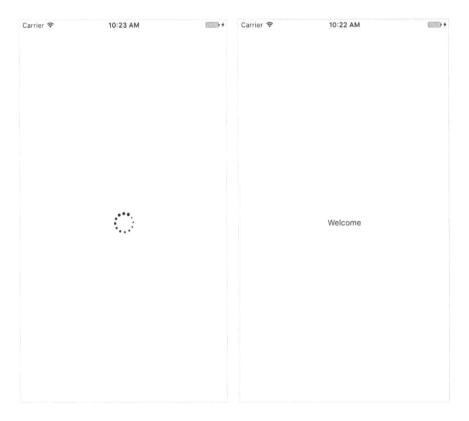

Figure 7.3   Creating a spinning loading indicator using interpolation and an animated loop

Listing 7.3   Creating an infinitely spinning loading animation

```
import React, { Component } from 'react';
import {
  Easing,
  StyleSheet,
  View,
  Animated,
  Button,
  Text,
} from 'react-native';

export default class RNAnimations extends Component {
  state = {
    loading: true,
  }
  componentDidMount() {
    this.animate();
```

Initializes the state with a Boolean loading value of true

Triggers the animation by calling this. animate, and invokes a setTimeout function to set loading to false in the state after 2 seconds

```
      setTimeout(() => this.setState({ loading: false }), 2000)
    }
    animatedRotation = new Animated.Value(0);        ◀── Sets an initial animatedRotation value of 0
    animate = () => {    ◀──────────────
      Animated.loop(                        Creates an animate class method that passes
        Animated.timing(                    Animated.timing into a call to Animated.loop
          this.animatedRotation,
          {
            toValue: 1,
            duration: 1800,
            easing: Easing.linear,
          }
        )
      ).start()
    }
    render() {
      const rotation = this.animatedRotation.interpolate({    ◀──────
        inputRange: [0, 1],
        outputRange: ['0deg', '360deg'],    ◀──────── Passes in the values for inputRange to map to
      });
      const { loading } = this.state;
      return (
        <View style={styles.container}>
          {
            loading ? (    ◀──────────────
              <Animated.Image
                source={require('./pathtoyourimage.png')}
                style={{ width: 40,
                         height: 40,
                         transform: [{ rotate: rotation }] }}
              />
            ) : (
              <Text>Welcome</Text>
            )
          }
        </View>
      );
    }
  }

  const styles = StyleSheet.create({
    container: {
      flex: 1,
      justifyContent: 'center',
      alignItems: 'center',
      padding: 10,
      paddingTop: 50,
    },
    input: {
      height: 50,
      marginHorizontal: 15,
      backgroundColor: '#ededed',
      marginTop: 10,
      paddingHorizontal: 9,
    },
  });
```

Passes in the animation's beginning and end values (0 and I)

Uses the animatedRotation value to create a new rotation value using the interpolate method

Checks whether loading is true, and responds accordingly

The animate class method passes Animated.timing into a call to Animated.loop. In the configuration, you set toValue to 1, duration to 1800, and easing to Easing.linear, to create a smooth spinning movement.

The animatedRotation value creates a new value called rotation, using the interpolate method. inputRange gives the animation's beginning and end values, and outputRange gives the values inputRange should map to: a beginning value of 0 degrees and a final value of 360 degrees, creating a full 360-degree rotation.

In the return statement, first check to see whether loading is true. If it is, show the animated loading indicator (update this path to that of the image in your application); if it's false, show a welcome message. Attach the rotation variable to the transform rotate value in the styling of Animated.Image.

7.4   *Creating multiple parallel animations*

Sometimes you need to create multiple animations at once and have them run simultaneously. The Animated library has a class method called parallel you can use to do this. parallel starts an array of animations at the same time.

For example, to make a welcome screen with two messages and a button all appear to move into the screen at once, you could create three separate animations and

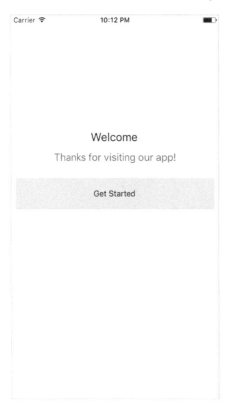

**Figure 7.4   Welcome screen using parallel animations
(shown after the animations are complete)**

call .start() on each of them. But a more efficient way would be to use the Animated. parallel function and pass in the array of animations to run at the same time.

In this example, you'll create a welcome screen that animates in two messages and a button when the component mounts (see figure 7.4). Because you're using Animated. parallel, all three animations will begin at exactly the same time. You'll add a delay property to the configuration to control the start time of two of the animations.

Listing 7.4 Creating an animated welcome screen

```
import React, { Component } from 'react';
import {
  Easing,
  StyleSheet,
  View,
  Animated,
  Text,
  TouchableHighlight,
} from 'react-native';

export default class RNAnimations extends Component {    When you create the class, also
  animatedTitle = new Animated.Value(-200);              create three new animated values.
  animatedSubtitle = new Animated.Value(600);
  animatedButton = new Animated.Value(800);

  componentDidMount() {      Calls the animate() method     Calls Animated.parallel and
    this.animate();          on componentDidMount           passes in three Animated.timing
  }                                                         animations to trigger all three
  animate = () => {                                         animations to start at once
    Animated.parallel([
      Animated.timing(
        this.animatedTitle,
        {
          toValue: 200,
          duration: 800,
        }
      ),
      Animated.timing(          Calls Animated.parallel and
        this.animatedSubtitle,  passes in three Animated.timing
        {                       animations to trigger all three
          toValue: 0,           animations to start at once
          duration: 1400,
          delay: 800,
        }
      ),
      Animated.timing(
        this.animatedButton,
        {
          toValue: 0,
          duration: 1000,
          delay: 2200,
        }
      )
    ]).start();
  }
```

```
    render() {                                    Attach the animated values to
      return (                                  each component you're animating.
        <View style={styles.container}>
          <Animated.Text style={[styles.title,
                                 { marginTop: this.animatedTitle}]}>
            Welcome
          </Animated.Text>        ◄───────────────────────────────────────┐
          <Animated.Text style={[styles.subTitle,                         │
                                 { marginLeft: this.animatedSubtitle }]}>  │
            Thanks for visiting our app!                                   │
          </Animated.Text>        ◄───────────────────────────────────────┤
          <Animated.View style={{ marginTop: this.animatedButton }}>  ◄───┘
            <TouchableHighlight style={styles.button}>
              <Text>Get Started</Text>
            </TouchableHighlight>
          </Animated.View>
        </View>
      );
    }
}

const styles = StyleSheet.create({
  container: {
    flex: 1,
  },
  title: {
    textAlign: 'center',
    fontSize: 20,
    marginBottom: 12,
  },
  subTitle: {
    width: '100%',
    textAlign: 'center',
    fontSize: 18,
    opacity: .8,
  },
  button: {
    marginTop: 25,
    backgroundColor: '#ddd',
    height: 55,
    justifyContent: 'center',
    alignItems: 'center',
    marginHorizontal: 10,
  }
});
```

7.5   *Creating an animated sequence*

An animated *sequence* is a series of animations that occur one after another, with each animation waiting for the previous animation to complete before it begins. You can create an animated sequence with sequence. Like parallel, sequence takes an array of animations:

```
Animated.sequence([
  animationOne,
```

```
    animationTwo,
    animationThree
]).start()
```

In this example, you'll create a sequence that drops the numbers 1, 2, and 3 into the screen, 500 milliseconds apart (figure 7.5).

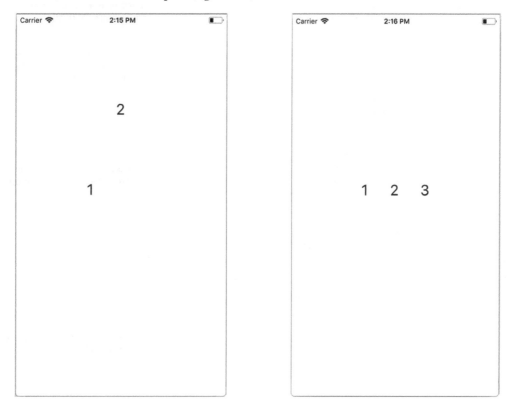

Figure 7.5   Creating an animated sequence of numbers

Listing 7.5   Creating a sequence of animations

```
import React, { Component } from 'react';
import {
  StyleSheet,
  View,                          Imports Animated from React Native
  Animated
} from 'react-native';

export default class RNAnimations extends Component {
  componentDidMount() {
    this.animate();            Calls the animate function
  }                             when the component mounts
```

```
AnimatedValue1 = new Animated.Value(-30);
AnimatedValue2 = new Animated.Value(-30);
AnimatedValue3 = new Animated.Value(-30);
animate = () => {
  const createAnimation = (value) => {
    return Animated.timing(
      value, {
        toValue: 290,
        duration: 500
      })
  }
  Animated.sequence([
    createAnimation(this.AnimatedValue1),
    createAnimation(this.AnimatedValue2),
    createAnimation(this.AnimatedValue3)
  ]).start()
}
render() {
  return (
    <View style={styles.container}>
      <Animated.Text style={[styles.text,
                      { marginTop: this.AnimatedValue1}]}>
        1
      </Animated.Text>
      <Animated.Text style={[styles.text,
                      { marginTop: this.AnimatedValue2}]}>
        2
      </Animated.Text>
      <Animated.Text style={[styles.text,
                      { marginTop: this.AnimatedValue3}]}>
        3
      </Animated.Text>
    </View>
  );
}
}

const styles = StyleSheet.create({
  container: {
    flex: 1,
    justifyContent: 'center',
    flexDirection: 'row',
  },
  text: {
    marginHorizontal: 20,
    fontSize: 26
  }
});
```

Creates three animated values, passing in -30 for the beginning value

Creates a createAnimation function as a helper for making a new timing animation

Starts the sequence, calling createAnimation once for each animated value

Passes the animated values to the three Animated.Text components

Passes the animated values to the three Animated.Text components

This example uses beginning animated values of -30 because they're the marginTop values for the text elements: the text is pulled off the top of the screen and hidden before the animation begins. The createAnimation function also receives an animated value as its argument.

7.6 *Using Animated.stagger to stagger animation start times*

The last type of animation we'll go over is `Animated.stagger`. Like `parallel` and `sequence`, `stagger` takes an array of animations. The array of animations starts in parallel, but the start time is staggered equally across all the animations. Unlike `parallel` and `sequence`, the first argument to `stagger` is the stagger time, and the second argument is the array of animations:

```
Animated.stagger(
  100,
  [
    Animation1,
    Animation2,
    Animation3
  ]
).start()
```

In this example, you'll dynamically create a large number of animations that are used to stagger a series of red boxes onto the screen (figure 7.6).

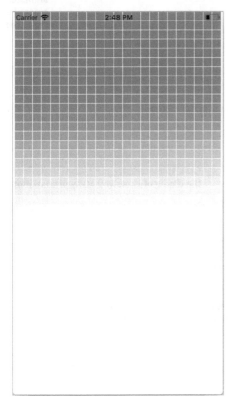

Figure 7.6   Using `Animated.stagger` to create an array of staggered animations

Listing 7.6   Using `Animated.stagger` to stagger a series of animations

```
import React, { Component } from 'react'
import {
  StyleSheet,                    Imports Animated from React Native
  View,
  Animated    ◄
} from 'react-native'

export default class RNAnimations extends Component {
  constructor () {
    super()                                            Creates an array
    this.animatedValues = []                           that will contain 1,000
    for (let i = 0; i < 1000; i++) {                   animated values of 0
      this.animatedValues[i] = new Animated.Value(0)
    }                                                  Creates an array of
    this.animations = this.animatedValues.map(value => {   Animated.timing
      return Animated.timing(                              animations
        value,                                             referencing the
        {                                                  animated values
          toValue: 1,                                      created in the
          duration: 6000                                   animatedValues array
        }
      )
    })
  }
  componentDidMount() {
    this.animate()    ◄──────── Calls the animate method
  }
  animate = () => {
    Animated.stagger(15, this.animations).start()    ◄
  }
  render() {                      Calls Animated.stagger().start(), passing in
    return (                      the timing of 15 ms and array of animations
      <View style={styles.container}>
        {
          this.animatedValues.map((value, index) => (    ◄
            <Animated.View key={index}
                        style={[{opacity: value},
                              styles.box]} />    ◄
          ))    ◄
        }
      </View>                   Maps over the animations, creating an
    );                          Animated.View for each item in the array
  }
}

const styles = StyleSheet.create({
  container: {
    flex: 1,
    justifyContent: 'center',
    flexDirection: 'row',
    flexWrap: 'wrap'
  },
  box: {
```

```
        width: 15,
        height: 15,
        margin: .5,
        backgroundColor: 'red'
    }
}))
```

7.7   *Other useful tips for using the Animated library*

In addition to the parts of the Animated API we've already covered, a few more techniques are useful to know about: resetting an animated value, invoking callbacks, offloading animations to the native thread, and creating custom animatable components. This section takes a quick look at each of these.

7.7.1   *Resetting an animated value*

If you're calling an animation, you can reset the value to whatever you want by using setValue(value). This is useful if you've already called an animation on a value and need to call the animation again, and you want to reset the value to either the original value or a new value:

```
animate = () => {
  this.animatedValue.setValue(300);
    #continue here with the new animated value
}
```

7.7.2   *Invoking a callback*

When an animation is completed, an optional callback function can be fired, as shown here:

```
Animated.timing(
  this.animatedValue,
  {
    toValue: 1,
    duration: 1000
  }
).start(() => console.log('animation is complete!'))
```

7.7.3   *Offloading animations to the native thread*

Out of the box, the Animated library performs animations using the JavaScript thread. In most cases, this works fine, and you shouldn't have many performance problems. But if anything is blocking the JavaScript thread, you may see issues like frames being skipped, causing laggy or jumpy animations.

There's a way around using the JavaScript thread: you can use a configuration Boolean called useNativeDriver. useNativeDriver offloads the animation to the native UI thread, and the native code can then update the views directly on the UI thread, as shown here:

```
Animated.timing(
  this.animatedValue,
```

```
  {
    toValue: 100,
    duration: 1000,
    useNativeDriver: true
  }
).start();
```

Not every animation can be offloaded using useNativeDriver, so be sure to check the Animated API documentation when you use it. As of this writing, only non-layout properties can be animated using this method; flexbox properties as well as properties like margins and padding can't be animated.

7.7.4   *Creating a custom animatable component using createAnimatedComponent*

We mentioned in section 7.1 that the only animatable components out of the box are View, Text, Image, and ScrollView. There's also a way to create an animated component from any existing or custom React Native element or component. You can do this by wrapping the component in a call to createAnimatedComponent. Here's an example:

```
const Button = Animated.createAnimatedComponent(TouchableHighlight)

<Button onPress={somemethod} style={styles.button}>
  <Text>Hello World</Text>
</Button>
```

Now you can use the button just like a regular React Native component.

Summary

- The built-in Animated API is the recommended way to create animations in React Native.
- Animated.timing is the main method to use to create animations using the Animated library.
- The only components that are animatable out of the box are View, Text, ScrollView, and Image, but you can create custom animatable components using createAnimatedComponent.
- To interpolate and reuse animated values, use the Animated interpolate method.
- To create and trigger an array of animations at the same time, use Animated .parallel.
- To create an infinitely looping animation, use Animated.loop.
- Use Animated.sequence to create a sequence of animations that execute one after another.
- Use Animated.stagger to create an array of animations that happen in parallel, but whose start times are staggered based on the time passed in.

Using the Redux data architecture library

This chapter covers

- How the React context API works
- Creating a Redux `store`
- How to use Redux actions and reducers to manage global state
- Reducer composition using `combineReducers`

When building React and React Native applications in the real world, you'll quickly learn that the data layer can become complex and unmanageable if it isn't handled very precisely and deliberately. One way to handle data is to keep it in component state and pass it around as props, as we've done throughout this book. Another way is to use a data architecture pattern or library. This chapter covers the Redux library: it's the most widely adopted method of handling data in the React ecosystem, and it's maintained by Facebook, the same team that maintains both React and React Native.

8.1 What is Redux?

In the Redux documentation, the library is described as "a predictable state container for JavaScript apps." Redux is basically a global state object that's the single source of truth in an application. This global state object is received as props into

React Native components. Any time a piece of data is changed in the Redux state, the entire application receives this new data as props.

Redux simplifies application state by moving it all into one place called a *store*; this makes it much easier to reason about and understand. When you need the value of something, you'll know exactly where to look in a Redux application and can expect the same value to be available and up-to-date elsewhere in the application, too.

So how does Redux work? It takes advantage of a React feature called *context*, a mechanism for creating and managing global state.

8.2   Using context to create and manage global state in a React application

Context is a React API that creates global variables that can be accessed anywhere in the application, as long as the component receiving the context is a child of the component that created it. Normally you'd have to do this by passing props down each level of the component structure. With context, you don't need to use props. You can use the context anywhere in the app and access it without passing it down to each level.

> **NOTE** Although context is good to understand and is used in numerous open source libraries, you probably won't need to use it in apps unless you're building an open source library or can't find another way around a problem. We're discussing it in order for you to fully understand how Redux works under the hood.

Let's look at how to create context in a basic component structure of three components: `Parent`, `Child1`, and `Child2`. This example shows how to apply application-wide theming from a parent level, which could make it possible to control the styling of an entire application if needed.

Listing 8.1   Creating context

```
const ThemeContext = React.createContext()          ◀── Creates a new variable called ThemeContext

class Parent extends Component {                      ◀── Creates a themeValue state
  state = { themeValue: 'light' }                        variable with the value 'light'
  toggleThemeValue = () => {
    const value = this.state.themeValue === 'dark' ? 'light' : 'dark'
    this.setState({ themeValue: value })
  }
  render() {                                                Checks the current theme value
    return (                                                and toggles it to 'light' or 'dark'
      <ThemeContext.Provider
        value={{
          themeValue: this.state.themeValue,
          toggleThemeValue: this.toggleThemeValue
        }}
      >
        <View style={styles.container}>
```

Provides the context to child components. Anything wrapped in a Provider is available to children of a component in a Consumer.

```
            <Text>Hello World</Text>
          </View>
          <Child1 />
      </ThemeContext.Provider>
    );
  }
}

const Child1 = () => <Child2 />
```

Stateless function that returns a component, demonstrating that you aren't passing props between Parent and Child2

```
const Child2 = () => (
  <ThemeContext.Consumer>
    {(val) => (
      <View style={[styles.container,
                    val.themeValue === 'dark' &&
                    { backgroundColor: 'black' }]}>
        <Text style={styles.text}>Hello from Component2</Text>
        <Text style={styles.text}
              onPress={val.toggleThemeValue}>
          Toggle Theme Value
        </Text>
      </View>
    )}
  </ThemeContext.Consumer>
)
```

Stateless function that returns a component wrapped in a ThemeContext.Consumer

```
const styles = StyleSheet.create({
  container: {
    flex: 1,
    justifyContent: 'center',
    alignItems: 'center',
    backgroundColor: '#F5FCFF',
  },
  text: {
    fontSize: 22,
    color: '#666'
  }
})
```

The `Child2` stateless function returns a component that's wrapped in a `ThemeContext.Consumer`. `ThemeContext.Consumer` requires a function as its child. The function receives an argument containing whatever context is available (in this case, the `val` object containing two properties). You can now use the context values in the component.

When you use Redux with React, you'll take advantage of a function called `connect`, which basically takes pieces of context and makes them available as props in the component. Understanding context should make learning Redux much easier!

8.3   *Implementing Redux with a React Native app*

Now that you've know the fundamentals of what Redux is and have seen what's going on under the hood with context, let's create a new React Native app and start adding

Redux. You'll be creating a basic list app you can use to keep up with books you've read (see figure 8.1). Follow these steps:

1 Create a new React Native application, and call it RNRedux:

```
react-native init RNRedux
```

2 Change into the new directory:

```
cd RNRedux
```

3 Install the Redux-specific dependencies you'll need:

```
npm i redux react-redux --save
```

4 In the root of the directory, create a folder called src, and add to it the following files: Books.js and actions.js. Also, in src, create a folder called reducers, containing two files: bookReducer.js and index.js. The src folder structure should now look like figure 8.2.

The next thing to do is create the first piece of Redux state. You'll do this in bookReducer.js. In section 8.1, I described Redux as a global object. To create this global object, you'll piece together smaller objects using what are known as *reducers*.

Figure 8.1   Completed book list application

▲ src

   ▲ reducers

      JS bookReducer.js

      JS index.js

   JS actions.js

   JS Books.js

Figure 8.2   RNRedux src folder structure

8.4 *Creating Redux reducers to hold Redux state*

A reducer is a function that returns an object; when combined with other reducers, they create the global state. Reducers can be more easily thought of as data stores. Each store contains a piece of data, which is exactly what reducers do in the Redux architecture.

In the reducers folder are two files: bookReducer.js and index.js. In index.js, you'll combine all the reducers in the app to create the global state. The app will have only one reducer to start with (bookReducer), so the global state object will look something like this:

```
{
  bookReducer: {}
}
```

You've yet to decide what to put in bookReducer. An array in which to store a list of books will be a good start. This reducer will create and return a piece of state that you'll access later from the Redux store. In reducers/bookReducer.js, create your first reducer. This code creates a function whose only purpose (for now) is to return the state.

Listing 8.2 Creating a reducer

```
const initialState = {    #A
  books: [{ name: 'East of Eden', author: 'John Steinbeck' }]    ◄─────────
}    #A
                                            Creates the initialState object

const bookReducer = (state = initialState) => {    ◄─────
  return state    ◄─────                         Takes a state argument and sets
}                │ Returns the state              the default to the initial state

export default bookReducer
```

The initialState object will hold the beginning state. In this case, that's an array of books that you'll populate with objects containing name and author props. You create a function that takes an argument, state, and sets the default value to the initial state. When this function is first called, state will be undefined and will return the initialState object. At this time, the function's only purpose is to return the state.

Now that you've created the first reducer, go into rootReducer (reducers/index.js) and create what will be the global state. The root reducer gathers all the reducers in the application and allows you to make a global store (state object) by combining them.

Listing 8.3 Creating a root reducer

```
import { combineReducers } from 'redux'    ◄─────────
import bookReducer from './bookReducer'
                                            Imports the combineReducers
                                            function from Redux
Imports the
bookReducer    const rootReducer = combineReducers({    ◄─────
reducer          bookReducer
               })                          Creates a root reducer containing
                                           all the reducers; in this case it contains
export default rootReducer                 the single property bookReducer
```

Next, to hook this all together, you'll go into App.js, create the Redux store, and make the store available to all child components using a couple of Redux and React-Redux helpers.

8.5   *Adding the provider and creating the store*

In this section, you'll add a *provider* to the app. A provider is usually a parent component that passes data of some kind along to all child components. In Redux, the provider passes the global state/store to the rest of the application. In App.js, update the code as follows.

Listing 8.4   Adding the provider and store

```
import React from 'react'

import Books from './src/Books'          ◀── Imports the Books component
import rootReducer from './src/reducers'  (created in listing 8.5)
                                         ◀─── Imports rootReducer
import { Provider } from 'react-redux'   ◀─── Imports the Provider wrapper from react-redux
import { createStore } from 'redux'      ◀──
                                             Imports createStore
const store = createStore(rootReducer)   ◀──
                                             Creates a store, passing
export default class App extends React.Component {  in the rootReducer
  render() {
    return (
      <Provider store={store} >
        <Books />              Returns the Books component wrapped
      </Provider>              in a Provider component, passing in the
    )                          store as a prop to the Provider
  }
}
```

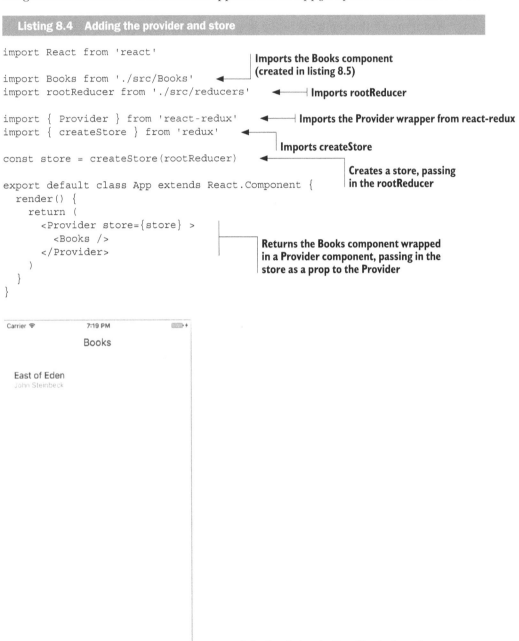

Figure 8.3   Rendering the list of books from the Redux store

The `Provider` wrapper is used to wrap the main component. Any child of `Provider` will have access to the Redux store. `createStore` is a utility from Redux that you use to create the Redux store by passing in the `rootReducer`. You're finished with the basic Redux setup, and you can now access the Redux store in the app.

In the `Books` component, you'll hook into the Redux store, pull out the `books` array, and map over the books, displaying them in the UI (figure 8.3). Because `Books` is a child of `Provider`, it can access anything in the Redux store.

8.6   *Accessing data using the connect function*

You access the Redux store from a child component by using the `connect` function from react-redux. The first argument to `connect` is a function that gives you access to the entire Redux state. You can then return an object with whatever pieces of the store you want access to.

`connect` is a *curried* function, meaning in the most basic sense a function that returns another function. You'll have two sets of arguments, and a blueprint that looks something like this: `connect(args)(args)`. The properties in the object returned from the first argument to `connect` are then made available to the component as props.

Let's see what this means by looking at the `connect` function you'll use in the Books.js component.

Listing 8.5   `connect` function in Books.js

```
connect(
    (state) => {          ◄────  Function that gives the
      return {                   global Redux state object
        books: state.bookReducer.books
      }
    }
) (Books)             ◄────  Passes in Books
```

Returns an object from this function

The first argument to `connect` is a function that gives the global Redux `state` object as an argument. You can then reference this `state` object and have access to anything in the Redux state. You return an object from this function. Whatever keys are returned in the object become available as props in the component you're wrapping: in this case, `Books`. You pass in `Books` as the only argument to the `connect` function's second function call.

Often, you'll separate this function and store it in a variable to make this easier to read:

```
const mapStateToProps = state => ({
  books: state.bookReducer.books
})
```

In this connected component is a new property called `this.props.books`, which is the `books` array from `bookReducer`. Tie all this together, access the `books` array, and map over the books to display them in the UI, as shown in the following listing (Books.js).

```
import React from 'react'
import {
  Text,
  View,
    ScrollView,
  StyleSheet
} from 'react-native'

import { connect } from 'react-redux'        ◀───  Imports connect from react-redux

class Books extends React.Component<{}> {
  render() {                                        Because the books array was returned
    const { books } = this.props      ◀───         from the connect function (at the bottom
                                                    of the code listing), you have access to it
                                                    as props.
    return (
      <View style={styles.container}>
        <Text style={styles.title}>Books</Text>
        <ScrollView
          keyboardShouldPersistTaps='always'
          style={styles.booksContainer}
        >                                               Maps over the array, displaying
          {                                             the name and author of each book
            books.map((book, index) => (
              <View style={styles.book} key={index}>
                <Text style={styles.name}>{book.name}</Text>
                <Text style={styles.author}>{book.author}</Text>
              </View>
            ))
          }
        </ScrollView>
      </View>
    )
  }
}

const styles = StyleSheet.create({
  container: {
    flex: 1
  },
  booksContainer: {
    borderTopWidth: 1,
    borderTopColor: '#ddd',
    flex: 1
  },
  title: {
    paddingTop: 30,
    paddingBottom: 20,
    fontSize: 20,
    textAlign: 'center'
  },
  book: {
    padding: 20
  },
  name: {
```

```
    fontSize: 18
  },
  author: {
    fontSize: 14,
    color: '#999'
  }
})
const mapStateToProps = (state) => ({          Takes the Redux state, and returns an object
  books: state.bookReducer.books              with a key containing the books array
})
                                                      Exports the connect function
export default connect(mapStateToProps)(Books)
```

You begin by importing `connect` from react-redux. In listing 8.5, you wrote the function returning the props inline. This listing separates it and names it `mapStateToProps`, following the convention of the Redux ecosystem. This naming convention makes a lot of sense, because you're essentially mapping Redux state to component props. This function takes the Redux state as an argument and returns an object with one key containing the `books` array from `bookReducer`. Finally, you export the `connect` function, passing in `mapStateToProps` as the first argument to `connect` and `Books` as the only argument in the second set of arguments to `connect`.

After launching the application, you should see a basic list of books, as shown earlier in figure 8.3.

8.7 Adding actions

Now that you have access to the Redux state, a logical next step is to add some functionality that will allow you to add books to the `books` array Redux store. To do this, you'll use *actions*. Actions are basically functions that return objects that send data to the store and update reducers; they're the only way to change the store. Each action should contain a `type` property in order for reducers to be able to use them. Here are a couple of examples of actions:

```
function fetchBooks() {
    return {
      type: 'FETCH_BOOKS'
    }
  }

  function addBook(book) {
    return {
      type: 'Add_BOOK',
      book: book
    }
  }
```

Actions, when called using a Redux `dispatch` function, are sent to all reducers in the application as the second argument to the reducer. (We'll cover how to attach the Redux `dispatch` function later in this chapter.) When the reducer receives the action, you check the action's type property and update what the reducer returns based on whether the action is one that it's listening for.

In this case, the only action you need for the next step is addBook, to add additional books to the array of books. In actions.js, create the following action.

Listing 8.7   Creating the first action

```
export const ADD_BOOK = 'ADD_BOOK'          ◄──────  Creates and exports an ADD_BOOK
                                                     constant for reuse in reducers
export function addBook (book) {     ◄──────
  return {                                   Creates the addBook function,
    type: ADD_BOOK,                          which takes a single book object
    book                                     and returns an object containing
  }                                          a type and the passed-in book
}
```

Next, wire up bookReducer to use the addBook action.

Listing 8.8   Updating bookReducer to use the addBook action

```
import { ADD_BOOK } from '../actions'    ◄──────
                                                  Imports the ADD_BOOK constant
const initialState = {                            from the actions file
  books: [{ name: 'East of Eden', author: 'John Steinbeck' }]         Adds a second
}                                                                      argument to
                                                                       bookReducer:
const bookReducer = (state = initialState, action) => {    ◄──────     the action
  switch(action.type) {      ◄──────
    case ADD_BOOK:                  Creates a switch statement that
      return {                      will switch on the action type
        books: [     ◄──────
          ...state.books,           If the action type equals ADD_BOOK,
          action.book               returns a new books array
        ]
      }
    default:     ◄──────            If the switch statement doesn't
      return state                  hit, returns the existing state
  }
}

export default bookReducer
```

In the listing, if the action type is equal to ADD_BOOK, you return a new books array containing all the previous items in the array. You do so by creating a new array, using the spread operator to add the contents of the existing books array to the new array, and adding to the array a new item that's the book property of the action.

That's all you need to do in the Redux configuration to get this working. The last step is to go into the UI and wire it all together. To get the user's book info, you need to create a form. Figure 8.4 shows what the UI will look like.

This form has two inputs: one for the book name and one for the author name. It also has a submit button. When the user types into the form, you need to keep up with the values in the local state. You can then pass those values on to the action when the user clicks the submit button.

Figure 8.4 UI with added text inputs to capture the book and the author name

Open Books.js, and import the additional components needed for this functionality, as well as the addBook function from the actions. You'll also create an initialState variable to use as the local component state.

Listing 8.9 Additional imports in Books.js

```
import React from 'react'
import {
  Text,
  View,
  ScrollView,
  StyleSheet,
  TextInput,
  TouchableOpacity
} from 'react-native'
import { addBook } from './actions'

import { connect } from 'react-redux'

const initialState = {
  name: '',
  author: ''
}

...
```

Imports TextInput and TouchableOpacity

Imports the addBook function from the actions file

Creates an initialState object containing name and author fields

Next, in the body of the class, you need to create three things: the component state, a method that keeps up with the component state when the `textInput` values change, and a method that will send the action to Redux containing the book values (name and author) when the submit button is pressed. Before the `render` method, add the following code.

Listing 8.10   Adding state and class methods to Books.js

```
class Books extends React.Component {

  state = initialState        ◄────────  Gives the component state the
                                          value of the initialState variable

  updateInput = (key, value) => {    ◄────  Creates an updateInput method that
    this.setState({                        takes two arguments: key and value.
      ...this.state,                       You'll update the state by using the
      [key]: value                         spread operators to add the existing
    })              Calls dispatchAddBook, state key-value pairs to the new state
  }                 accessible as props from and then adding the new key-value pair.
                    the connect function

  addBook = () => {    ◄─────────
    this.props.dispatchAddBook(this.state)
    this.setState(initialState)
  }
}
```

. . .

The `addBook` method calls a function that you have access to as props from the `connect` function: `dispatchAddBook`. This function accepts the entire state as an argument, which is an object with `name` and `author` properties. After the dispatch action has been called, you then clear the component state by resetting it to the `initialState` value.

With the functionality in place, you can create the UI and hook these methods up to it. Under the closing tag of the `ScrollView` in Books.js, add the form UI.

Listing 8.11   Adding the UI for the form

```
class Books extends React.Component {
    ...                                   Receives the updateInput method as the
    render() {                            property of onChangeText, passing 'name'
      ...                                 or 'author' as the first argument and the
    </ScrollView>                         value of TextInput as the second argument
    <View style={styles.inputContainer}>
      <View style={styles.inputWrapper}>
        <TextInput    ◄────────────────────────────
          value={this.state.name}
          onChangeText={value => this.updateInput('name', value)}
          style={styles.input}
          placeholder='Book name'
        />
        <TextInput    ◄────────────────────────────
          value={this.state.author}
          onChangeText={value => this.updateInput('author', value)}
          style={styles.input}
          placeholder='Author Name'
        />
      </View>
```

```
      <TouchableOpacity onPress={this.addBook}>
        <View style={styles.addButtonContainer}>
          <Text style={styles.addButton}>+</Text>
        </View>
      </TouchableOpacity>
    </View>
    </View>
  }
}
```

Calls the addBook method. TouchableOpacity wraps the View component, allowing it to respond properly to touches.

```
const styles = StyleSheet.create({            Adds new styles
  inputContainer: {
    padding: 10,
    backgroundColor: '#ffffff',
    borderTopColor: '#ededed',
    borderTopWidth: 1,
    flexDirection: 'row',
    height: 100
  },
  inputWrapper: {
    flex: 1
  },
  input: {
    height: 44,
    padding: 7,
    backgroundColor: '#ededed',
    borderColor: '#ddd',
    borderWidth: 1,
    borderRadius: 10,
    flex: 1,
    marginBottom: 5
  },
  addButton: {
    fontSize: 28,
    lineHeight: 28
  },
  addButtonContainer: {
    width: 80,
    height: 80,
    backgroundColor: '#ededed',
    marginLeft: 10,
    justifyContent: 'center',
    alignItems: 'center',
    borderRadius: 20
  },
  ...
}
```

Creates a mapDispatchToProps object

```
const mapDispatchToProps = {
  dispatchAddBook: (book) => addBook(book)
}
```

Passes in mapDispatchToProps as the second argument to connect

```
export default connect(mapStateToProps, mapDispatchToProps)(Books)

}
```

In the `mapDispatchToProps` object, you can declare functions you want access to as props in the component. You create a new function called `dispatchAddBook` and have it call the `addBook` action, passing in `book` as an argument. Similar to how `mapStateTo-Props` maps state to component props, `mapDispatchToProps` maps actions (that need to be dispatched to reducers) to component props. In order for an action to be recognized by the Redux reducers, it must be declared in this `mapDispatchToProps` object. You pass in `mapDispatchToProps` as the second argument to the `connect` function.

Now you should be able to easily add books to the book list.

8.8 *Deleting items from a Redux store in a reducer*

The next logical step is to add a way to remove books you've already read. Given everything you've put together, this won't require too much more work (figure 8.5).

The first thing to think about when removing an item from an array such as this is how to identify a book as being unique. Right now, a user could have multiple books with the same author or multiple books with the same name, so using the existing properties won't work. Instead, you can use a library such as uuid to create unique identifiers on the fly. To begin setting this up, from the command line, install the uuid library into node_modules:

```
npm i uuid --save
```

Figure 8.5 Adding the Remove button to the Books.js UI

Next, you'll implement a unique identifier in the reducer for the items in the `initialState` books array. In reducers/bookReducer.js, update the imports and `initialState` to look like the next listing.

Listing 8.12 Importing and using uuid

```
import uuidV4 from 'uuid/v4'
import { ADD_BOOK } from '../actions'

const initialState = {
  books: [{ name: 'East of Eden', author: 'John Steinbeck', id: uuidV4() }]
}
```

Imports the v4 algorithm

Adds an id property to initialState and generates a new unique identifier

The uuid library has a few algorithms to choose from. Here, you import only the v4 algorithm, which creates a random 32-character string. Then you add a new property to the `initialState` books array, `id`, and generate a new unique identifier by calling `uuidV4()`.

Now that you have a way to uniquely identify the items in the `books` array, you're ready to move forward with the rest of the functionality. The next step is to create a new action in actions.js; you'll call it when you want to remove a book. You also need to update the `addBook` action to add an ID to newly created books.

Listing 8.13 Creating the `removeBook` action

```
export const ADD_BOOK = 'ADD_BOOK'
export const REMOVE_BOOK = 'REMOVE_BOOK'
import uuidV4 from 'uuid/v4'

export function addBook (book) {
  return {
    type: ADD_BOOK,
    book: {
      ...book,
      id: uuidV4()
    }
  }
}

export function removeBook (book) {
  return {
    type: REMOVE_BOOK,
    book
  }
}
```

Creates a reusable constant, REMOVE_BOOK, used here and in the reducer

Imports the uuid library

Adds a new key to the book, assigning id a property of a newly created unique identifier using the uuidV4 function

Creates a new removeBook function that returns an object with a type and the book parameter that's passed in

Next, the reducer needs to be aware of the new action. In reducers/bookReducer.js, create a new type listener, this one for REMOVE_BOOK, and add the necessary functionality to remove a book from the array of books stored in the Redux state.

```
import uuidV4 from 'uuid/v4'
import { ADD_BOOK, REMOVE_BOOK } from '../actions'        ◄─── Imports the new REMOVE_BOOK
                                                               constant from the actions folder
const initialState = {
  books: [{ name: 'East of Eden', author: 'John Steinbeck', id: uuidV4() }]
}
const bookReducer = (state = initialState, action) => {
  switch(action.type) {
    ...                      Adds a new case to the switch statement that
    case REMOVE_BOOK:    ◄── listens for the REMOVE_BOOK action type
      const index = state.books.findIndex(
                        book => book.id === action.book.id)   ◄──────────────┐
      return {                      Finds the index of the book to be deleted │
        books: [
          ...state.books.slice(0, index),
          ...state.books.slice(index + 1)
        ]
      }
    ...
  }
}

export default bookReducer
```

Returns a new array containing the first and second half of the existing books array, leaving out the index of the book to be removed

The last thing to do is implement this new `removeBook` functionality in the UI of the Books component (Books.js). You'll import the `removeBook` action, add a remove button to each rendered item, and wire the remove button up to the `removeBook` action.

```
...
import { addBook, removeBook } from './actions'       ◄─── Adds removeBook as an import
...                                                         from the actions file
  removeBook = (book) => {
    this.props.dispatchRemoveBook(book)        ─┐
  }                                             │  Creates a new class method removeBook,
...                                             │  calling this.props.dispatchRemoveBook
                                                └─ as a new key in mapDispatchToProps
{
            books.map((book, index) => (
              <View style={styles.book} key={index}>
                <Text style={styles.name}>{book.name}</Text>
                <Text style={styles.author}>{book.author}</Text>
                <Text onPress={() => this.removeBook(book)}>
                    Remove
                </Text>
              </View>
            ))
          }                                    Returns a new Text component and
                                         attaches removeBook to its onPress event
...
```

```
const mapDispatchToProps = {
  dispatchAddBook: (book) => addBook(book),
  dispatchRemoveBook: (book) => removeBook(book)
}
...
```

**Adds the new dispatchAddBook
function to mapDispatchToProps**

Summary

- With context, you can pass properties and data to children in a React Native application without explicitly passing the properties to each individual child.
- Reducers are similar to a traditional data store in the sense that they keep up with and return data, but also allow you to update data in the store.
- You can create and use actions to update a Redux store.
- With the connect function, you can access data from the Redux state as props and also create dispatch functions that interact with reducers using actions.
- Any time data needs to be changed in a reducer, it must be done by using an action.

Part 3

API reference

React Native offers a wealth of APIs. The chapters in this part cover cross-platform APIs as well as APIs that are specific to the iOS and Android platforms.

In chapter 9, we explore using React Native's cross-platform APIs: APIs that can be used on either iOS or Android to create alerts; detect whether the app is in the foreground, is in the background, or is inactive; persist, retrieve, and remove data; store and update text to the device clipboard; and perform a number of other useful tasks. In chapters 10 and 11, we'll look at React Native's APIs that are specific to either the iOS platform or the Android platform.

Implementing
cross-platform APIs

This chapter covers

- Creating native application alert dialogs

- Detecting whether the app is in the foreground, background, or inactive

- Storing and updating text to the device clipboard

- Using geolocation to retrieve and use latitude, longitude, speed, and altitude of the user's device

- Detecting device attributes such as the height and width of the screen and the connection type

One of the key benefits of using React Native is the ease with which native APIs can be accessed and used with JavaScript. In this chapter, we'll cover most of the cross-platform APIs available in the framework. When accessing these APIs, you'll be able to use a single codebase to implement platform-specific behavior on both iOS and Android.

The main difference between the native APIs discussed in this chapter and native components is that native components usually have something to do with the UI, such as showing a specific UI element. APIs, on the other hand, are more about accessing native features and hardware in the phone, such as interacting with or accessing data held in the device (geolocation, application state, and so on).

This chapter covers the following cross-platform APIs:

- Alert
- AppState
- AsyncStorage
- Clipboard
- Dimensions
- Geolocation
- Keyboard
- NetInfo
- PanResponder

Although React Native offers other cross-platform APIs, you'll find these to be the most useful.

In addition to its cross-platform APIs, React Native also offers platform-specific APIs (that is, APIs that work only on either iOS or Android). We'll cover iOS-specific APIs in chapter 10 and Android-specific APIs in chapter 11.

> **NOTE**   You can find the code for this chapter at www.manning.com/books/react-native-in-action and also at https://github.com/dabit3/react-native-in-action/tree/chapter9.

9.1   *Using the Alert API to create cross-platform notifications*

Alert launches a platform-specific alert dialog with a title, a message, and optional methods that can be called when an alert button is pressed. Alert can be triggered by calling the `alert` method (`Alert.alert`), which takes four arguments (see table 9.1):

```
Alert.alert(title, message, buttons, options)
```

Table 9.1   `Alert.alert` method arguments

Argument	Type	Description
`title`	String	Main message of the alert button
`message`	String	Secondary message of the alert button
`buttons`	Array	Array of buttons, each of which is an object with two keys: `title` (string) and `onPress` (function)
`options`	Object	Object containing a cancelable Boolean (options: `{ cancelable: true }`)

9.1.1   *Use cases for alerts*

An alert is a common UI pattern across both the web and mobile devices, and it's an easy way to let the user know about something happening in the application such as an error or success. Many times, an alert is used if a download has finished, an error has occurred, or an asynchronous process (such as logging in) has completed.

9.1.2 Example of using alerts

You can trigger an alert by calling the `Alert.alert()` method and passing in one or more arguments. In this example, you'll create an alert with two options: Cancel and Show Message (see figure 9.1). If cancel is pressed, you'll dismiss the alert; if Show Message is pressed, you'll update the state to show the message.

Listing 9.1 Binding an alert to a touch event

```
import React, { Component } from 'react'
import { TouchableHighlight, View, Text, StyleSheet, Alert }
    from 'react-native'                  ◀——  Imports alert from React Native
let styles = {}

export default class App extends Component {
  constructor () {
    super()
    this.state = {                             Instantiates the state with
      showMessage: false                       showMessage set to false
    }
    this.showAlert = this.showAlert.bind(this)
  }
  showAlert () {      ◀——      Defines the showAlert method,
    Alert.alert(                passing in a title of 'Title', a message
      'Title',                  of 'Message!', and two buttons
      'Message!',
      [
        {
          text: 'Cancel',
          onPress: () => console.log('Dismiss called...'),
          style: 'destructive'
        },                                  If Show Message is pressed, updates
        {                                   the state to showMessage being true
          text: 'Show Message',
          onPress: () => this.setState({ showMessage: true })
        }
      ]
    )
  }
  render () {
    const { showMessage } = this.state
    return (
      <View style={styles.container}>
        <TouchableHighlight onPress={this.showAlert} style={styles.button}>
          <Text>SHOW ALERT</Text>
        </TouchableHighlight>
        {
          showMessage && <Text>Showing message - success</Text>
        }
      </View>                              Hides the message unless
    )                                      showMessage is set to true
  }
}
```

```
  }
styles = StyleSheet.create({
  container: {
    justifyContent: 'center',
    flex: 1
  },
  button: {
    height: 70,
    justifyContent: 'center',
    alignItems: 'center',
    backgroundColor: '#ededed'
  }
})
```

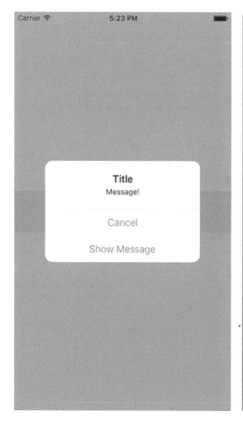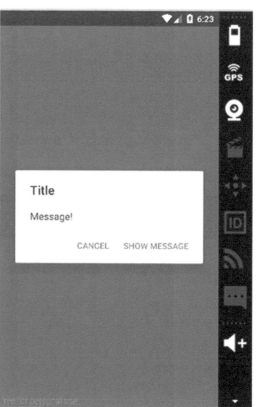

Figure 9.1   `onPress` alert with two options: Cancel and Show Message (left: iOS, right: Android)

9.2   *Using the AppState API to detect the current application state*

AppState will tell you whether the app is active, inactive, or in the background. It basically calls a method whenever the app state changes, allowing you to perform actions or call other methods based on the state of the app.

AppState triggers whenever the app state changes and then returns active, inactive, or background. To respond to app state changes, add an event listener and call a method when the event is fired. The events that AppState uses to respond are change and memorywarning. This section's example uses change because it's what you'll primarily use in a real-world scenario.

9.2.1 Use cases for AppState

AppState is a useful API, and frequently comes in handy. Many times, when the app is pulled into the foreground, you may want to do things such as fetch fresh data from your API—and that's a great use case for AppState.

Another use case is authentication. When the app is set into the foreground, you may want to add another layer of security, such as a PIN or fingerprint.

If you're doing polling, such as hitting a database every 15 seconds or so to check for new data, you may want to disable the polling when the user pushes the app into the background. AppState is a great use case for this as well.

9.2.2 Example of using AppState

In this example, you'll add an event listener that listens for the change event in componentDidMount and then displays the current state in the console.

Listing 9.2   Using AppState to log out the current app state

```
import React, { Component } from 'react'
import { AppState, View, Text, StyleSheet } from 'react-native'    ◀──────┐
let styles = {}
                                                        Imports the AppState
                                                        API from React Native
class App extends Component {
  componentDidMount () {
    AppState.addEventListener('change', this.handleAppStateChange)
  }
  handleAppStateChange (currentAppState) {                       Calls AppState.
    console.log('currentAppState:', currentAppState)      addEventListener, passing
  }                                                          in the type of event to
  render () {                                                listen for (change) and a
    return (                                                      callback function
      <View style={styles.container}>                     (handleAppStateChange)
        <Text>Testing App State</Text>
      </View>
    )
  }
}

styles = StyleSheet.create({
  container: {
    justifyContent: 'center',
    flex: 1
  }
})

export default App
```

Logs the currentAppState

Run the project, and test it by either pressing CMD-Shift-H in iOS Simulator or pressing the home button in the Android emulator. The console should log the current app state (active, inactive, or background).

9.3   *Using the AsyncStorage API to persist data*

Next up is AsyncStorage. AsyncStorage is a great way to persist and store data: it's asynchronous, meaning you can retrieve data using a promise or `async await`, and it uses a key-value system to store and retrieve data.

When you use an application and then close it, its state will be reset the next time you open it. One of the main benefits of AsyncStorage is that it lets you store the data directly to the user's device and retrieve it whenever you need it!

AsyncStorage's methods and arguments are listed in table 9.2.

Table 9.2   **AsyncStorage methods and arguments**

Method	Arguments	Description
`setItem`	`key, value, callback`	Stores an item in AsyncStorage
`getItem`	`key, callback`	Retrieves an item from AsyncStorage
`removeItem`	`key, callback`	Removes an item from AsyncStorage
`mergeItem`	`key, value, callback`	Merges an existing value with another existing value (both values must be stringified JSON)
`clear`	`callback`	Erases all values in AsyncStorage
`getAllKeys`	`callback`	Gets all keys stored in your app
`flushGetRequests`	None	Flushes any pending requests
`multiGet`	`[keys], callback`	Allows you to get multiple values using an array of keys
`multiSet`	`[keyValuePairs], callback`	Allows you to set multiple key-value pairs at once
`multiRemove`	`[keys], callback`	Allows you to delete multiple values using an array of keys
`multiMerge`	`[keyValuePairs], callback`	Allows you to merge multiple key-value pairs into one method

9.3.1   *Use cases for AsyncStorage*

AsyncStorage is often used for authentication purposes, persisting user data and information that you don't want lost when the application is closed. For example, when a user logs in and you get their name, user ID, avatar, and so on from the API, you don't want to force that user to log in every time they open the app. You can save their information to AsyncStorage when they log in the first time, and from then on, use the original information and only update it when necessary.

Another use case is when you're working with large data sets or slow APIs and don't want to wait for them more than once. For example, if a data set takes a few seconds to retrieve, you may want to cache that data in AsyncStorage, show it to the user when they open the app, and refresh the data in a background process so the user doesn't have to wait to begin interacting with the data or the UI.

9.3.2 *Example of using AsyncStorage*

In this example, you'll take a user object and store it into the AsyncStorage in component-DidMount. You'll then use a button to extract the data from AsyncStorage, populate the state with the data, and render it to the view.

Listing 9.3 Persisting and retrieving data using AsyncStorage

```
import React, { Component } from 'react'
import { TouchableHighlight, AsyncStorage, View,          Imports AsyncStorage
      Text, StyleSheet } from 'react-native'              from React Native
let styles = {}
                                                    Creates a person object and
const person = {                                    stores the information in it
  name: 'James Garfield',
  age: 50,
  occupation: 'President of the United States'
}

const key = 'president'          Creates a key you'll use to add and
                                 remove data from AsyncStorage

export default class App extends Component {
  constructor () {
    super()
    this.state = {          Creates a person object in the state
      person: {}
    }
    this.getPerson= this.getPerson.bind(this)
  }
  componentDidMount () {
    AsyncStorage.setItem(key, JSON.stringify(person))
      .then(() => console.log('item stored...'))
      .catch((err) => console.log('err: ', err))
  }
  getPerson () {
    AsyncStorage.getItem(key)
      .then((res) => this.setState({ person: JSON.parse(res) }))
      .catch((err) => console.log('err: ', err))
  }
  render () {
    const { person } = this.state
    return (
      <View style={styles.container}>
        <Text style={{textAlign: 'center'}}>Testing AsyncStorage</Text>
        <TouchableHighlight onPress={this.getPerson}
```

Creates the getPerson method

Calls AsyncStorage.setItem, passing in the key as well as the person. Calls JSON.stringify because the value stored in AsyncStorage needs to be a string; JSON.stringify turns objects and arrays into strings.

Calls AsyncStorage.getItem, passing in the key created earlier. You receive a callback function with the data retrieved from AsyncStorage.

Calls JSON.parse, which turns the returned data back into a JavaScript object; and populates the state

```
                              style={styles.button}>
                <Text>Get President</Text>
              </TouchableHighlight>
              <Text>{person.name}</Text>
              <Text>{person.age}</Text>
              <Text>{person.occupation}</Text>
            </View>
          )
        }
      }

      styles = StyleSheet.create({
        container: {
          justifyContent: 'center',
          flex: 1,
          margin: 20
        },
        button: {
          justifyContent: 'center',
          marginTop: 20,
          marginBottom: 20,
          alignItems: 'center',
          height: 55,
          backgroundColor: '#dddddd'
        }
      })
```

Wires up getPerson to a TouchableHighlight in the view. When the TouchableHighlight is pressed, the data from AsyncStorage is rendered to the View.

As you can see, promises are used to set and return the values from AsyncStorage. There's also another way to do this: let's look at async await.

Listing 9.4 Using `async await to fetch data asynchronously`

```
async componentDidMount () {
  try {
    await AsyncStorage.setItem(key, JSON.stringify(person))
    console.log('item stored')
  } catch (err) {
    console.log('err:', err)
  }
}
async getPerson () {
  try {
    var data = await AsyncStorage.getItem(key)
    var person = await data
    this.setState({ person: JSON.parse(person) })
  } catch (err) {
    console.log('err: ', err)
  }
}
```

async await first requires you to mark the function as async by adding the async keyword before the function name. You're then able to use the await keyword to wait for the returned value of a function, allowing you to write promise-based code as if it were synchronous. When you await a promise, the function waits until the promise settles, but it does so in a nonblocking way; it then assigns the value to the variable.

9.4 Using the Clipboard API to copy text into the user's clipboard

Clipboard lets you save and retrieve content from the clipboard on both iOS and Android. Clipboard has two methods: `getString()` and `setString()` (see table 9.3).

Table 9.3 Clipboard methods

Method	Arguments	Description
`getString`	None	Gets the contents of the clipboard
`setString`	`content`	Sets the contents of the clipboard

9.4.1 Use cases for Clipboard

The most common use case for Clipboard is when a user needs to copy a string of text. Rather than have to remember it, the user can copy it to the clipboard using Clipboard and then paste it anywhere they want to use the information!

9.4.2 Example of using Clipboard

In this example, you'll set an initial clipboard value of "Hello World" in `component-DidMount` and then use a method attached to a `TextInput` to update the clipboard. You'll add a button that pushes the current `ClipboardValue` to an array and renders it to the View.

Listing 9.5 Saving and replacing clipboard content

```
import React, { Component } from 'react'
import { TextInput, Clipboard, TouchableHighlight, View,         ◀── Imports Clipboard
        Text, StyleSheet } from 'react-native'                       from React Native
let styles = {}

export default class App extends Component {
  constructor() {
    super()
    this.state = {                  ┐ Sets an empty array called
      clipboardData: []        ◀──┘ clipboardData in the state
    }
    this.pushClipboardToArray = this.pushClipboardToArray.bind(this)
  }
  componentDidMount () {                         ┐ Updates the Clipboard
    Clipboard.setString('Hello World! ');   ◀──┘ value to "Hello World"
  }
  updateClipboard (string) {            ┐ Adds an updateClipboard method that
    Clipboard.setString(string);   ◀──┘ will replace the existing slipboard value
  }
  async pushClipboardToArray() {    ◀── ┐ Adds an async method pushClipboardToArray,
    const { clipboardData } = this.state └ using the async await syntax from listing 9.4
    var content = await Clipboard.getString();
```

Stores the clipboard value in a variable named content

Attaches the TextInput with the updateClipboard method

Pushes to the clipboardData array

Resets the array's state

Attaches the pushClipboardToArray method to be called when the TouchableHighlight is pressed

Maps through the items in the clipboardData array and renders them to the screen

```
          clipboardData.push(content)
          this.setState({clipboardData})
        }
        render () {
          const { clipboardData } = this.state
          return (
            <View style={styles.container}>
              <Text style={{textAlign: 'center'}}>Testing Clipboard</Text>
              <TextInput style={styles.input}
                         onChangeText={
                             (text) => this.updateClipboard(text)
                         } />
              <TouchableHighlight onPress={this.pushClipboardToArray}
                                  style={styles.button}>
                <Text>Click to Add to Array</Text>
              </TouchableHighlight>
              {
                clipboardData.map((d, i) => {
                  return <Text key={i}>{d}</Text>
                })
              }
            </View>
          )
        }
      }

      styles = StyleSheet.create({
        container: {
          justifyContent: 'center',
          flex: 1,
          margin: 20
        },
        input: {
          padding: 10,
          marginTop: 15,
          height: 60,
          backgroundColor: '#dddddd'
        },
        button: {
          backgroundColor: '#dddddd',
          justifyContent: 'center',
          alignItems: 'center',
          height: 60,
          marginTop: 15,
        }
      })
```

9.5 *Using the Dimensions API to get the user's screen information*

Dimensions gives you a way to get the device screen's height and width. This is a good way to perform calculations based on the screen's dimensions.

9.5.1   Use cases for the Dimensions API

Many times, you want to know the exact dimensions of the user's device, in order to create the perfect UI. When creating a global theme, having the width and the height to set global variables (such as font sizes) is a great way to provide consistent styling across your app, regardless of device size. Using the width of the device to make consistent grid elements is another easy way to create a consistent experience. Bottom line: whenever you need the device screen's height and width, use Dimensions.

9.5.2   Example of using the Dimensions API

To use Dimensions, import the API from React Native, and then call the `get()` method, passing in either `window` or `screen` as a parameter. Return `width`, `height`, or both.

> **Listing 9.6   Using Dimensions to retrieve the width and height of the device**

```
import React, { Component } from 'react'
import { View, Text, Dimensions, StyleSheet } from 'react-native'
let styles = {}

const { width, height } = Dimensions.get('window')
const windowWidth = Dimensions.get('window').width

const App = () => (
  <View style={styles.container}>
    <Text>{width}</Text>
    <Text>{height}</Text>
    <Text>{windowWidth}</Text>
  </View>
)

styles = StyleSheet.create({
  container: {
    flex: 1,
    justifyContent: 'center',
    alignItems: 'center'
  }
})
```

Imports Dimensions from React Native

Destructures the width and height

Accesses the width object property directly

In the View, render the dimensions that were stored in the variables you retrieved off the Dimensions.get method.

One way to access the dimensions is to destructure what's returned from calling `Dimensions.get` on the window, in this case `width` and `height`. You can also get the scale of the window. Another way is to call `Dimensions.get` and access the object property directly, calling `.width` on `Dimensions.get`.

9.6   Using the Geolocation API to get the user's current location information

Geolocation is achieved in React Native using the same API used in the browser, with the `navigator.geolocation` global variable available anywhere in the app. You don't need to import anything to begin using this, because it's again available as a global.

9.6.1 Use cases for the Geolocation API

If you're building an application that requires the user's latitude and longitude, then you'll need to use geolocation. `react-native-maps`, the map component that was created and open sourced by Airbnb, is a great use case for geolocation. Many times you'll want to have the map load to the user's current location; to do that, you have to pass in the correct coordinates. Use Geolocation to get those coordinates.

9.6.2 Example of using Geolocation

To get started with Geolocation, you must enable it to be used in the app if you're developing for Android (iOS is enabled by default):

```
<uses-permission android:name="android.permission.ACCESS_FINE_LOCATION" />
```

Table 9.4 lists the available methods.

Table 9.4   Geolocation methods

Method	Arguments	Description
getCurrentPosition	successcallback, errcall-back, optionsobject{enable-HighAccuracy: Boolean, timeout: number, maximum-Age: number}	Gets the current position. Success returns an object with a coords object and a timestamp.
watchPosition	successcallback, errcallback, optionsobject{enable-HighAccuracy: Boolean, timeout: number, maximum-Age: number}	Gets the current position and is automatically called when the device position changes.
clearWatch	watchId	Cancels a watch. Store the watchPosition method in a variable when created to have access to the watchId.
stopObserving	None	Cancels all geolocation watches that have been set up.

getCurrentPosition and watchPosition return coordinates as an object with information about the current user's location (see figure 9.2). The information returned contains not only the latitude and longitude, but also the speed and altitude as well as a few other data points.

To see this in action, you'll set up an instance of Geolocation getCurrentPosition and watchPosition. You'll also have a button to call clearWatch, which will clear the watch position functionality enabled by the call to watchPosition.

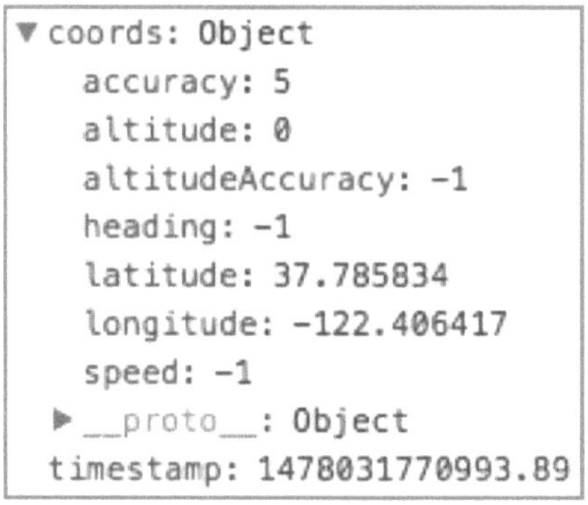

```
▼ coords: Object
    accuracy: 5
    altitude: 0
    altitudeAccuracy: -1
    heading: -1
    latitude: 37.785834
    longitude: -122.406417
    speed: -1
  ▶ __proto__: Object
  timestamp: 1478031770993.89
```

Figure 9.2   Coordinates object returned from Geolocation

watchPosition will only change if you physically change the coordinates. For example, if you run this on a device and walk around, you should see the coordinates update. This watch can be cancelled at any time by calling navigator.geolocation.clearWatch(id), passing in the ID of the watch you want to cancel. You'll then display both the original coordinates as well as the updated coordinates (latitude and longitude).

Listing 9.7   Retrieving user coordinates using the Geolocation API

```
import React, { Component } from 'react'
import { TouchableHighlight, View, Text, StyleSheet } from 'react-native'
let styles = {}

export default class App extends Component {
  constructor () {
    super()
    this.state = {
      originalCoords: {},
      updatedCoords: {},
      id: ''
    }
    this.clearWatch = this.clearWatch.bind(this)
  }
  componentDidMount () {
    navigator.geolocation.getCurrentPosition(
      (success) => {
        this.setState({originalCoords: success.coords})
      },
      (err) => console.log('err:', err)
    )
    let id = navigator.geolocation.watchPosition(
      (success) => {
        this.setState({
          id,
          updatedCoords: success.coords
        })
      },
      (err) => console.log('err:', err)
    )
  }
  clearWatch () {
    navigator.geolocation.clearWatch(this.state.id)
  }
  render () {
    const { originalCoords, updatedCoords } = this.state
    return (
      <View style={styles.container}>
        <Text>Original Coordinates</Text>
        <Text>Latitude: {originalCoords.latitude}</Text>
        <Text>Longitude: {originalCoords.longitude}</Text>
        <Text>Updated Coordinates</Text>
        <Text>Latitude: {updatedCoords.latitude}</Text>
        <Text>Longitude: {updatedCoords.longitude}</Text>
        <TouchableHighlight
```

Creates an initial state with originalCoords and updatedCoords set as an empty object and id set as an empty string

Calls getCurrentPosition on navigator.geolocation

Sets the state of originalCoords to success.coords

Calls watchPosition, and stores the result of the function in a variable named id that you'll use later to clear the watch

Resets the state with the id

Creates a clearWatch method to clear the watch

Displays the latitude and longitude from both the original coordinates as well as the updated coordinates

```
                onPress={this.clearWatch}
                style={styles.button}>
                <Text>Clear Watch</Text>
            </TouchableHighlight>
          </View>
        )
      }
    }

    styles = StyleSheet.create({
      container: {
        flex: 1,
        justifyContent: 'center',
        padding: 20,
      },
      button: {
        height: 60,
        marginTop: 15,
        backgroundColor: '#ededed',
        justifyContent: 'center',
        alignItems: 'center'
      }
    })
```

9.7   Using the Keyboard API to control the location and functionality of the native keyboard

The Keyboard API gives you access to the native keyboard. You can use this to either listen to keyboard events (and call methods based on these events) or dismiss the keyboard. The Keyboard methods are listed in table 9.5.

Table 9.5   Keyboard methods

Method	Arguments	Description
addListener	event, callback	Connects a method to be called based on native keyboard events such as keyboardWillShow, keyboardDidShow, keyboardWillHide, keyboardDidHide, keyboardWillChangeFrame, and keyboardDidChangeFrame
removeAllListeners	eventType	Removes all listeners of the type specified
dismiss	None	Dismisses the keyboard

9.7.1   Use cases for the Keyboard API

Many times, the default behavior of text inputs and the keyboard is exactly what you want, but not always. If you simulate a text input using some other type of component, the keyboard won't slide up. In this case, you can import Keyboard and get manual and granular control over when the keyboard is shown and hidden.

In some cases, you may want to manually dismiss the keyboard even when the text input is in focus. For example, if a PIN number input accepts four numbers and automatically checks to see if the input value is correct on the last input value, you may want to provide a UI that fetches or checks after the last value is typed in. Hiding the keyboard may make sense, and you can achieve this using the Keyboard API.

9.7.2   Example of using the Keyboard API

In this example, you'll set up a text input and have listeners for all available events. When the event is fired, you'll log the event to the console. You'll also have two buttons: one to dismiss the keyboard and another to remove all event listeners set up in `componentWillMount`.

Listing 9.8   Controlling the device keyboard using the Keyboard API

```
import React, { Component } from 'react'
import { TouchableHighlight, Keyboard, TextInput, View,
       Text, StyleSheet } from 'react-native'          ◀── Imports the Keyboard
                                                            API from React Native

let styles = {}

export default class App extends Component {
  componentWillMount () {   ◀──── Sets up event listeners for all
    this.keyboardWillShowListener =    available keyboard events, and
       Keyboard.addListener('keyboardWillShow',      then calls the logEvent method
                        () => this.logEvent('keyboardWillShow'))   ◀── to log out the event name
    this.keyboardDidShowListener =
       Keyboard.addListener('keyboardDidShow',
                        () => this.logEvent('keyboardDidShow'))    ◀───
    this.keyboardWillHideListener =
       Keyboard.addListener('keyboardWillHide',
                        () => this.logEvent('keyboardWillHide'))   ◀───
    this.keyboardDidHideListener =
       Keyboard.addListener('keyboardDidHide',
                        () => this.logEvent('keyboardDidHide'))    ◀───
    this.keyboardWillChangeFrameListener =
       Keyboard.addListener('keyboardWillChangeFrame',
                        () => this.logEvent('keyboardWillChangeFrame'))  ◀───
    this.keyboardDidChangeFrameListener =
       Keyboard.addListener('keyboardDidChangeFrame',
                        () => this.logEvent('keyboardDidChangeFrame'))   ◀───
  }
  logEvent(event) {
    console.log('event: ', event)    │ Takes in the event name, and
  }                                  │ logs out the name of the event
  dismissKeyboard () {
    Keyboard.dismiss()    │ Dismisses the keyboard if it's in view
  }
```

```
      removeListeners () {
        Keyboard.removeAllListeners('keyboardWillShow')
        Keyboard.removeAllListeners('keyboardDidShow')
        Keyboard.removeAllListeners('keyboardWillHide')
        Keyboard.removeAllListeners('keyboardDidHide')
        Keyboard.removeAllListeners('keyboardWillChangeFrame')
        Keyboard.removeAllListeners('keyboardDidChangeFrame')
      }
      render () {
        return (
          <View style={styles.container}>
            <TextInput style={styles.input} />
            <TouchableHighlight
              onPress={this.dismissKeyboard}
              style={styles.button}>
              <Text>Dismiss Keyboard</Text>
            </TouchableHighlight>
            <TouchableHighlight
              onPress={this.removeListeners}
              style={styles.button}>
              <Text>Remove Listeners</Text>
            </TouchableHighlight>
          </View>
        )
      }
    }

    styles = StyleSheet.create({
      container: {
        flex: 1,
        marginTop: 150,
      },
      input: {
        margin: 10,
        backgroundColor: '#ededed',
        height: 50,
        padding: 10
      },
      button: {
        height: 50,
        backgroundColor: '#dddddd',
        margin: 10,
        justifyContent: 'center',
        alignItems: 'center'
      }
    })
```

Calls Keyboard .removeAllListeners, passing in each of the listeners declared in componentWillMount

Wires up the dismissKeyboard method to a button in the UI

Wires up the removeListeners method to a button in the UI

9.8   Using NetInfo to get the user's current online/ offline status

NetInfo is an API that allows you to access data describing whether the device is online or offline. In order to use the NetInfo API on Android, you need to add the required permission to AndroidManifest.xml:

```
<uses-permission android:name="android.permission.ACCESS_NETWORK_STATE"/>
```

iOS and Android have different connectivity types, listed in table 9.6. Access to them depends on the actual connectivity type of the user's connection. To determine the connection, you can use the methods in table 9.7.

Table 9.6   Cross platform and Android specific connectivity types

Cross platform (iOS and Android)	Android
none	bluetooth
wifi	ethernet
cellular	wimax
unknown	

Table 9.7   NetInfo methods

Method	Arguments	Description
isConnectionExpensive	None	Returns a promise that returns a Boolean specifying whether the connection is or isn't expensive
isConnected	None	Returns a promise that returns a Boolean specifying whether the device is or isn't connected
addEventListener	eventName, callback	Adds an event listener for the specified event
removeEventListener	eventName, callback	Removes an event listener for the specified event
getConnectionInfo	None	Returns a promise that returns an object with type and effectiveType.

9.8.1   Use cases for NetInfo

NetInfo is often used to prevent other API calls from happening, or to provide an offline UI that provides some but not all features of an online application. For example, suppose you have a feed of items that, when pressed, shows a new view with fetched information about that item. You can show some indication of the application being offline and not navigate to the item detail when the device is offline. NetInfo will give you this type of device information, allowing you to interact with the user in a useful way.

Another use case is to set different API configurations based on the type of connection. For example, on Wi-Fi you may want to be more generous about the amount of data you allow to be requested and sent: if the user is on a cellular network, you may fetch only 10 items at a time; but on Wi-Fi, you'll bump that to 20. With NetInfo, you can determine what type of connection the user has, if any.

9.8.2   *Example of using NetInfo*

Let's set up a `NetInfo.getConnectionInfo` method to get the initial connection information. Then you'll set up a listener to log out the current NetInfo if and when it changes.

Listing 9.9   Fetching and displaying the user connection type using NetInfo

```
import React, { Component } from 'react'
import { NetInfo, View, Text, StyleSheet } from 'react-native'    ◄─── Imports NetInfo from React Native

class App extends Component {
  constructor () {                                Sets the initial state of connectionInfo
    super()                                       to an empty object
    this.state = {
      connectionInfo: {}
    }
    this.handleConnectivityChange =
        this.handleConnectivityChange.bind(this)
  }                                                          Gets the initial connection
  componentDidMount () {                                     type, and sets the state
    NetInfo.getConnectionInfo().then((connectionInfo) => {   ◄───
      console.log('type: ' + connectionInfo.type +
                  ', effectiveType: ' + connectionInfo.effectiveType)
      this.setState({connectionInfo})
    })
    NetInfo.addEventListener('connectionChange',             Creates an event listener to
        this.handleConnectivityChange)    ◄────────          call handleConnectivityChange
  }                                                          when the connection changes
  handleConnectivityChange (connectionInfo) {
    console.log('new connection:', connectionInfo)
    this.setState({connectionInfo})
  }                                                          Updates the state with the
  render () {                                                new connection information
    return (
      <View style={styles.container}>
        <Text>{this.state.connectionInfo.type}</Text>    ◄───
      </View>
    )                                         Renders the connection
  }                                           information to the view
}

const styles = StyleSheet.create({
  container: {
    flex: 1,
    justifyContent: 'center',
    alignItems: 'center'
  }
})
```

9.9   *Getting information about touch and gesture events with PanResponder*

The PanResponder API offers a way to use data from touch events. With it, you can granularly respond to and manipulate the application state based on single and multiple touch events, such as swiping, tapping, pinching, scrolling, and more.

9.9.1 Use cases for the PanResponder API

Because the fundamental functionality of PanResponder is to determine the current touches happening on the user's device, the use cases are unlimited. In my experience, I've used this API often to do things like the following:

- Create a swipeable stack of cards where an item is removed from the stack when swiped out of view (think Tinder)
- Create an animatable overlay that the user can close by clicking a button or move out of view by swiping down
- Give the user the ability to rearrange items in a list by pressing part of a list item and moving to the desired location

The use cases for PanResponder are many, but the most apparent and frequently used let the user move items around in the UI based on their press/swipe position.

Let's look at a basic gesture event using `onPanResponderMove(event, gestureState)`, which gives you data about the current position of the touch event, including current position, accumulated difference between current position and original position, and more:

```
onPanResponderMove(evt, gestureState) {
  console.log(evt.nativeEvent)
  console.log(gestureState)
}
```

To use this API, you first create an instance of `PanResponder` in the `componentWill-Mount` method. In this instance, you can then set all the configuration and callback methods for the `PanResponder`, using the methods to manipulate the state and `View`.

Let's look at the `create` method, which is the only available method for PanResponder. It creates the configuration for the `PanResponder` instance. Table 9.8 shows the configuration options available to the create method.

Table 9.8 Configuration arguments for the PanResponder `create` method

Configuration property	Description
onStartShouldSetPanResponder	Determines whether to enable the PanResponder. Gets called after the element is touched.
onMoveShouldSetPanResponder	Determines whether to enable the PanResponder. Gets called after the initial touch has first move.
onPanResponderReject	Gets called if the PanResponder does not register.
onPanResponderGrant	Gets called if the PanResponder does register.
onPanResponderStart	Gets called after the PanResponder registers.
onPanResponderEnd	Gets called after the PanResponder has finished.
onPanResponderMove	Gets called when the PanResponder moves.
onPanResponderTerminationRequest	Gets called when something else wants to become responder.
onPanResponderRelease	Gets called when the touch has been released.
onPanResponderTerminate	This responder has been taken by another one.

Each configuration option is supplied with the Native Event and Gesture State. Table 9.9 describes all the available properties of both `evt.nativeEvent` and `gestureState`.

Table 9.9   `evt` and `gestureState` properties

evt.nativeEvent properties	Description
changedTouches	Array of all touch events that have changed since the last event
identifier	ID of the touch
locationX	X position of the touch, relative to the element
locationY	Y position of the touch, relative to the element
pageX	X position of the touch, relative to the root element
pageY	Y position of the touch, relative to the root element
target	Node ID of the element receiving the touch event
timestamp	Time identifier for the touch; useful for velocity calculations
touches	Array of all current touches on the screen
gestureState properties	**Description**
stateID	ID of the `gestureState`, persisted as long as there is at least one touch on the screen
moveX	Latest screen coordinates of the recently moved touch
moveY	Latest screen coordinates of the recently moved touch
x0	Screen coordinates of the responder
y0	Screen coordinates of the responder
dx	Accumulated distance of the gesture since the touch started
dy	Accumulated distance of the gesture since the touch started
vx	Current velocity of the gesture
vy	Current velocity of the gesture
numberActiveTouches	Number of touches currently on screen

9.9.2   *Example of using PanResponder*

For this example, you'll create a draggable square and display its x and y coordinates in the view. The result is shown in figure 9.3.

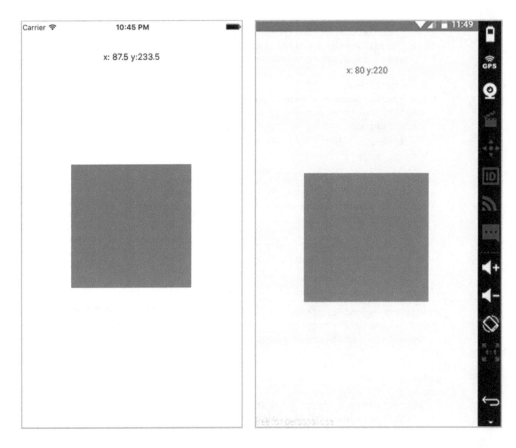

Figure 9.3   PanResponder used to make the square draggable

Listing 9.10   Using PanResponder to create a draggable element

```
import React, { Component }  from 'react'
import { Dimensions, TouchableHighlight, PanResponder, TextInput,
      View, Text, StyleSheet } from 'react-native'
const { width, height } = Dimensions.get('window')
let styles = {}

class App extends Component {
  constructor () {
    super()
    this.state = {
      oPosition: {
        x: (width / 2) - 100,
        y: (height / 2) - 100,
      },
      position: {
        x: (width / 2) - 100,
        y: (height / 2) - 100,
      },
    }
  }
```

> **Imports Dimensions, PanResponder, and everything else needed for this component**

> **Stores the window width and height in variables for later use**

> **Creates an object called oPosition to store the original square position x and y axes to center the square, and stores it into the state**

> **Creates an object called position to store the actual square position x and y axes to center the square, and stores it into the state**

```
    this._handlePanResponderMove = this._handlePanResponderMove.bind(this)
    this._handlePanResponderRelease =
        this._handlePanResponderRelease.bind(this)
  }
  componentWillMount () {
    this._panResponder = PanResponder.create({
      onStartShouldSetPanResponder: () => true,
      onPanResponderMove: this._handlePanResponderMove,
      onPanResponderRelease: this._handlePanResponderRelease
    })
  }
  _handlePanResponderMove (evt, gestureState) {
    let ydiff = gestureState.y0 - gestureState.moveY
    let xdiff = gestureState.x0 - gestureState.moveX
    this.setState({
      position: {
        y: this.state.oPosition.y - ydiff,
        x: this.state.oPosition.x - xdiff
      }
    })
  }
  _handlePanResponderRelease () {
    this.setState({
      oPosition: this.state.position
    })
  }
  render () {
    return (
      <View  style={styles.container}>
        <Text style={styles.positionDisplay}>
            x: {this.state.position.x} y:{this.state.position.y}
        </Text>
        <View
          {...this._panResponder.panHandlers}
          style={[styles.box,
                 { marginLeft: this.state.position.x,
                   marginTop: this.state.position.y } ]}
        />
      </View>
    )
  }
}

styles = StyleSheet.create({
  container: {
    flex: 1,
  },
  positionDisplay: {
    textAlign: 'center',
    marginTop: 50,
    zIndex: 1,
    position: 'absolute',
    width
  },
  box: {
```

Creates a new PanResponder, returning true for onStartShouldSetPanResponder, and setting up onPanResponderMove and onPanResponderRelease methods

Finds the total movement of x and y by calculating the difference between the location that the pan started and the current total of movement since the pan started. Updates the state position with these values.

Sets the state of oPosition with the updated position in the view

Attaches the PanResponder to the view by passing in {...this._panResponder. panHandlers} as props

Displays the current position values in the view

Attaches the position x and y values to the view to update the margins, making the item draggable

```
      position: 'absolute',
      width: 200,
      height: 200,
      backgroundColor: 'red'
    }
  })
```

Summary

- Alert gives you the ability to prompt or alert the user to important information or events in the app.
- AppState provides information about whether the current app is in use. You can then use this information in the app in a useful way.
- AsyncStorage lets you persist data to the user's device, so that if the user closes the app, you can still access the data.
- Clipboard copies information to the user's device clipboard so they can access it later.
- Dimensions provides useful information about the user's device, most importantly the screen width and height.
- Geolocation provides the location as well as other important information about the user's device, and allows you to check the location data when the user moves.
- NetInfo provides the user's current connection information, including the type of connection and whether they're currently connected.
- PanResponder provides the current touch location(s) happening on the user's device. You can use this information to enhance the UX and UI.

Implementing iOS-specific components and APIs

This chapter covers

- Strategies for effectively targeting platform-specific code

- Using the picker components, `DatePickerIOS`, and `PickerIOS`

- Showing loading progress using `ProgressViewIOS`

- Choosing views using `SegmentedControlIOS` and `TabBarIOS`

- Calling and choosing items in an action sheet using `ActionSheetIOS`

One of the end goals of the React Native project is to have a minimal amount of platform-specific logic and code. Most APIs can be built so the platform-specific code is abstracted away by the framework, giving you a single way to interact with them and easily create cross-platform functionality.

Unfortunately, there will always be platform-specific APIs that can't be completely abstracted away using an approach that makes sense cross-platform. Therefore, you'll need to use at least a handful of platform-specific APIs and components.

In this chapter, we cover iOS-specific APIs and components, discuss their props and methods, and create examples that mimic functionality and logic that will get you up to speed quickly.

10.1 Targeting platform-specific code

The main idea of platform-specific code is writing components and files in a way that renders iOS- or Android-specific code based on the platform you're on. There are a few techniques that can be implemented to show components based on what platform the app is running, and we cover the two most useful of those techniques here: using the correct file extension, and using the Platform API.

10.1.1 iOS and Android file extensions

The first way to target platform-specific code is to name the file with the correct file extension, depending on the platform you wish to target. For example, one component that differs quite a bit between iOS and Android is DatePicker. If you want specific styling around DatePicker, writing all the code in the main component may become verbose and difficult to maintain. Instead, you create two files—DatePicker.ios.js and DatePicker.android.js—and import them into the main component. When you run the project, React Native will automatically choose the correct file and render it based on the platform you're using. Let's look at a basic example in listings 10.1, 10.2, and 10.3. (Note that this example will throw an error as is—DatePicker requires both props and methods to function correctly.)

Listing 10.1 iOS platform-specific code

```
import React from 'react'
import { View, Text, DatePickerIOS } from 'react-native'

export default () => (
  <View>
    <Text>This is an iOS specific component</Text>
    <DatePickerIOS />
  </View>
)
```

Listing 10.2 Android platform-specific code

```
import React from 'react'
import { View, Text, DatePickerAndroid } from 'react-native'

export default () => (
  <View>
    <Text>This is an Android specific component</Text>
    <DatePickerAndroid />
  </View>
)
```

```
import React from 'react'
import DatePicker from './DatePicker'

const MainComponent = () => (
  <View>
    ...
    <DatePicker />
    ...
  </View>
)
```

You import the date picker without giving a specific file extension. React Native knows which component to import depending on the platform. From there, you can use it in the application without having to worry about which platform you're on.

10.1.2   *Detecting the platform using the Platform API*

Another way to detect and perform logic based on the platform is to use the Platform API. Platform has two properties. The first is an OS key that reads either ios or android, depending on the platform.

```
import React from 'react'
import { View, Text, Platform } from 'react-native'

const PlatformExample = () => (
  <Text
    style={{ marginTop: 100, color: Platform.OS === 'ios' ? 'blue' : 'green'
    }}
  >
    Hello { Platform.OS }
  </Text>
)
```

Here, you check whether the value of Platform.OS is equal to the string 'ios' and, if it is, return a color of 'blue'. If it isn't, you return 'green'.

The second property of Platform is a method called select. select takes in an object containing the Platform.OS strings as keys (either ios or android) and returns the value for the platform you're running.

```
import React from 'react'
import { View, Text, Platform } from 'react-native'

const ComponentIOS = () => (
  <Text>Hello from IOS</Text>
)
```

```
const ComponentAndroid = () => (
  <Text>Hello from Android</Text>
)

const Component = Platform.select({
  ios: () => ComponentIOS,
  android: () => ComponentAndroid,
})();


const PlatformExample = () => (
  <View style={{ marginTop: 100 }}>
    <Text>Hello from my App</Text>
    <Component />
  </View>
)
```

You can also use the ES2015 spread syntax to return objects and use those objects to apply styling. You may recall seeing the `Platform.select` function used in a couple of examples in chapter 4.

Listing 10.6 Using `Platform.select` to apply styles based on Platform

```
import React from 'react'
import { View, Text, Platform } from 'react-native'

let styles = {}

const PlatformExample = () => (
  <View style={styles.container}>
    <Text>
        Hello { Platform.OS }
    </Text>
  </View>
)

styles = {
  container: {
    marginTop: 100,
    ...Platform.select({
      ios: {
        backgroundColor: 'red'
      }
    })
  }
}
```

10.2 *DatePickerIOS*

DatePickerIOS provides an easy way to implement a native date picker component on iOS. It has three modes that come in handy when working with dates and times: date, time, and dateTime, shown in figure 10.1.

Figure 10.1   DatePickerIOS with date mode, time mode, and datetime mode

DatePickerIOS has the props listed in table 10.1. The minimum props that need to be passed are date (the date that's the beginning or current date choice) and an onDateChange method. When any of the date values are changed, onDateChange is called, passing the function the new date value.

Table 10.1   DatePickerIOS props and method

Prop	Type	Description
date	Date	Currently selected date
maximumDate	Date	Maximum allowed date
minimumDate	Date	Minimum allowed date
minuteInterval	Enum	Interval at which minutes can be selected
mode	String: date, time, or datetime	Date picker mode
onDateChange	Function: on DateChange(date) { }	Function called when the date changes
timeZoneOffsetInMinutes	Number	Time zone offset in minutes; overrides the default (the device time zone)

10.2.1 *Example of using DatePickerIOS*

In the following example, you'll set up a DatePickerIOS component and display the time in the view. You won't pass in a mode prop, because the mode defaults to datetime. Figure 10.2 shows the result.

Figure 10.2   DatePickerIOS rendering chosen date and time

Listing 10.7   Using `DatePicker` to show and update time values

```
import React, { Component } from 'react'
import { Text, View, DatePickerIOS } from 'react-native'

class App extends Component {

  constructor() {
    super()
    this.state = {
      date: new Date(),
    }
    this.onDateChange = this.onDateChange.bind(this)
  }

  onDateChange(date) {
    this.setState({date: date});
  };
```

◄── Imports DatePickerIOS from React Native

Creates a date value, and stores it in the state

Creates a method called onDateChange that updates the state with the new date value

```
render() {
  return (
    <View style={{ marginTop: 50 }}>
      <DatePickerIOS
        date={this.state.date}
        onDateChange={this.onDateChange}
      />
      <Text style={{ marginTop: 40, textAlign: 'center' }}>
        { this.state.date.toLocaleDateString() } { this.state.date.
  toLocaleTimeString() }
      </Text>
    </View>)
  }
}
```

> **Returns the DatePickerIOS component, and passes in the date and onDateChange as props**

> **Renders the date value as text**

10.3   *Using PickerIOS to work with lists of values*

Using `PickerIOS`, you can access the native iOS `Picker` component. This component basically allows you to scroll through and choose from a list of values using the native UI (see figure 10.3). `PickerIOS` has the methods and props listed in table 10.2.

Table 10.2   `PickerIOS` methods and props

Prop	Type	Description
itemStyle	Object (style)	The text style for items within the container
onValueChange	Function (value)	Called when the `PickerIOS` value changes
selectedValue	Number or string	Currently selected `PickerIOS` value

`PickerIOS` wraps a list of items to be rendered as children. Each child item must be a `PickerIOS.Item`:

```
import { PickerIOS } from 'react-native'
const PickerItem = PickerIOS.Item

<PickerIOS>
  <PickerItem />
  <PickerItem />
  <PickerItem />
</PickerIOS>
```

It's possible to declare each `PickerIOS.Item` individually as done here, but most of the time you'll be mapping over elements in an array and returning a `PickerIOS.Item` for each item in the array. The following listing shows an example.

Figure 10.3   PickerIOS rendering a list of people

Listing 10.8   Using `PickerIOS` with an array of `PickerIOS.Items`

```
const people = [    #an array of people ];

render() {
  <PickerIOS>
    {
      people.map((p, i) =>(
        <PickerItem key={i} value={p} label={p}/>
      ))
    }
  <PickerIOS>

  }
```

PickerIOS and PickerIOS.Item receive their own props. For PickerIOS, the main props are onValueChange and selectedValue. The onValueChange method is called whenever the picker is changed. The selectedValue is the value the picker shows as selected in the UI.

For `PickerIOS.Item`, the main props are key, value, and label. key is a unique identifier, value is what will be passed to the onValueChange method of the `PickerIOS` component, and label is what is displayed in the UI as the label for the `PickerIOS.Item`.

10.3.1 *Example of using PickerIOS*

In this example, you'll render an array of people in the `PickerIOS`. When the value changes, you'll update the UI to show the new value.

Listing 10.9   Using `PickerIOS` to render an array of people

```
import React, { Component } from 'react'
import { Text, View, PickerIOS } from 'react-native'        ◄———  Imports PickerIOS
                                                                   from React Native
const people = [        ◄———┐
  {
    name: 'Nader Dabit',        Creates an array of people that's used to
    age: 36                     populate the PickerItem values
  },
  {
    name: 'Christina Jones',
    age: 39
  },
  {
    name: 'Amanda Nelson',
    age: 22
  }
];

const PickerItem = PickerIOS.Item

class App extends Component {
                                      Creates an initial value in the state to
  constructor() {                              hold the chosen picker value
    super()
    this.state = {
      value: 'Christina Jones'
    }
    this.onValueChange = this.onValueChange.bind(this)
  }

  onValueChange(value) {                  Creates an onValueChange method to
    this.setState({ value });            update the state value with the new
  };                                     value from the PickerIOS
  render() {
    return (
      <View style={{ marginTop: 50 }}>
        <PickerIOS
          onValueChange={this.onValueChange}        Renders the PickerIOS, passing on
          selectedValue={this.state.value}          ValueChange and selectedValue as props
        >
          {
            people.map((p, i) => {        ◄———
              return (                          Renders a PickerIOS.Item for every
                <PickerItem                     person in the people array
```

```
                    key={i}
                    value={p.name}
                    label={p.name}
                />
            )
        })
    }
</PickerIOS>
<Text style={{ marginTop: 40, textAlign: 'center' }}>
    {this.state.value}
</Text>
</View>)
    }
}
```

Renders the value of
this.state.value in the UI

10.4 Using ProgressViewIOS to show loading indicators

ProgressViewIOS lets you render the native UIProgressView in the UI. Basically, it's a
native way to show a loading-percentage indication, download-percentage indication,
or any indication of a task that's being completed (see figure 10.4). It has the props
shown in table 10.3.

Figure 10.4   Rendering ProgressViewIOS in the UI

Table 10.3   `ProgressViewIOS` **methods and props**

Prop	Type	Description
`progress`	Number	Progress value (between 0 and 1)
`progressImage`	Image source	Stretchable image to display as the progress bar
`progressTintColor`	String (color)	Tint color of the progress bar
`progressViewStyle`	Enum (default or bar)	Progress bar style
`trackImage`	Image source	Stretchable image to display behind the progress bar
`trackTintColor`	String	Tint color of the progress bar track

10.4.1 Use cases for ProgressViewIOS

The most common use case for `ProgressViewIOS` is working with an external API that tells you how much information has been passed across the wire when you're fetching or posting data or working with a local API that does the same. For example, if you're saving a video to the user's camera roll, you can use `ProgressViewIOS` to show the user how much longer the download will take and how much has been completed.

10.4.2 Example of using ProgressViewIOS

The main prop you need to know about to create this functionality is `progress`. `progress` takes a number between 0 and 1 and fills the `ProgressViewIOS` with a percentage fill between 0% and 100%.

In this example, you'll simulate some data loading by setting a `setInterval` method that's called in `componentDidMount`. You'll increment the state value by 0.01 every 0.01 seconds until you're at 1, starting with the initial value 0.

Listing 10.10   Using `ProgressViewIOS` to increment progress bar from 0% to 100%

```
import React, { Component } from 'react'
import { Text, View, ProgressViewIOS } from 'react-native'
```
Imports ProgressViewIOS from React Native

```
class App extends Component {

  constructor() {
    super()
    this.state = {
      progress: 0,
    }
  }
```
Creates an initial state value of progress, set to 0

```
  componentDidMount() {
    this.interval = setInterval(() => {
      if (this.state.progress >= 1) {
        return clearInterval(this.interval)
      }
      this.setState({
        progress: this.state.progress + .01
      })
    }, 10)
```
Stores a setInterval method in a variable, and increments the state value of progress every 1/100 of a second by .01. If this.state.progress is greater than or equal to 1, you clear and cancel the interval by calling clearInterval and return.

```
  }

  render() {
    return (
      <View style={{ marginTop: 50 }}>
        <ProgressViewIOS
          progress={this.state.progress}
        />
        <Text style={{ marginTop: 10, textAlign: 'center' }}>
          {Math.floor(this.state.progress * 100)}% complete
        </Text>
      </View>)
  }
}
```

Renders the ProgressViewIOS, passing in this.state.progress as the progress prop

Rounds and renders the value of this. state.progress in the UI

10.5 Using SegmentedControlIOS to create horizontal tab bars

SegmentedControlIOS allows you to access the native iOS UISegmentedControl component. It's a horizontal tab bar made up of individual buttons, as shown in figure 10.5.

Figure 10.5 Basic SegmentedControlIOS implementation with two values (one and two)

SegmentedControlIOS has the methods and props in table 10.4. At a minimum, it takes an array of values to render the control values, a selectedIndex as the index of the control selected, and an onChange method that will be called when a control is pressed.

Table 10.4 SegmentedControlIOS **methods and props**

Prop	Type	Description
enabled	Boolean	If false, the user can't interact with the control. Default value is true.
momentary	Boolean	If true, selecting a segment won't persist visually. onValueChange will still work as expected.
onChange	Function (event)	Callback called when the user taps a segment; passes the event as an argument.
onValueChange	Function (value)	Callback called when the user taps a segment; passes the segment's value as an argument.
selectedIndex	Number	Index in props.values of the segment to be (pre)selected.
tintColor	String (color)	Accent color of the control.
values	Array of strings	Labels for the control's segment buttons, in order.

10.5.1 Use cases for SegmentedControlIOS

SegmentedControlIOS is a good place to separate and display certain filterable/sortable data in the UI. For example, if an app had information listed and viewable by week, you could use SegmentedControlIOS to separate that data even further by day of the week, with a separate view for each day.

10.5.2 Example of using SegmentedControlIOS

In this example, you'll render an array of three items as a SegmentedControlIOS. You'll also show a value in the UI based on which item is selected.

Listing 10.11 SegmentedControlIOS **rendering three values**

Imports SegmentedControlIOS from React Native

Creates an array of values to use in the SegmentedControlIOS

```
import React, { Component } from 'react'
import { Text, View, SegmentedControlIOS } from 'react-native'

const values = ['One', 'Two', 'Three']

class App extends Component {

  constructor() {
    super()
    this.state = {
      selectedIndex: 0,
    }
  }
}
```

Creates a state value of selectedIndex set to 0

```
render() {
  const { selectedIndex } = this.state
  let selectedItem = values[selectedIndex]
  return (
    <View style={{ marginTop: 40, padding: 20 }}>
      <SegmentedControlIOS
        values={values}
        selectedIndex={this.state.selectedIndex}
        onChange={(event) => {
          this.setState({selectedIndex:
                event.nativeEvent.selectedSegmentIndex});
        }}
      />
      <Text>{selectedItem}</Text>
    </View>)
  }
}
```

Creates a variable called selectedItem, set to the value of the selectedIndex of the values array

Renders the SegmentedControlIOS component, passing in the values array as the values prop, this.state.selectedIndex as the selectedIndex, and an onChange method that updates the selectedIndex state value with the index of the pressed item

Renders the value of selectedItem in the UI

10.6 Using TabBarIOS to render tabs at the bottom of the UI

TabBarIOS allows you to access the native iOS tab bar. It renders tabs at the bottom of the UI, as shown in figure 10.6, giving you a nice, easy way to separate an application into sections. Its methods and props are listed in table 10.5.

Table 10.5 TabBarIOS props

Prop	Type	Description
barTintColor	String (color)	Background color of the tab bar.
itemPositioning	Enum ("fill", "center", "auto")	Tab bar item positioning. fill distributes items across the entire width of the tab bar. center centers items in the available tab bar space. auto (default) distributes items dynamically according to the UI idiom; in a horizontally compact environment, defaults to fill; otherwise defaults to center.
style	Object (style)	Style of the TabBarIOS.
tintColor	String (color)	Color of the currently selected tab icon.
translucent	Boolean	Indicates whether the tab bar is translucent.
unselectedItemTintColor	String (color)	Color of unselected tab icons (available since iOS 10).
unselectedTintColor	String (color)	Color of the text on unselected tabs.

TabBarIOS takes a list of TabBarIOS.Item components as children:

```
const Item = TabBarIOS.Item

<TabBarIOS>
  <Item>
```

```
  <View>    #some content here </View>
  </Item>
  <Item>
    <View>    #some other content here </View>
  </Item>
</TabBarIOS>
```

To show the content in the `TabBarIOS.Item`, the selected prop of the `TabBarIOS.Item` must be true:

```
<Item
  selected={this.state.selectedComponent === 'home'}
>
    #your content here
</Item>
```

10.6.1 *Use cases for TabBarIOS*

Figure 10.6   `TabBarIOS` with two tabs: History and Favorites

The main use case for `TabBarIOS` is for navigation. Many times, on mobile, the best type of navigation is a tab bar. Separating the UI and displaying content in sections separated by tabs is a common pattern and is encouraged because it delivers a good user experience.

10.6.2 *Example of using TabBarIOS*

In this example, you'll create an app with two views: History and Favorites. When the `TabBarIOS.Item` is pressed, you'll switch between views by calling an `onPress` method to update the state.

Listing 10.12   Rendering tabs using `TabBarIOS`

```
import React, { Component } from 'react'
import { Text, View, TabBarIOS } from 'react-native'          ◄──── Imports TabBarIOS
                                                                    from React Native
const Item = TabBarIOS.Item   ◄──
                                   │ Creates a variable called Item to
class App extends Component {      │ hold the TabBarIOS.Item component

  constructor() {
    super()                              Creates an initial state value of
    this.state = {                       selectedTab, and sets it to history
      selectedTab: 'history',   ◄──
    }
    this.renderView = this.renderView.bind(this)
  }
                               │ Creates a reusable renderView method
                               │ that takes in tab as an argument
  renderView(tab) {   ◄──
    return (
      <View style={{ flex: 1, justifyContent: 'center',
                     alignItems: 'center' }}>
        <Text>Hello from {tab}</Text>
      </View>
    )                          Renders a TabBarIOS in the UI, passing in
  }                            two Item components as children

                                     Sets the systemIcon prop to history
  render() {
    return (                                    Attaches an onPress method to the item,
      <TabBarIOS>   ◄──                          updating the selectedTab value in the state
        <Item                                   with the value passed in to this.setState({})
          systemIcon="history"   ◄──
          onPress={() => this.setState({ selectedTab: 'history' })}
          selected={this.state.selectedTab === 'history'}
        >
          {this.renderView('History')}   ◄──
        </Item>                                Renders the view by
        <Item                                  calling this.renderView
          systemIcon='favorites'
          onPress={() => this.setState({ selectedTab: 'favorites' })}
          selected={this.state.selectedTab === 'favorites'}
        >
          {this.renderView('Favorites')}
        </Item>
      </TabBarIOS>
    )
  }
}
```

You can set icons either with a system icon or by passing in an icon prop and requiring a local image. For a list of all system icons, see http://mng.bz/rYNJ.

10.7   *Using ActionSheetIOS to show action or share sheets*

ActionSheetIOS allows you to access the native iOS UIAlertController to show a native iOS action sheet or share sheet (see figure 10.7).

The two main methods that you can call on ActionSheetIOS are showAction-SheetWithOptions and showShareActionSheetWithOptions; these methods have the options listed in tables 10.6 and 10.7, respectively. showActionSheetWithOptions lets you pass an array of buttons and attach methods to each of the buttons. It's called with two arguments: an options object and a callback function. showShareAction-SheetWithOptions displays the native iOS share sheet, passing in a URL, message, and subject to share. It's called with three arguments: an options object, a failure callback function, and a success callback function.

Table 10.6   ActionSheetIOS showActionSheetWithOptions **options**

Option	Type	Description
options	Array of strings	List of button titles (required)
cancelButtonIndex	Integer	Index of the Cancel button in options
destructiveButtonIndex	Integer	Index of the Destructive button in options
title	String	Title to show above the action sheet
message	String	Message to show below the title

Figure 10.7   ActionSheetIOS **rendering an action sheet (left) and a share sheet (right)**

Table 10.7 `ActionSheetIOS showShareActionSheetWithOptions` **options**

Option	Type	Description
`url`	String	URL to share
`message`	String	Message to share
`subject`	String	Subject for the message
`excludedActivityTypes`	Array	Activities to exclude from the action sheet

10.7.1 Use cases for ActionSheetIOS

The main use case for `ActionSheetIOS` is to give the user a set of options to choose from and then call a function based on their selection. For example, in the Twitter app, the action sheet is used when the Retweet button is pressed, giving the user a few options including retweet, quote retweet, and cancel. This is a common use case, displaying an action sheet after a user presses a button and giving the user a set of options to choose from.

10.7.2 Example of using ActionSheetIOS

In this example, you'll create a view with two buttons. One button will call `showActionSheetWithOptions`, and the other will call `showShareActionSheetWithOptions`.

Listing 10.13 Using `ActionSheetIOS` to create action sheets and share sheets

```
import React, { Component } from 'react'
import { Text, View, ActionSheetIOS,            ◄──── Imports ActionSheetIOS
         TouchableHighlight } from 'react-native'        from React Native

const BUTTONS = ['Cancel', 'Button One', 'Button Two', 'Button Three']   ◄──┐
                                                      Creates an array of buttons
class App extends Component {        ┌─ Creates a variable clicked    to use in the action sheet
  constructor() {                    │  and sets it to null
    super()
    this.state = {              ─┐
      clicked: null              │
    }                            │
    this.showActionSheet = this.showActionSheet.bind(this)
    this.showShareActionSheetWithOptions =
        this.showShareActionSheetWithOptions.bind(this)
  }

  showActionSheet() {    ◄──── Creates a showActionSheet method
    ActionSheetIOS.showActionSheetWithOptions({
      options: BUTTONS,
      cancelButtonIndex: 0,
    },
    (buttonIndex) => {
      if (buttonIndex > 0) {
        this.setState({ clicked: BUTTONS[buttonIndex] });
```

```
      }
    });
  }

  showShareActionSheetWithOptions() {
    ActionSheetIOS.showShareActionSheetWithOptions({
      url: 'http://www.reactnative.training',
      message: 'React Native Training',
    },
    (error) => console.log('error:', error),
    (success, method) => {
      if (success) {
        console.log('successfully shared!', success)
      }
    });
  };
  render() {
    return (
      <View style={styles.container}>
        <TouchableHighlight onPress={this.showActionSheet}
                            style={styles.button}>
          <Text style={styles.buttonText}>
              Show ActionSheet
          </Text>
        </TouchableHighlight>
        <TouchableHighlight onPress={this.showShareActionSheetWithOptions}
                            style={styles.button}>
          <Text style={styles.buttonText}>
              Show ActionSheet With Options
          </Text>
        </TouchableHighlight>
        <Text>
          {this.state.clicked}
        </Text>
      </View>
    )
  }
}

styles = {
  container: {
    flex: 1,
    justifyContent: 'center',
    padding: 20,
  },
  button: {
    height: 50,
    marginBottom: 20,
    justifyContent: 'center',
    alignItems: 'center',
    backgroundColor: 'blue'
  },
  buttonText: {
    color: 'white'
  }
}
```

Creates a showShareActionSheetWithOptions method

The success callback takes a Boolean signifying success or failure, and a string that indicates the method of sharing.

Creates two buttons in the view, and attaches the showActionSheet and showShareActionSheetWithOptions to them

In the `showActionSheet` method, you pass in the buttons as the options. Setting `cancelButtonIndex` to zero positions Cancel at the bottom of the action sheet. The callback method takes the button index as an argument; if the button index is greater than 0, the `clicked` state value is set to the new button value. When you create the `showShareActionSheetWithOptions` method, you pass in `url` and a `message` to share. The first callback function checks to see if there's an error, and the second checks whether success is `true`.

Summary

- To import cross-platform files, use platform-specific android.js and ios.jsfile extensions.
- To render platform-specific code, use the Platform API.
- Use `DatePickerIOS` to choose and save dates in your app.
- Use `PickerIOS` to render and save values from a list.
- Use `ProgressViewIOS` to show loading progress.
- Use `SegmentedControlIOS` to choose from an array of options.
- Use `TabBarIOS` to create and switch between tabs in your app.
- With `ActionSheetIOS`, you can call a native iOS action sheet or share sheet in an app.

Implementing Android-specific components and APIs

This chapter covers

- Using `DrawerLayoutAndroid` to create a side menu
- Creating a native toolbar with `ToolbarAndroid`
- Create paging views using `ViewPagerAndroid`
- Create date/time pickers using `DatePickerAndroid` and `TimePickerAndroid`
- Creating toasts using `ToastAndroid`

In this chapter, we'll implement the most used Android-specific APIs and components, discuss their props and methods, and create examples that will mimic functionality and logic that will get you up to speed quickly. To see how these work, you'll create a demo app with a menu, a toolbar, scrollable paging, a date picker, and a time picker. The app will also implement Android toasts. As you implement each of these features, you'll learn the capabilities of the most commonly used Android-specific APIs and components.

> **NOTE** Section 10.1 covered how to target platform-specific code. If you skipped that chapter on iOS-specific components and APIs and don't already know how to target platform-specific code, you should read that section before continuing.

242

11.1   Creating a menu using DrawerLayoutAndroid

To get started, you'll first create a slide-out menu (see figure 11.1). This menu will link to each of the app's pieces of functionality. It will basically serve as a way to navigate between components. You'll create this menu using the DrawerLayoutAndroid component.

The first thing to do is create a new Android application. From the command line in the folder you'll be working in, create a new application, replacing YourApplication in the following command with whatever application name you choose:

```
react-native init YourApplication
```

Next, create the files you'll use to create all this functionality. In the root of the application, add a folder named app and four files: App.js, Home.js, Menu.js, and Toolbar.js.

Now you need to update index.android.js to use your first Android-specific component, DrawerLayoutAndroid, which is a sliding toolbar from the left side of the screen. Edit index.android.js to include and implement this component.

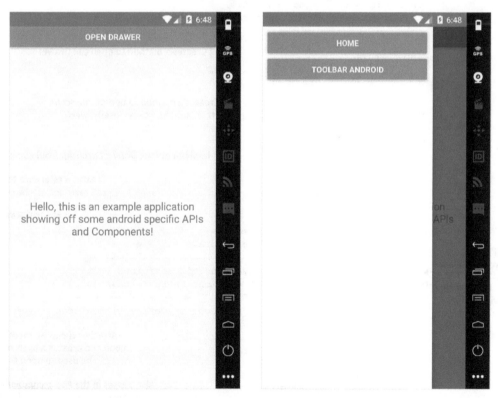

Figure 11.1   Initial layout of the application using DrawerLayoutAndroid. **The button at the top in the first screen, Open Drawer, will call a method that opens the drawer. The second screen is the opened drawer.**

```
import React from 'react'
import {
  AppRegistry,               Imports DrawerLayoutAndroid
  DrawerLayoutAndroid,       from React Native
  Button,
  View                       Imports the Menu component
} from 'react-native'        (not yet created)

import Menu from './app/Menu'     Imports the App component
import App from './app/App'       (not yet created)

class mycomponent extends React.Component {

  constructor () {
    super()
    this.state = {            Creates a component state
      scene: 'Home'           setting scene to 'Home'
    }
    this.jump = this.jump.bind(this)
    this.openDrawer = this.openDrawer.bind(this)
  }

  openDrawer () {                      Creates a method to open the Drawer
    this.drawer.openDrawer()
  }

  jump (scene) {                       Creates a method to update the scene
    this.setState({                    state, and then calls closeDrawer()
      scene
    })
    this.drawer.closeDrawer()          Implements the DrawerLayoutAndroid component
  }
                                                Creates a reference to the drawer to
                                                call methods on the component
  render () {
    return (                                        Gives the drawer a width of 300
      <DrawerLayoutAndroid
        ref={drawer => this.drawer = drawer}
        drawerWidth={300}
        drawerPosition={DrawerLayoutAndroid.positions.Left}
        renderNavigationView={() => <Menu onPress={this.jump} />}
        <View style={{ margin: 15 }}>
          <Button onPress={() => this.openDrawer()} title='Open Drawer' />
        </View>
        <App
          openDrawer={this.openDrawer}
          jump={this.jump}
          scene={this.state.scene} />
      </DrawerLayoutAndroid>
    )
  }
}

AppRegistry.registerComponent('mycomponent', () => mycomponent)
```

Positions the drawer to the left

Renders the navigation view, which is the Menu component

Attaches the jump method to the menu and creates a button that will be used to open the drawer

Also passes in the App component as a child, giving the openDrawer, jump, and scene as props

Next, create the menu you'll use in the drawer, in app/Menu.js.

Listing 11.2   Creating the `DrawerLayoutAndroid` menu component

```
import React from 'react'
import { View, StyleSheet, Button } from 'react-native'

let styles

const Menu = ({onPress }) => {
  const {
    button
  } = styles

  return (
    <View style={{ flex: 1 }}>
      <View style={button} >
        <Button onPress={() => onPress('Home')} title='Home' />
      </View>
      <View style={button} >
        <Button onPress={() => onPress('Toolbar')} title='Toolbar Android' />
      </View>
    </View>
  )
}

styles = StyleSheet.create({
  button: {
    margin: 10,
    marginBottom: 0
  }
})

export default Menu
```

Now, in app/App.js, create the following component, which basically takes in a scene as a prop and returns a component based on the prop.

Listing 11.3   Creating the `DrawerLayoutAndroid` App component

```
import React from 'react'                      Imports the Home component (not yet created)

import Home from './Home'
import Toolbar from './Toolbar'                Imports the Toolbar component (not yet created)

function getScene (scene) {                     Creates a getScene method that checks the
  switch (scene) {                              scene and returns the correct component
    case 'Home':
      return Home
    case 'Toolbar':
      return Toolbar
    default:
      return Home
  }
}

const App = (props) => {                         Creates a component based on
  const Scene = getScene(props.scene)            the current scene prop
```

```
  return (
    <Scene openDrawer={props.openDrawer} jump={props.jump} />
  )
}

export default App
```

> **Renders the component, passing in openDrawer and jump as props**

Now you can start creating components to interact with the menu. For the current setup to work, you need to create a Home component and a Toolbar component. Although you've seen the imports, you haven't actually created those components yet. In app/Home.js, create the following component, which is a basic introduction page.

Listing 11.4   Creating the `DrawerLayoutAndroid` Home component

```
import React, { Component } from 'react'
import {
  View,
  Text,
  StyleSheet
} from 'react-native'

let styles

class Home extends Component {
  render () {
    return (
      <View style={styles.container}>
        <Text style={styles.text}>
          Hello, this is an example application showing off some
          android-specific APIs and Components!
        </Text>
      </View>
    )
  }
}

styles = StyleSheet.create({
  container: {
    flex: 1,
    justifyContent: 'center',
    alignItems: 'center'
  },
  text: {
    margin: 20,
    textAlign: 'center',
    fontSize: 18
  }
})

export default Home
```

In app/Toolbar.js, create the following component, which will show that you're in the toolbar by displaying a "Hello from Toolbar" message.

Listing 11.5 Creating the `DrawerLayoutAndroid` Toolbar component

```
import React from 'react'
import {
  View,
  Text
} from 'react-native'

class ToolBar extends React.Component {
  render () {
    return (
      <View style={{ flex: 1 }}>
        <Text>Hello from Toolbar</Text>
      </View>
    )
  }
}

export default ToolBar
```

Start the application, and you should see the menu shown in figure 11.1.

11.2 *Creating a toolbar with ToolbarAndroid*

With everything set up, let's add a new component, `ToolbarAndroid`. `ToolbarAndroid` is a React Native component that wraps the native Android toolbar. This component can display a variety of things, including a title, a subtitle, a log, a navigation icon, and action buttons.

In this example, you'll implement `ToolbarAndroid` with a title, a subtitle, and two actions (Options and Menu; see figure 11.2). When Menu is clicked, you'll trigger the `openDrawer` method, which will open the menu.

In app/Toolbar.js, update the code as follows to implement the toolbar.

Listing 11.6 Implementing `ToolbarAndroid`

```
import React from 'react'
import {
  ToolbarAndroid,          ◀──── Imports the ToolbarAndroid component
  View
} from 'react-native'

class Toolbar extends React.Component {
  render () {
    const onActionSelected = (index) => {
      if (index === 1) {
        this.props.openDrawer()
      }
    }

    return (
      <View style={{ flex: 1 }}>
        <ToolbarAndroid          ◀──── Returns ToolbarAndroid
          subtitleColor='white'
          titleColor='white'
          style={{ height: 56, backgroundColor: '#52998c' }}
```

Creates an onActionSelected method. This method takes in an index and calls this.props.openDrawer if index is l. You'll have an array of actions, each of which will call this method when clicked, passing in its own index.

```
                title='React Native in Action'
                subtitle='ToolbarAndroid'
                actions={[ { title: 'Options', show: 'always' },
                           { title: 'Menu', show: 'always' } ]}
                onActionSelected={onActionSelected}
            />
          </View>
        )
      }
    }
    export default Toolbar
```

> Passes in an array of actions. Pressing these actions calls them with their array index as an argument.

> Passes in the onActionSelected function to the onActionSelected property

When you refresh your device, you should not only see the `ToolbarAndroid` but also be able to open the `DrawerLayoutAndroid` menu by pressing the button labeled Menu.

Figure 11.2 `ToolbarAndroid` with title, subtitle, and two actions. This menu is configurable, but you're only working with the default settings in this example.

11.3 *Implementing scrollable paging with ViewPagerAndroid*

Next, you'll create a new example page and component using `ViewPagerAndroid`. This component allows you to easily swipe left and right between views. Every child of `ViewPagerAndroid` is treated as its own separate, swipeable view (see figure 11.3).

To get started, create an app/ViewPager.js file and add the code in listing 11.7 to implement the `ViewPagerAndroid` component.

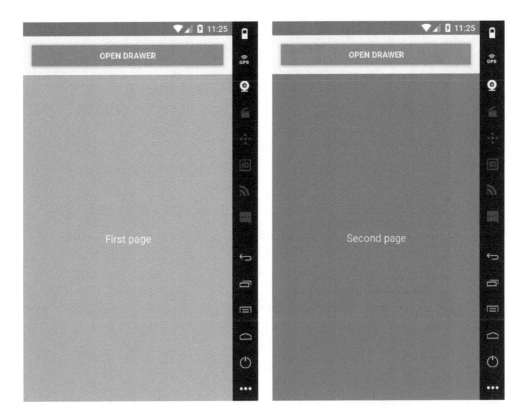

Figure 11.3 `ViewPagerAndroid` with two child views. When you swipe the pages, they scroll left and right to show the next page.

Listing 11.7 Using `ViewPagerAndroid` to enable a scrollable paging view

```
import React, { Component } from 'react'
import {
  ViewPagerAndroid,        ◄──────── Imports ViewPagerAndroid from React Native
  View,
  Text
} from 'react-native'

let styles

class ViewPager extends Component {
  render () {
    const {
      pageStyle,
      page1Style,
      page2Style,
      textStyle              Returns ViewPagerAndroid with two child
    } = styles                views, one with an orange background and
    return (                  one with a red background
      <ViewPagerAndroid   ◄──────
        style={{ flex: 1 }}
```

```
              initialPage={0}>
              <View style={[ pageStyle, page1Style ]}>
                <Text style={textStyle}>First page</Text>
              </View>
              <View style={[ pageStyle, page2Style ]}>
                <Text style={textStyle}>Second page</Text>
              </View>
          </ViewPagerAndroid>
      )
    }
}

styles = {
  pageStyle: {
    justifyContent: 'center',
    alignItems: 'center',
    padding: 20,
    flex: 1,
  },
  page1Style: {
    backgroundColor: 'orange'
  },
  page2Style: {
    backgroundColor: 'red'
  },
  textStyle: {
    fontSize: 18,
    color: 'white'
  }
}

export default ViewPager
```

Next, update Menu.js to add the button to view the new component. In Menu.js, add this button below the Toolbar Android button:

```
<View style={button} >
  <Button onPress={() => onPress('ViewPager')} title='ViewPager Android' />
</View>
```

Finally, import the new component and update the `switch` statement in App.js to render the component.

Listing 11.8   App.js with the new `ViewPager` component

```
import React from 'react'

import Home from './Home'
import Toolbar from './Toolbar'
import ViewPager from './ViewPager'

function getScene (scene) {
  switch (scene) {
    case 'Home':
      return Home
    case 'Toolbar':
      return Toolbar
```

```
      case 'ViewPager':
        return ViewPager
      default:
        return Home
    }
  }

const App = (props) => {
  const Scene = getScene(props.scene)
  return (
    <Scene openDrawer={props.openDrawer} jump={props.jump} />
  )
}

export default App
```

Run the app. You should see the new ViewPager Android button in the side menu, and you can view and interact with the new component.

11.4 *Using the DatePickerAndroid API to show a native date picker*

DatePickerAndroid lets you open and interact with the native Android date-picker dialog as shown in figure 11.4. To open and use the DatePickerAndroid component, import DatePickerAndroid and call DatePickerAndroid.open(). To get started, create app/DatePicker.js and then the DatePicker component in it (listing 11.9).

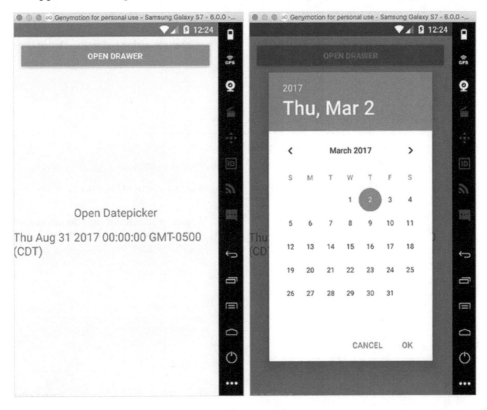

Figure 11.4 **DatePickerAndroid** **with a button that opens the date picker and then shows the selected date in the view**

Listing 11.9   Implementing a `DatePicker` component

```
import React, { Component } from 'react'
import { DatePickerAndroid, View, Text } from 'react-native'
```
Imports DatePickerAndroid
from React Native

```
let styles

class DatePicker extends Component {

  constructor() {
    super()
    this.state = {
      date: new Date()
    }
    this.openDatePicker = this.openDatePicker.bind(this)
  }
```
Creates the state, setting the
date as a new Date()

Creates the openDatePicker method that
will be used when the button is pressed

```
  openDatePicker () {
    DatePickerAndroid.open({
      date: this.state.date
    })
    .then((date) => {
      const { year, month, day, action } = date
      if (action === 'dateSetAction') {
        this.setState({ date: new Date(year, month, day) })
      }
    }) }
```
DatePickerAndroid.open returns a promise,
giving you an object with the selected day,
month, year, and the action that was chosen.

If you choose a date, then the action is
dateSetAction. If the modal is dismissed,
then the action is dismissedAction.

```
  render() {
    const {
      container,
      text
    } = styles

    return (
      <View style={container}>
        <Text onPress={this.openDatePicker} style={text}>
          Open Datepicker
        </Text>
        <Text style={text}>{this.state.date.toString()}</Text>
      </View>
    )
  }
}
```
Creates a button that calls the openDatePicker
method and displays the date in the view.

```
styles = {
  container: {
    flex: 1,
    justifyContent: 'center',
    alignItems: 'center'
  },
  text: {
    marginBottom: 15,
    fontSize: 20
  }
}

export default DatePicker
```

Now that you have the component, update app/App.js to include it.

Listing 11.10   app/App.js with the new `DatePicker` component

```
import React from 'react'

import Home from './Home'
import Toolbar from './Toolbar'
import ViewPager from './ViewPager'
import DatePicker from './DatePicker'

function getScene (scene) {
  switch (scene) {
    case 'Home':
      return Home
    case 'Toolbar':
      return Toolbar
    case 'ViewPager':
      return ViewPager
    case 'DatePicker':
      return DatePicker
    default:
      return Home
  }
}

const App = (props) => {
  const Scene = getScene(props.scene)
  return (
    <Scene openDrawer={props.openDrawer} jump={props.jump} />
  )
}

export default App
```

Finally, update the menu to add the new button that will open the DatePicker component. In app/Menu.js, add the following button below the ViewPager Android button:

```
<View style={button} >
  <Button onPress={() => onPress('DatePicker')} title='DatePicker Android' />
</View>
```

11.5 *Creating a time picker with TimePickerAndroid*

Next up is TimePickerAndroid. It's like DatePickerAndroid in that you import it and call the open method to interact with it. This component brings up a time picker dialog that allows you to choose a time and use it in your application (figure 11.5).

To standardize the time formats, you'll use a third party library called moment.js. To get started with this library, you must first install it. In the root directory of the project, install moment using either npm or yarn (your preference—both npm and yarn will work exactly the same here):

```
npm install moment -save
```

or

```
yarn add moment
```

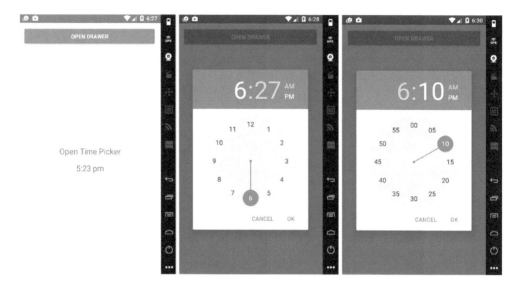

Figure 11.5 `TimePickerAndroid` **with both hour and minute views**

Next, in app/TimePicker.js, create the following `TimePicker` component.

Listing 11.11 `TimePickerAndroid` **using moment.js**

Imports TimePickerAndroid from React Native

```
import React, { Component } from 'react'
import { TimePickerAndroid, View, Text } from 'react-native'
import moment from 'moment'          ◀── Imports moment from moment.js

let styles

class TimePicker extends Component {

  constructor () {
    super()
    this.state = {
      time: moment().format('h:mm a')
    }
    this.openTimePicker = this.openTimePicker.bind(this)
  }

  openTimePicker () {
    TimePickerAndroid.open({
      time: this.state.time
    })
    .then((time) => {
      const { hour, minute, action } = time
      if (action === 'timeSetAction') {
        const time = moment().minute(minute).hour(hour).format('h:mm a')
        this.setState({ time })
      }
```

Creates an initial time and stores it in the state with a format 'h:mm a', hour:minutes a.m. or p.m.

Creates the openTimePicker method

The TimePickerAndroid.open method returns a promise, with a time object that contains hour, minute, and action.

Check to see if the action is timeSetAction, and if so, update the state to reflect the new time.

```
      })
    }

    render () {
      const {
        container,
        text
      } = styles
```

**Creates a button to call openTimePicker
and display the time in the view**

```
      return (
        <View style={container}>
          <Text onPress={this.openTimePicker} style={text}>Open Time Picker</
      Text>
          <Text style={text}>{this.state.time.toString()}</Text>
        </View>
      )
    }
  }

  styles = {
    container: {
      flex: 1,
      justifyContent: 'center',
      alignItems: 'center'
    },
    text: {
      marginBottom: 15,
      fontSize: 20
    }
  }

  export default TimePicker
```

Next, update app/App.js to include the new component.

```
import React from 'react'

import Home from './Home'
import Toolbar from './Toolbar'
import ViewPager from './ViewPager'
import DatePicker from './DatePicker'
import TimePicker from './TimePicker'

function getScene (scene) {
  switch (scene) {
    case 'Home':
      return Home
    case 'Toolbar':
      return Toolbar
    case 'ViewPager':
      return ViewPager
    case 'DatePicker':
      return DatePicker
    case 'TimePicker':
      return TimePicker
```

```
      default:
        return Home
    }
}

const App = (props) => {
  const Scene = getScene(props.scene)
  return (
    <Scene openDrawer={props.openDrawer} jump={props.jump} />
  )
}

export default App
```

Finally, update the menu to add the button that will open the new `TimePicker` component. In app/Menu.js, add the following below the DatePicker Android button:

```
<View style={button} >
  <Button onPress={() => onPress('TimePicker')} title='TimePicker Android' />
</View>
```

11.6   *Implementing Android toasts using ToastAndroid*

`ToastAndroid` allows you to easily call native Android toasts from a React Native application. An Android *toast* is a popup with a message that goes away after a given period of time (see figure 11.6). To get started building out this component, create app/Toast.js, as shown in the next listing.

> **Listing 11.13   Implementing `ToastAndroid`**

```
import React from 'react'
import { View, Text, ToastAndroid } from 'react-native'      ◄──── Imports ToastAndroid from React Native

let styles

const Toast = () => {
  let {
    container,
    button
  } = styles
                                                    Creates a basicToast
                                                    method that will call
  const basicToast = () => {                        ToastAndroid.show()
    ToastAndroid.show('Hello World!', ToastAndroid.LONG)
  }
                                          Creates a gravityToast method that will
  const gravityToast = () => {         ◄── call ToastAndroid.showWithGravity()
    ToastAndroid.showWithGravity('Toast with Gravity!',
                        ToastAndroid.LONG, ToastAndroid.CENTER)
  }
                                   Creates two buttons in the view: Open
  return (                         basic toast and Open gravity toast
    <View style={container}>    ◄──
      <Text style={button} onPress={basicToast}>    ◄──── Opens the basicToast
        Open basic toast                                  popup when the
      </Text>                                             button is pressed
```

```
        <Text style={button} onPress={gravityToast}>
          Open gravity toast
        </Text>
      </View>
    )
  }

styles = {
  container: {
    flex: 1,
    justifyContent: 'center',
    alignItems: 'center'
  },
  button: {
    marginBottom: 10,
    color: 'blue'
  }
}

export default Toast
```

Opens the gravityToast popup
when the button is pressed

The `ToastAndroid.show()` takes two arguments: a message and a length of time to show the toast. The time can be either SHORT (about 2 seconds) or LONG (about 4 seconds); this example uses LONG. The `ToastAndroid.showWithGravity()` method is like `ToastAndroid.show()`, but you can pass it a third argument to position the toast at the

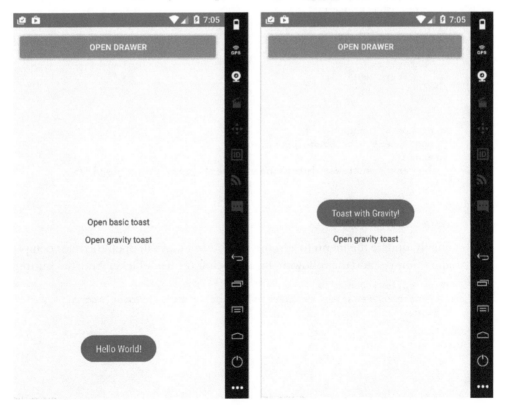

Figure 11.6 `ToastAndroid` **with toasts in the default and middle positions**

top, bottom, or center of the view. In this case, you're positioning the toast in the middle of the screen with ToastAndroid.CENTER as the third argument.

Now, update app/App.js to include the new component.

Listing 11.14   Adding the toast component to the app

```
import React from 'react'

import Home from './Home'
import Toolbar from './Toolbar'
import ViewPager from './ViewPager'
import DatePicker from './DatePicker'
import TimePicker from './TimePicker'
import Toast from './Toast'

function getScene (scene) {
  switch (scene) {
    case 'Home':
      return Home
    case 'Toolbar':
      return Toolbar
    case 'ViewPager':
      return ViewPager
    case 'DatePicker':
      return DatePicker
    case 'TimePicker':
      return TimePicker
    case 'Toast':
      return Toast
    default:
      return Home
  }
}

const App = (props) => {
  const Scene = getScene(props.scene)
  return (
    <Scene openDrawer={props.openDrawer} jump={props.jump} />
  )
}

export default App
```

Finally, update the menu to add the new button that will open the toast component. In app/Menu.js, add the following button below the TimePicker Android button:

```
<View style={button} >
  <Button onPress={() => onPress('Toast')} title='Toast Android' />
</View>
```

Summary

- You can use `DrawerLayoutAndroid` to create the main menu of an application.
- You can use `ToolbarAndroid` to create an interactive app toolbar.
- You can use `ViewPagerAndroid` to create swipeable views.
- With `DatePickerAndroid`, you can access the native date picker, allowing you to create and manipulate dates in the application.
- `TimePickerAndroid` lets you access the native time picker, making it possible to create and manipulate time in the application.
- You can easily create native Android toast notifications with `ToastAndroid`.

Part 4

Bringing it all together

This part of the book pulls together everything covered in the previous chapters—styling, navigation, animations, and some of the cross-platform components—into a single app. We'll start by looking at the final design and walking through a basic overview of what the app will do.

You'll create a new React Native application and install the React Navigation library, dive deep into styling both the components as well as the navigation UI, work with data from external network resources by using the Fetch API, and ultimately build out an application that allows users to view information about their favorite *Star Wars* characters.

Building a Star Wars app using cross-platform components

12

This chapter covers

- The basics of fetching data using the Fetch API

- Using a `Modal` component to show and hide views

- Creating a list using the `FlatList` component

- Using the `ActivityIndicator` to show loading state

- Using React Navigation in a real-world project to handle navigation

React Native ships with many components that are ready to use in your apps. Some of these components work cross-platform: that is, they work regardless of whether you're running an app on iOS or Android. Other components are platform-specific: for example, `ActionSheetIOS` only runs on iOS, and `ToolbarAndroid` only runs on the Android platform (cross-platform components were covered in Chapters 10 and 11).

This chapter covers some of the most-used cross-platform components and how to implement each one as you build a demo application. For this purpose, you'll implement the following cross-platform components and APIs by building a cross-platform *Star Wars* information app:

- Fetch API
- Modal
- ActivityIndicator
- FlatList
- Picker
- React-Navigation

This app will access SWAPI, the Star Wars API (https://swapi.co), and return information about *Star Wars* characters, starships, home planets, and more, as shown in figure 12.1. When a user clicks People, the app fetches the movie's main cast from https://swapi.co/api/people and displays their information. In the process, the app uses several React Native cross-platform components. In this chapter, you'll learn how to use these components as you do the following:

1. Set up a new React Native application and install dependencies
2. Import the People component and create the Container component
3. Create the Navigation component and register routes
4. Create the main class for the view
5. Create the People component
6. Use the cross-platform components FlatList, Modal, and Picker to create the state and set up a fetch call to retrieve data

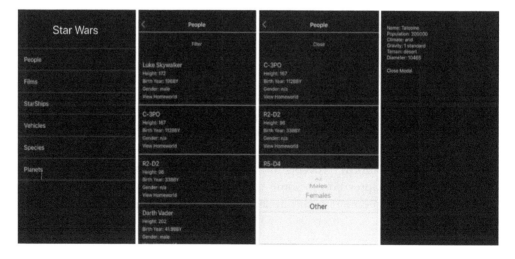

Figure 12.1   The completed *Star Wars* app that you'll build with React Native cross-platform components. You'll focus on the first link: People.

> **NOTE** You can download this chapter's code from the book's website (www. manning.com/books/react-native-in-action) and also from GitHub (https:// github.com/dabit3/react-native-in-action/tree/chapter12/StarWars).

12.1 Creating the app and installing dependencies

The first thing you need to do is set up a new React Native application and install any dependencies required to build this app. Go to the command line, and create a React Native app by typing in the following:

```
react-native init StarWarsApp
```

Next, change into the newly created StarWarsApp directory:

```
cd StarWarsApp
```

The only thing you'll need to install for this app is react-navigation, so install it using either npm or yarn:

- Using npm: `npm i react-navigation`
- Using yarn: `yarn add react-navigation`

Now that the project is created, open App.js and create the components needed for the screen shown in figure 12.2. At the top of the file, import the components shown next.

Listing 12.1 Importing the initial components

```
import React, { Component } from 'react';
import {
  StyleSheet,
  Text,
  FlatList,
  TouchableHighlight
} from 'react-native';
import { createStackNavigator } from 'react-navigation';
```

In this listing you import the required React Native components, as well as createStackNavigator from react-navigation. FlatList is a component that will allow you to render performant lists in an app using any array of data. createStackNavigator is a navigator from react-navigation that provides an easy way to navigate between scenes; each scene is pushed on top of a route stack. All the animations are configured for you and give the default iOS and Android feel and transitions.

12.1.1 Importing the People component and creating the Container component

Next, you need to import the two views you'll use in this app. Take another look at the first screen in figure 12.2. As you can see, there are links for People, Films, and so on. When the user clicks People, the app should navigate to a component that lists the people (main characters) in the *Star Wars* films. To do this, you'll create a `People` component in section 12.2—you'll import the component now and create it later. Below the last `import` in listing 12.1, import the yet-to-be-created `People` component:

```
import People from './People'
```

Because the design uses a black color background and you don't want to repeat styling code across components, let's create a `Container` component that you'll use as a wrapper for your views. This `Container` component will be strictly used for styling. In the root of the app, create a new file called Container.js, and enter the following code.

Figure 12.2   The initial view of the app

Listing 12.2   Creating a reusable `Container` component

```
import React from 'react'
import { StyleSheet, View } from 'react-native'

const styles = StyleSheet.create({
  container: {
    flex: 1,
    backgroundColor: 'black',
  },
})

const Container = ({ children }) => (
  <View style={styles.container}>
    {children}
  </View>
)

export default Container
```

Stylesheet, covered in chapter 4, lets you create a set of reusable styles.

Container takes a single property, children—in this case, the component wrapped in the Container.

Wraps the children component in a View and assigns it a style of container, which will give the component a black background and a flex property of I

Import the `Container` into the App.js file, below the last `import` of the `People` component:

```
import Container from './Container'
```

Below the `Container` import, create an array of data that you'll use for the links. The items in the array will be passed to the `FlatList` component to create the list of links. This array should contain objects, and each object should contain a `title` key. You need the `title` key to display the name of the link:

```
const links = [
  { title: 'People' },
  { title: 'Films' },
  { title: 'StarShips' },
  { title: 'Vehicles' },
  { title: 'Species' },
  { title: 'Planets' }
]
```

12.1.2 *Creating the navigation component and registering routes*

At the bottom of the App.js file, you'll next create the main navigation component and pass it to the `AppRegistry`. You're using `createStackNavigator` as the navigation component, and you need to register the routes you'll use in the application.

Initialize `createStackNavigator` and pass the navigator to the `AppRegistry` method, replacing the default `StarWars` component with the navigation component as shown in the following listing. `createStackNavigator` provides a way for the app to transition between screens: each new screen is placed on top of a stack and is a cross-platform component.

> **Listing 12.3 Using `createStackNavigator`**

The first key is automatically rendered as the initial route. In this case, you pass in the StarWars component (created in listing 12.4) as the initial route.

```
const App = createStackNavigator({
  StarWars: {
    screen: StarWars
  },
  People: {
    screen: People
  }
})
export default App
```

The first argument to createStackNavigator is the route configuration: an object with the routes you want to define. The route name is defined by the key, and the value passed to the key defines the component you want to use for the named route.

The other route in the app is People: you pass in the People component (created in listing 12.5).

12.1.3 *Creating the main class for the initial view*

In App.js, below the links array you created in section 12.1.1, add the main class for the view (listing 12.4). This class returns a list that will render all the movie characters who come back from the API. You'll also set the header title using the `navigationOptions` static property and set the logo in the header. You'll render this list using `FlatList` from React Native. It's a built-in interface for rendering simple lists in a React Native app.

Listing 12.4   Creating the main `StarWars` component

```
class StarWars extends Component {

  static navigationOptions = {

  headerTitle: <Text
    style={{
      fontSize: 34, color: 'rgb(255,232,31)'
    }}
    >Star Wars</Text>,
    headerStyle: { backgroundColor: "black", height: 110 }
  }
  navigate = (link) => {
    const { navigate } = this.props.navigation
    navigate(link)
  }
  renderItem = ({ item, index }) => {
    return (
      <TouchableHighlight
        onPress={() => this.navigate(item.title)}
        style={[ styles.item, { borderTopWidth: index === 0 ? 1 : null} ]}>
        <Text style={styles.text}>{item.title}</Text>
      </TouchableHighlight>
    )
  }

  render() {
    return (
      <Container>
        <FlatList
          data={links}
          keyExtractor={(item) => item.title}
          renderItem={this.renderItem}
        />
      </Container>
    )
  }
}

const styles = StyleSheet.create({
  item: {
    padding: 20,
    justifyContent: 'center',
    borderColor: 'rgba(255,232,31, .2)',
    borderBottomWidth: 1
  },
  text: {
    color: '#ffe81f',
    fontSize: 18
  }
});
```

Creates a static navigationOptions object, and passes in a headerTitle component and a headerStyle object

Creates a navigate method that takes a link as an argument

Loops through the data array and returns an item and an index for each item

Returns the Container, wraps the FlatList component in it, and passes in links, renderItem, and a keyExtractor method

Because you're using `createStackNavigator` from `react-navigation`, you can pass in configuration for each route. In this route, you want to change the default header configuration and styling. To do so, you create a static `navigationOptions` object, and in it you pass in a `headerTitle` component containing a title and a `headerStyle` object containing some specific styling. The `headerTitle` is the text you'll use as the logo, and `headerStyle` sets the background color to black and gives a set height to fit the text.

The `navigate` method takes a link as an argument. Any component rendered by `StackNavigation` receives the navigation object as a prop. You use this prop to destructure the `navigate` method and then navigate to the link passed in. The link, in this case the `title` property in the links array, correlates with the keys passed in to `createStackNavigator`.

`FlatList` takes a `renderItem` method that loops through the array of data passed in as the `data` property and returns an object with an `item` and an `index` for each item in the array. The `item` is the actual item with all its properties, and the `index` is the index of the item. You destructure these as arguments, pass `item` as an argument to `navigate` to display the title, and use `index` to apply a `borderTop` style if it's the first array item.

`render()` returns the `Container`, and in it you wrap the `FlatList` passing in links as the data and the `renderItem` method you created earlier. You also pass in a `keyExtractor` method. If there's no item labeled `key` in the array, you have to tell the `FlatList` which item to use as its key; otherwise it will throw an error. Figure 12.3 shows the initial application view with its components. The final code for App.js is at www.manning.com/books/react-native-in-action and on GitHub at https://github.com/dabit3/react-native-in-action/blob/chapter12/StarWars/App.js.

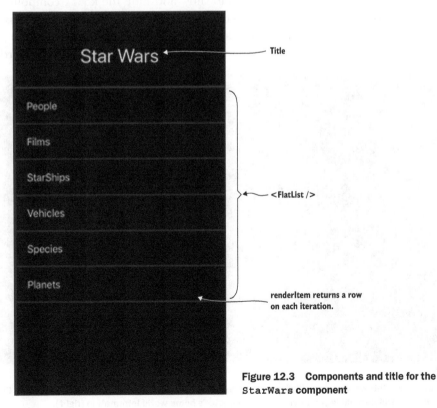

Figure 12.3 Components and title for the StarWars component

12.2 *Creating the People component using FlatList, Modal, and Picker*

Next you'll create a `People` component to fetch and display information about the *Star Wars* cast that you get from the Star Wars API (figure 12.4). As part of this component, you'll use the React Native cross-platform components `Modal` and `Picker`. `Modal` lets you display an element on top of whatever view you're currently working in. `Picker` displays a scrollable list of options or values; this component provides a convenient means of capturing input from a user and making their selection available to the rest of the application.

When the `People` component loads, it will start with an empty data array, a `loading` state of `true`, and with a few other pieces of state:

```
state = {
    data: [],
    loading: true,
    modalVisible: false,
    gender: 'all',
    pickerVisible: false
}
```

When the component mounts, you'll fetch the data you need from the Star Wars API at https://swapi.co/api/people; and when this data returns, you'll populate the data array with the returned data, and set the `loading` Boolean to `false`.

You'll use the `modalVisble` Boolean to show and hide the `Modal` component that will fetch information about the character's home world. You'll use `pickerVisible` to show and hide a `Picker` component that will let you choose the gender of the person you want to view, and will pass the result to a filter that will filter the results accordingly.

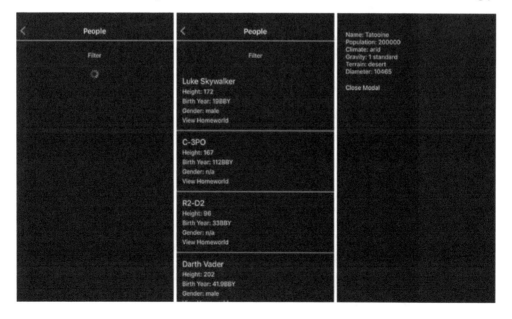

Figure 12.4   This component will display the `Loading` (left) and `Loaded` (middle) state of the People. js screen. It will also allow you to view each character's home world information (right).

Creating a new file, People.js, and begin coding.

Listing 12.5 People.js imports

```
import React, { Component } from 'react'
import {
  StyleSheet,                    ◄──────  Imports components from React Native
  Text,
  View,
  Image,                         ◄──────  Imports the lodash utility library
  TouchableHighlight,
  ActivityIndicator,                       Imports the Container component used in App.js,
  FlatList,                                because you'll need the same styling here
  Modal,
  Picker                                   Imports the HomeWorld component
} from 'react-native'                      (not yet created) that will populate
import _ from 'lodash'         ◄──────     with a character's information when
                                           you click View Homeworld
import Container from './Container'  ◄──┘
import HomeWorld from './HomeWorld'  ◄──
```

The Lodash utility library provides many convenience functions. You'll need to install it via npm or yarn prior to importing it here.

The next step is to create the main class for the component and set up the `navigationOptions` to give the header a title as well as some styling. Under the last import in People.js, create the following `People` class.

Listing 12.6 Creating the `People` class and setting up the page title

```
export default class People extends Component {
  static navigationOptions = {      ◄───────
    headerTitle: 'People',                      Creates the static navigationOptions property
    headerStyle: {                ◄──────
      borderBottomWidth: 1,                     headerStyle is the style object for the title header.
      borderBottomColor: '#ffe81f',
      backgroundColor: 'black'                  Sets the color to use the "material
    },                                          ripple" animation used when the button
    headerTintColor: '#ffe81f',                 is pressed (Android >= 5.0 only)
    pressColorAndroid: 'white'    ◄──────┘
  }
}
```

The static `navigationOptions` property is created here, as in the App.js file, but instead of passing in a component as the `headerTitle`, you pass in the string "People". You also add some styling.

12.2.1 *Creating the state and setting up a fetch call to retrieve data*

Now you'll create the state and set up a `fetch` call on `componentDidMount`. Fetch is a cross-platform API for fetching network resources that's supplanting `XMLHttpRequest`. Fetch isn't yet 100% compatible with all internet browsers, but React Native provides a polyfill (an API that mimics the behavior of the original API, in this case Fetch). The Fetch API is an easy-to-use-out-of-the-box way to work with network requests, including

GET, POST, PUT, and DELETE. fetch returns a promise, which makes it easy to work with asynchronously.

A fetch request usually looks something like this:

```
fetch('https://swapi.co/api/people/')
  .then(response => response.json())
  .then(json => {
      #do something with the returned data / json
  })
  .catch(err => {
      #handle error here
  })
```

In the example, the fetch call will hit the Star Wars API at https://swapi.co/api/people and return an object containing a results array. This results array will contain the characters to display on this page. To view this dataset, open the URL in a browser to check out the data structure.

The data set looks like the following, with results being the array of movie characters you're interested in using:

```
{
  "count": 87,
  "next": "http://swapi.co/api/people/?page=2",
  "previous": null,
  "results": [
      {    "name": "Luke Skywalker",
           "height": "172",
           "mass": "77",
           ...
      },
      ...
}
```

Once the data is returned from the API, you update the data array in the state with the results.

Below the navigationOptions object in People.js, create the state and the component-DidMount fetch call.

Listing 12.7   Setting up the initial state and fetching data

```
state = {
    data: [],
    loading: true,
    modalVisible: false,
    gender: 'all',
    pickerVisible: false
  }
  componentDidMount() {
    fetch('https://swapi.co/api/people/')
      .then(res => res.json())
      .then(json => this.setState({ data: json.results, loading: false }))
      .catch((err) => console.log('err:', err))
  }
```

In componentDidMount, you fetch the data from the API using fetch(). fetch returns a promise. You then take the returned data and call the .json() method to read the response and transform the data. .json() returns a promise containing the JSON data. Finally, you set the state again, updating the data and loading variables.

12.2.2 Adding the remaining class methods

At this point in the app, if you load this page, the data should be loaded into the state and ready to use. Next up, you need to create the rest of the functionality to display this data, as well as a render method to display the data. To create the rest of the methods used in this component, add the following code after componentDidMount in People.js.

Listing 12.8   Remaining methods for component functionality

```
renderItem = ({ item }) => {          ◄─────  renderItem method that will be passed
  return (                                    to the FlatList
    <View style={styles.itemContainer}>
      <Text style={styles.name}>{item.name}</Text>
      <Text style={styles.info}>Height: {item.height}</Text>
      <Text style={styles.info}>Birth Year: {item.birth_year}</Text>
      <Text style={styles.info}>Gender: {item.gender}</Text>
      <TouchableHighlight
        style={styles.button}
        onPress={() => this.openHomeWorld(item.homeworld)}
      >
        <Text style={styles.info}>View Homeworld</Text>
      </TouchableHighlight>
    </View>
  )
}
openHomeWorld = (url) => {        ◄─────  Updates the URL and the modalVisible
  this.setState({                         Boolean in the state, opening the
    url,                                  HomeWorld modal
    modalVisible: true
  })
}
closeModal = () => {          ◄─────  Closes the modal by setting
  this.setState({ modalVisible: false })    modalVisible in the state to false
}
togglePicker = () => {          ◄─────  Toggles the pickerVisible Boolean
  this.setState({ pickerVisible: !this.state.pickerVisible })
}

filter = (gender) => {          ◄─────  Updates the filter value in the state to the passed-in
  this.setState({ gender })            value used to filter the data in the render method
}
```

The renderItem method is what you'll pass to FlatList to render the data in the state. Every time an item is passed through this method, you get an object with two keys: item and key. You destructure the item when the method is called and use the item properties to display the data for the user (item.name, item.height, and so on). Note the onPress method passed to the TouchableHighlight component: this method passes the item.homeworld property to the openHomeWorld method. item.homeworld is a URL you'll use to fetch the movie character's home planet information.

The togglePicker method toggles the pickerVisible Boolean. This Boolean shows and hides a picker from which you can choose a filter to view characters by gender: all, female, male, or other (robots and so on).

12.2.3 *Implementing the render method*

With all the methods set up, the last thing to do is implement the UI in the render method. In People.js, you'll introduce a new component called the ActivityIndicator: a cross-platform circular loading indicator that will indicate the loading state (you can see a list of properties in table 12.1). After the filter method, add the render method as shown next.

Listing 12.9   render method

Destructures the data array from the state for easier access

Checks whether the filter is set to all: if so, skips this function; if not, performs a filter based on the gender of the character vs. the gender set in the state

```
render() {
  let { data } = this.state
  if (this.state.gender !== 'all') {
    data = data.filter(f => f.gender === this.state.gender)
  }

  return (
    <Container>
      <TouchableHighlight style={styles.pickerToggleContainer}
                          onPress={this.togglePicker}>
        <Text style={styles.pickerToggle}>
          {this.state.pickerVisible ? 'Close Filter' : 'Open Filter'}
        </Text>
      </TouchableHighlight>
      {
        this.state.loading ? <ActivityIndicator color='#ffe81f' /> : (
          <FlatList
            data={data}
            keyExtractor={(item) => item.name}
            renderItem={this.renderItem}
          />
        )
      }
    }
```

Creates a button: Close Filter or Open Filter, based on the value of this.state.pickerVisible

Checks whether the data is loading by evaluating this.state.loading: if so, shows an ActivityIndicator to indicate loading is taking place; if not, renders the FlatList, passing in the data, this.renderItem, and keyExtractor

The Modal component stays hidden until modalVisible is set to true and then slides up into view.

If this.state .pickerVisible is set to true, renders the Picker component

```
<Modal
  onRequestClose={() => console.log('onrequest close called')}
  animationType="slide"
  visible={this.state.modalVisible}>
  <HomeWorld closeModal={this.closeModal}
             url={this.state.url} />
</Modal>
{
  this.state.pickerVisible && (
    <View style={styles.pickerContainer}>
      <Picker
        style={{ backgroundColor: '#ffe81f' }}
        selectedValue={this.state.gender}
        onValueChange={(item) => this.filter(item)}>

        <Picker.Item itemStyle={{ color: 'yellow' }}
                     label="All"
                     value="all" />
        <Picker.Item label="Males" value="male" />
        <Picker.Item label="Females" value="female" />
        <Picker.Item label="Other" value="n/a" />
      </Picker>
    </View>
  )
}
    </Container>
  );
}
```

Animation type of the Modal; could also be none or fade

onRequestClose is a required property. You don't need to do anything, so just logs to the console when called.

Renders the Picker, passing in a value, a style, and an onValueChange method

When the Close Filter / Open Filter button is clicked, the `togglePicker` method is called and the picker is shown or hidden. The `onValueChange` method fires every time the picker value is updated, which then updates the state, triggering a rerender of the component, and updating the filtered list of items in the view.

Table 12.1 `ActivityIndicator` **properties**

Property	Type	Description (some from docs)
animating	Boolean	Animates the `ActivityIndicator` icon
color	Color	Color of the `ActivityIndicator`
size	String (small or large)	Size of the `ActivityIndicator`

The last thing you need is the styling for this component. This code goes below the class definition in People.js.

Listing 12.10 `People` **component styling**

```
const styles = StyleSheet.create({
  pickerToggleContainer: {
    padding: 25,
    justifyContent: 'center',
```

```
      alignItems: 'center'
    },
    pickerToggle: {
      color: '#ffe81f'
    },
    pickerContainer: {
      position: 'absolute',
      bottom: 0,
      right: 0,
      left: 0
    },
    itemContainer: {
      padding: 15,
      borderBottomWidth: 1, borderBottomColor: '#ffe81f'
    },
    name: {
      color: '#ffe81f',
      fontSize: 18
    },
    info: {
      color: '#ffe81f',
      fontSize: 14,
      marginTop: 5
    }
});
```

You can find the final code for this component at www.manning.com/books/react-native-in-action and also on GitHub at https://github.com/dabit3/react-native-in-action/blob/chapter12/StarWars/People.js.

12.3 Creating the HomeWorld component

To finish the app, you'll create the final component: HomeWorld. In People.js, you created a Modal, and this HomeWorld component was the Modal's content:

```
<Modal
  onRequestClose={() => console.log('onrequest close called')}
  animationType="slide"
  visible={this.state.modalVisible}>
  <HomeWorld closeModal={this.closeModal} url={this.state.url} />
</Modal>
```

You'll use the HomeWorld component to fetch data about a character's home planet and display this information to the user in the modal, as shown in figure 12.5.

This component will fetch the url prop that's passed in when the modal opens in a fetch call placed in componentDidMount. This happens because componentDidMount is called every time the visible property of the modal is set to true: it's basically reloading the component when the modal is shown.

12.3.1 Creating the HomeWorld class and initializing state

Create a new file: HomeWorld.js. Then, import the components you'll need, create the class definition, and create the initial state, as shown next.

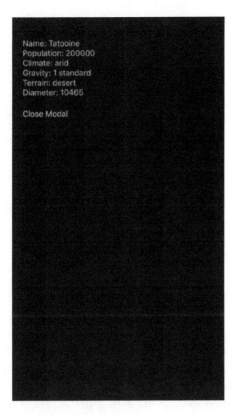

Name: Tatooine
Population: 200000
Climate: arid
Gravity: 1 standard
Terrain: desert
Diameter: 10465

Close Modal

Figure 12.5 `HomeWorld` component displaying data after fetching from the API. The Close Modal button calls the `closeModal` function passed in as a prop.

Listing 12.11 `HomeWorld` component class, imports, and initial state

```
import React from 'react'
import {
  View,
  Text,
  ActivityIndicator,
  StyleSheet,
} from 'react-native'

export default class HomeWorld extends React.Component {
  state = {
    data: {},
    loading: true              Initial state
  }
}
```

The initial state holds only two things: an empty `data` object and a `loading` Boolean set to `true`. When the component loads, you'll show a loading indicator while you wait for the data to come back from the API. Once the data loads, you'll update the `loading` Boolean to `false` and render the data that came back from the API.

12.3.2 *Fetching data from the API using the url prop*

You'll call the API using the `url` property in `componentDidMount`, which will be called once the component loads. Below the state declaration in HomeWorld.js, create the following `componentDidMount` method.

> **Listing 12.12   Fetching data and uploading state in `componentDidMount`**

Makes sure there's a URL; if not, returns out of the function to not cause an error

Updates the API URL to use HTTPS

Calls fetch on the URL passed in as a prop

```
componentDidMount() {
  if (!this.props.url) return
  const url = this.props.url.replace(/^http:\/\//i, 'https://')
  fetch(url)
    .then(res => res.json())
    .then(json => {
      this.setState({ data: json, loading: false })
    })
    .catch((err) => console.log('err:', err))
}
```

You update the API URL to use HTTPS because React Native doesn't allow unsecure HTTP requests out of the box (although it can be configured to work if necessary). You call `fetch` on the URL and, when the response comes back, transform the data into JSON, update the state to set `loading` to `false`, and add the data to the state by updating the `data` value of `state` with the returned JSON.

Finally, you need to create the `render` method and the styling. In the `render` method, you'll display some properties relating to the character's home world, such as its name, population, climate, and so on. These styles will be repetitive. In React and React Native, it's best to create and reuse a component rather than creating and reusing styling, if it's something you'll be doing more than a handful of times.

In this case, it makes sense to create a custom `TextContainer` component to use in the `render` method to display data. Above the class declaration in HomeWorld.js, create the following `TextContainer` component.

> **Listing 12.13   Creating a reusable `TextContainer` component**

```
const TextContainer = ({ label, info }) => (
  <Text style={styles.text}>{label}: {info}</Text>
)
```

In this component, you return a basic `Text` component and receive two props that you'll use: `label` and `info`. The static `label` is the description of the field, and `info` is the information you get when the API returns the home world data.

12.3.3 *Wrapping up the HomeWorld component*

Now that the `TextContainer` is ready to go, finish the component by creating the render method and the styling in HomeWorld.js.

Listing 12.14 `render` method and styling

```
export default class HomeWorld extends React.Component {
  ...
  render() {
    const { data } = this.state            ◄——  Destructures the data
    return (                                     object from the state
      <View style={styles.container}>          Check whether loading is true; if so, shows
        {                                        an ActivityIndicator to indicate loading
          this.state.loading ? (   ◄——┘
            <ActivityIndicator color='#ffe81f' />
          ) : (
              <View style={styles.HomeworldInfoContainer}>  ◄————————┐
                <TextContainer label="Name" info={data.name} />
                <TextContainer label="Population" info={data.population} />
                <TextContainer label="Climate" info={data.climate} />
                <TextContainer label="Gravity" info={data.gravity} />
                <TextContainer label="Terrain" info={data.terrain} />
                <TextContainer label="Diameter" info={data.diameter} />
                <Text
                  style={styles.closeButton}
                  onPress={this.props.closeModal}>
                  Close Modal
                </Text>
              </View>
          )
      }
      </View>
    )
  }
}
```

Creates a button that calls
this.props.closeModal to let
the user close the modal

If loading isn't true, returns the main
View component that wraps the
TextContainers and displays the data
returned from the API, now stored as the
data object in the state

```
const styles = StyleSheet.create({
  container: {
    flex: 1,
    backgroundColor: '#000000',
    paddingTop: 20
  },
  HomeworldInfoContainer: {
    padding: 20
  },
  text: {
    color: '#ffe81f',
  },
  closeButton: {
    paddingTop: 20,
    color: 'white',
    fontSize: 14
  }
})
```

Summary

- React Native ships with cross-platform components: components that work on both the iOS and Android platforms.
- Use the `Modal` component to show overlays by setting the `visible` prop to `true` or `false`.
- Use the `Picker` component to easily allow user selections. The `selectedValue` prop defines which value is selected.
- Use the Fetch API to work with network requests and use the response data. `fetch` will return a promise with data you can use in the app.
- The `FlatList` component lets you easily and efficiently render lists of data by passing in a `renderItem` method as well as a data array as props.
- `ActivityIndicator` is a great, easy way to indicate a loading state in your app. An indicator is shown or hidden based on the loading state.
- Create reusable containers by wrapping the `children` prop in two React Native `View` components.

appendix
Installing and running
React Native

A.1 Developing for iOS devices

At the time of this this writing, if you want to develop for iOS you must have a Mac, because Linux and Windows aren't supported for developing for the iOS platform.

A.1.1 Getting started

To get started, you must have a Mac, and you need the following installed on it:

- Xcode
- Node.js
- Watchman
- React Native command-line interface

Follow these steps:

1. Install Xcode, which is available through the App Store.
2. The React Native docs and I recommend installing Node and Watchman via Homebrew. If you don't already have Homebrew installed, go to http://brew.sh and install it on your machine.
3. Open a command line, and install Node and Watchman using Homebrew:

```
brew install node
brew install watchman
```

4. Once Node.js is installed, install the React Native command-line tools by running the following from the command line:

```
npm install -g react-native-cli
```

If you get a permission error, try again with sudo:

```
sudo npm install -g react-native-cli
```

A.1.2 *Testing the installation on iOS*

Check to see if React Native is properly installed by creating a new project. In the terminal or on your command line of choice, run the following commands, replacing *MyProjectName* with the project name:

```
react-native init MyProjectName
cd MyProjectName
```

Now that you've created the project and changed into the new directory, you can run the project a couple of different ways:

- From within the MyProjectName directory, run the command `react-native run-ios`.
- Open the project in Xcode by opening the MyProjectName.xcodeproj file located at MyProjectName/ios/MyProjectName.xcodeproj.

A.2 *Developing for Android devices*

You can develop React Native for Android with a Mac, Linux, or Windows environment.

A.2.1 *Mac and Android*

To get started on a Mac, you need the following installed on your machine:

- Node.js
- React Native command-line tools
- Watchman
- Android Studio

Follow these steps:

1 The React Native docs and I recommend installing Node and Watchman via Homebrew. If you don't already have Homebrew installed, go to http://brew.sh and install it on your machine.

2 Open a command line, and install Node and Watchman using Homebrew:

```
brew install node
brew install watchman
```

3 Once Node.js is installed, install the React Native command-line tools by running the following from the command line:

```
npm install -g react-native-cli
```

4 Install Android Studio at https://developer.android.com/studio/install.html.

When everything is installed, go to section A.2.4 to create your first project.

A.2.2 Windows and Android

The following must be installed on your machine:

- Node.js
- Python2
- React Native command-line tools
- Watchman
- Android Studio

Follow these steps:

1 Watchman is in the alpha stage for Windows, but it's working fine so far in my experience. To install Watchman, go to https://github.com/facebook/watchman /issues/19 and download the alpha build via the link in the first comment.

2 React Native recommends installing Node.js and Python2 via Chocolatey, a package manager for Windows. To do so, install Chocolatey (https://chocolatey.org), open a command line as admin, and then run these commands:

```
choco install nodejs.install
choco install python2
Install the React Native command-line interface:
npm install –g react-native-cli
```

3 Download and install Android Studio from https://developer.android.com/studio /install.html.

4 When everything is installed, go to section A.2.4 to create your first project.

A.2.3 Linux and Android

The following must be installed on your machine:

- Node.js
- React Native command-line tools
- Watchman
- Android Studio

Follow these steps:

1 If you don't already have Node.js installed, go to https://nodejs.org/en/download /package-manager and follow the instructions for your Linux distribution.

2 Run the following command to install the React Native command-line tools:

```
npm install -g react-native-cli
```

3 Download and install Android Studio from https://developer.android.com/studio /install.html.

4 Download and install Watchman from https://facebook.github.io/watchman /docs/install.html#installing-from-source.

Once everything is installed, continue to the next section to create your first project.

A.2.4   *Creating a new project (Mac/Windows/Linux)*

Once your development environment is set up and react-native-cli is installed, you create new React Native projects from the command line. Navigate to the folder in which you want to create a project, and issue the following command, replacing *MyProject-Name* with the project name:

```
react-native init MyProjectName
```

A.2.5   *Running a project (Mac/Windows/Linux)*

To run a React Native project, change directories into the project from the command line, and run this command for Android:

```
react-native run-android
```

index

RELATED MANNING TITLES

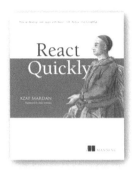

React Quickly
Painless web apps with React, JSX, Redux, and GraphQL
by Azat Mardan

    ISBN: 9781617293344
    528 pages, $49.99
    August 2017

React in Action
by Mark Tielens Thomas

    ISBN: 9781617293856
    360 pages, $44.99
    May 2018

Secrets of the JavaScript Ninja, Second Edition
by John Resig, Bear Bibeault, and Josip Maras

    ISBN: 9781617292859
    464 pages, $44.99
    August 2016

Get Programming with JavaScript Next
New features of ECMAScript 2015, 2016, and beyond
by JD Isaacks

    ISBN: 9781617294204
    376 pages, $39.99
    April 2018

For ordering information go to www.manning.com

Angular 2 Development with TypeScript
by Yakov Fain and Anton Moiseev

ISBN: 9781617293122
456 pages, $44.99
December 2016

Angular in Action
by Jeremy Wilken

ISBN: 9781617293313
320 pages, $44.99
March 2018

Testing Angular Applications
by Jesse Palmer, Corinna Cohn, Michael
   Giambalvo, Craig Nishina

ISBN: 9781617293641
240 pages, $44.99
November 2018

Usability Matters
Mobile-first UX for developers and other accidental designers
by Matt Lacey

ISBN: 9781617293931
392 pages, $44.99
July 2018

For ordering information go to www.manning.com

YOU MAY ALSO BE INTERESTED IN

Vue.js in Action
by Erik Hanchett with Benjamin Listwon

ISBN: 9781617294624
304 pages, $44.99
September 2018

Testing Vue.js Applications
by Edd Yerburgh

ISBN: 9781617295249
272 pages, $44.99
December 2018

RxJava for Android Developers
by Timo Tuominen

ISBN: 9781617293368
450 pages, $44.99
April 2019

iOS Development with Swift
by Craig Grummitt

ISBN: 9781617294075
568 pages, $49.99
November 2017